Trekking in Spain

Marc Dubin

Trekking in Spain
1st edition

Published by
Lonely Planet Publications
Head Office: PO Box 617, Hawthorn, Victoria 3122, Australia
US Office: PO Box 2001A, Berkeley, CA 94702, USA

Printed by
Colorcraft Ltd, Hong Kong

Photographs by
Marc Dubin
Front cover: Picos de Europa - Naranjo de Bulnes
Back cover: Picos de Europa - descending from Los Urrielles

Published
May 1990

Although the author and publisher have tried to make the information as accurate as possible, they accept no responsibility for any loss, injury or inconvenience sustained by any person using this book.

National Library of Australia Cataloguing in Publication Data

Dubin, Marc S.
    Trekking in Spain
    1st ed.

    Includes index.
    ISBN 0 86442 088 9.

    1. Hiking – Spain – Guide-books. 2. Spain – Description
    and travel – 1981 –   – Guide-books. I. Title.

914.60483

Marc S Dubin

Marc was born and educated in California, interrupting university studies in 1976 to teach English in South America, where he perfected his Spanish. Eventually finishing his formal schooling, he developed a travel habit which became a profession. Travel journalist and author since 1979, Marc wrote *Greece on Foot: Mountain Treks, Island Trails* (Seattle/Leicester, The Mountaineers/Cordee) and, with Enver Lucas, Lonely Planet's *Trekking in Turkey*. He is co-author of the Greek, Spanish and Turkish volumes of the Rough/Real Guides. An accomplished photographer with numerous publication credits, he currently divides his time between London and a hide-out somewhere in the Aegean.

Lonely Planet Credits

Editor	Frith Pike
Maps	Valerie Tellini
	Vicki Beale
Cover design	Valerie Tellini
Design & Illustrations	Margaret Jung

Thanks also to Chris Lee Ack for additional mapping, to Peter Turner for help with Ventura and the indexing, and to Vicki Beale for help with design.

A Warning & a Request

Things change – prices go up, schedules change, good places go bad and bad places go bankrupt -- nothing stays the same. So if you find things better or worse, recently opened or long since closed, please write and tell us and help make the next edition better!

Your letters will be used to help update future editions and, where possible, important changes will also be included as a Stop Press section in reprints.

All information is greatly appreciated and the best letters will receive a free copy of the next edition, or any other Lonely Planet book of your choice.

Acknowledgments

I would first of all like to express my appreciation to Antonio Manera and Jaime Gomera of the *Fomento de Turismo de Mallorca* for arranging my stay at the delightful Hotel El Guía in Soller, whose staff also deserves recognition. In the Picos de Europa, the warden of Vega Redonda refuge, Tomás Fernández López, graciously fielded my numerous questions about the area and provided me with ideas for hiking in the future. Xavier Massó i Ferrés, José Danes, and José and Ramón Salamaña, all of Santa Coloma de Farners (Girona), were lively and welcome company for three days in the central Picos de Europa, and Antonio and Rocio Brufau of Lleida spared me much pain getting up to the Valarties trailhead and laid on a memorable picnic. Matt the Welshman, whose last name I still don't know, appeared and disappeared as mysteriously on Mulhacén as he had in the Turkish Kaçkar range in 1987! Thanks for lending me the ice axe and good luck, Matt, in South America where you were headed...

Once more thanks are due John Chapple in Athens for extended storage of research materials and mail, and also to the people at the Rough Guides in London for answering mail and phone calls and tinkering with computer interface cards and cables.

Sandra Klein succeeded in capturing the essence of the generally unphotogenic author, and Emil Moryannidhis once again produced industrial-grade black & whites despite a busted drum processor and negatives that hadn't had the benefit of a yellow filter.

Disclaimer

Although the author and publisher have done their utmost to ensure the accuracy and currency of all information in this guide, they cannot accept responsibility for any loss, injury or inconvenience sustained by any person using this book. For example, we cannot guarantee that paths described have not been destroyed in the interval between research and publication. All hiking times given exclude rest stops, and unless otherwise stated, assume a trail surface unobstructed by snow. The fact that a trip or area is described in this guide does not mean that it is necessarily a safe one for you or your group. While technical rock-climbing is practised in most of the regions covered, the actual itineraries included have been deliberately selected to avoid the necessity of engaging in these activities. You are finally responsible for judging your own capabilities in the light of the conditions you encounter.

Contents

Introduction

Having written two previous hiker's guides (to Greece and Turkey), and having spent time as a tourist in Spain between 1978 and 1986, it was with a sense of excitement, and a relatively open mind, that I set out to research this book in 1988. It might initially seem strange to prepare a single hiking volume for the land that, spurred by British travel agencies, pioneered the package vacation, but it is precisely this creaky stereotype which has until recently both protected the Spanish countryside from exploitation by tourism, and allowed this to be the first comprehensive English-language trail guide to appear.

But Spain shatters preconceived notions and the current pace of change is dizzying.

Woe betide anyone who thinks of going there because it is 'cheap' or full of quaintly dressed peasants, because it no longer is – if it ever was. This is a nation which in the past three decades (but particularly since Franco's death) has been dragged or pushed, kicking and screaming, into the latter half of the 20th century. Economically it is a sleeping giant awakened, on the make and perhaps a little overconfident. The Barcelona Olympics and Sevilla Expo of 1992 will formalise Spain's big-league status, and will coincide symbolically with the frontier-less European Community (EC) of which it is the newest full member.

Some of the reform is doubtless superficial; habits and frames of mind of a millennium do not disappear overnight. But enough has gone by the board so that an aficionado is in some ways no longer at a substantial advantage over a novice visitor. Mindful of the less savoury aspects of '*Costa de...*' tourism, and determined to take advantage of the entire Spanish patrimony, the National Tourist Office has launched an aggressive publicity campaign to attract a 'quality' second generation of tourists, interested in the astounding range of art, architecture, cuisine, public cultural events, and sports to be enjoyed here.

In light of all this tumult, why should the day-hiker or serious trekker visit? Most importantly, for the sake of the countryside: large tracts of it, despite the best efforts of the road and dam builders, hunters, and chalet and ski-lift contractors, are still superb. In one season of touring six major mountain groups, I saw more wild animals than during the combined seven previous summers spent in Greece and Turkey. Walkers' amenities, whether maps, trails, alpine shelters, or information from tourist offices, are of or near the quality available in the rest of western Europe. Yet the Spanish wilderness is, and will be at least for the next few years, comparatively empty and unspoiled. All this should be sufficient endorsement, and inducement.

I have chosen to concentrate on those parts of walkable Spain which already have an international reputation and, in some cases, a limited coverage in the English-language hiking literature. This guide is aimed primarily at the overnight trekker, and also the day-hiker, but not the technical climber, although I have described routes where modest equipment (ie crampons and axe) is seasonally advisable. High-quality paths have been emphasised, with both cross-country scrambles and road-walking (that bane of trekkers, mother of blisters and bad tempers) kept to an absolute minimum. Where bulldozer interference became too outrageous, readers were directed elsewhere; there are still far too many beautiful trails in

Spain to indulge in masochism. Coverage of the more obscure corners of the country is reserved for future editions.

MAP LEGEND

—.—.	International Boundaries		⊥ ⊥ ⊥	Swamps
—..—..	Internal Boundaries			Glacier
—..—..	National Park Boundaries		—750—	Contour, Contour Interval
——	Major Roads		●	Settlements
------	Unsealed Roads, Tracks		⸸ ⸸	Church, Monastery
+++++++	Railways		☼	Lookout
....	Walking Trail		⚐	Camping Area
....	Cross Country Route		⌂	Hut
– – – –	Ferry Routes		▲	Mountain, Peak
+++++++	Cable Car		⟋⟍	Mountain Pass
⌐⌐⌐	Rivers, Creeks		⟋∤⟍	Bridge
	Lakes		⌒⌒⌒	Escarpment or Cliff
∽	Spring			Built up areas
—#—	Waterfall			

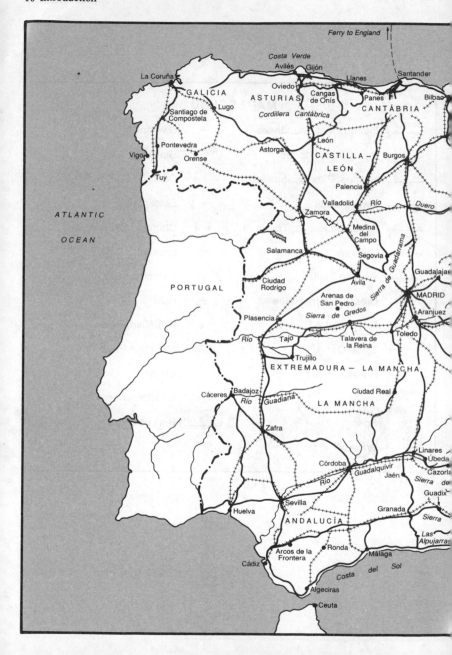

Facts about the Country

GEOGRAPHY

Spain and Portugal share the Iberian peninsula, a vaguely square shaped realm at the far south-western corner of the European continent, separated from France by the formidable Pyrenees mountains. It is by now a truism (albeit a useful one) that, except for Switzerland, Spain is the European country with the highest mean altitude with more than a third of its area exceeding 800 metres. The ruggedness of the topography has nurtured a unique flora and fauna, strong – often problematic – regional differences, and ample opportunities for walkers and trekkers.

The centre of the peninsula is occupied by the *meseta*, a bleak expanse (except for occasional *dehesa* – oak-studded grasslands) with broiling summers, harsh winters, and limited interest for hiking. This is broken up, however, by various mountain and river systems.

The Sierra de Gredos, the Sierra de Guadarrama and various lesser ranges of lower Aragón array themselves in a vast semicircle around the capital, Madrid; they contain the headwaters of the Río Tajo (Tagus), the Río Duero (Douro), and the Río Guadiana. North of another stretch of *meseta* watered by the Duero rises the Cordillera Cantábrica, extending from near the Atlantic almost to the Basque country, cutting off central Spain from the Mar Cantábrico (Bay of Biscay) and another possible maritime moderator of the inland climate. Here too springs the Río Ebro, the only major Spanish river to flow from west to east, with tributaries also draining the Pyrenees to the north.

South of Madrid and the Guadiana, a ring around the *meseta* is all but completed by the so-called Sierra Penibética, which includes the lofty Sierra Nevada, highest in mainland Spain, and its unusual south-to-north spur, the Sierra de Cazorla, the source of the Río Guadalquivir. The Balearic Islands, with the exception of Menorca, are a continuation of the Andalucian chains.

Yet this rather schematic description of rivers and sierras cannot possibly do justice to the staggering variety of landscapes in Spain. True, the country is big – it's almost 20 hours by the fastest train from any coast to the opposite one – but size alone still fails to prepare you for the coexistence of, say, almost-Scandinavian Galicia, an Asturias and Cantábria reminiscent of Oregon, and Almería (Europe's only true desert) – location for many a 'spaghetti Western'.

Spain's coastal lowlands are also evocative, if less than ideal for walkers. Much has been spoiled by runaway touristic and agricultural development, but the Guadalquivir delta is still one of Europe's great bird sanctuaries, and the *huerta* (market garden) of Valencia is the country's most fertile patch. The Ebro delta presents an almost south-east Asian aspect with its fish traps and rice paddies, plus magnificent, isolated beaches as an added bonus.

Geologically, Spain is a relatively old land mass, with little or no ongoing mountain-building, nor is there much geothermal, volcanic or seismic activity (except for some spas in the Pyrenees). However it is far from static or homogeneous. Rivers great and small cut amazing gorges – most notable at El Chorro in Andalucía, the Cares in Asturias, the Miño in Galicia, the Sierra de Guara in Aragón, and the Serranía de Cuenca – through strata that vary from limestone to granite, mica-schist to sandstone.

CLIMATE & SEASONS

With such variations in terrain, it should come as little surprise that Spain boasts a myriad of climates. Whatever month of the year you plan to visit, there is somewhere in the country that is tolerable if not ideal. More specific pointers are given in the season briefing for most hike write-ups, but the following outline will serve as a general overview.

Andalucía is most pleasant in late spring

and *very* early summer, when the landscape is still green from winter rains and temperatures have not soared to impossible levels. As the weather warms up, you're best off heading north to the mountains of central Spain.

Pyrenean trails and passes emerge from most snowpack by mid-July in a normal year, but day-to-day weather here is notoriously unstable even in summer and you should be prepared for anything. The first snow flurries can arrive in early October, when most of the staffed alpine refuges close until the winter climbing season (during February and March).

Galicia is the second wettest corner of the country, with perennial drizzle and mist except for some bright days in July and August; Asturias, Cantábria and the Basque provinces are similarly damp and green, but with better defined, if slightly muggy, summers when the heat will lure you to a sea most comfortable from July to September.

By early autumn you might again consider visiting central Spain, Andalucía and the eastern coast where the Mediterranean will certainly be at its warmest. Winters in the extreme south of Andalucía, and in Mallorca, are short and rarely severe, and then (or early spring when the fruit trees blossom) would be an excellent time to visit.

Most, though by no means all, of the major festivals take place in late winter and early spring: the Cádiz carnival and the *fallas* of Valencia are respectively the highlights of February and March; Easter in any Andalucian city, or the April *feria* in Sevilla, make excellent complements to a walking vacation; and Corpus Christi (in June) is similarly elaborate.

Be warned, though, that during Easter accommodation is at a premium; summer is infinitely worse in this respect, with the touristified mainland *costas* and the Balearic Islands a teeming, squalid mass of superheated humanity. By mid-July, Spaniards desert the cities (particularly Madrid) in droves, and make for the more salubrious coasts and hills of Galicia, Asturias, and Cantábria. Similarly the Pyrenees become a popular destination, particularly for the Aragonese and the Catalans.

In high season you might imitate the locals, but bear in mind that you face stiff competition in getting services of any sort. Purchase train and bus tickets a few days in advance, and if at all possible *take a tent*, wherever you go and whatever your budget. In any resort of repute, and at not a few lesser ones (as well as at many alpine refuges), there will not be a bed to be had; throwing money at the problem is not going to work, since all rooms, of every price category, will have been reserved by Spaniards months in advance! A tent will also save you a great deal of cash, particularly if you're alone, since accommodation (though not food) prices are jacked up enormously during the summer.

One exception to this pattern is in Galicia, when there are even enough rooms to go around for the 25 July festival at Santiago de Compostela, but abandon all hope of staying in, for example, Pamplona during the July *San Fermines* (running of the bulls) or during the San Sebastián and Santander jazz festivals of the same month.

Don't hesitate to plan a trip to Spain over Christmas; facilities stay open and you'll have some company, mostly other foreigners. Spaniards pretty much ignore *Navidad*, preferring to emphasise *Día de los Tres Reyes* (Day of the Three Magi, 6 January).

AN UNNATURAL HISTORY OF THE COUNTRYSIDE: USES & ATTITUDES

Various excellent field guides to the flora and fauna of Spain are available (see Books) so their coverage will not be duplicated here. Just as pertinent to the walker are the conflicting efforts of humans to destroy or preserve the Spanish wilderness in the past few decades.

It is a well-worn axiom, but one worth repeating, that the inhabitants of a suddenly developing society tend to throw any sort of preservation ethic out the window, despising the low-tech and traditional in the desire for pell-mell modernisation. This has certainly been true of Spain since the early 20th century, and only recently has there been any sort of homegrown conservationist backlash. Not to imply that Spain was some sort of ecological paradise 70 years ago; the physical condition of much of the *meseta* and Andalucía in particular was pretty dire, following years of maltreatment and neglect of agricultural tracts – particularly the age-old depredations by huge flocks of wandering sheep. The effects of this were shortly to be aggravated by one of the worst droughts in living memory, during the 1940s and 1950s. Much of Spain is arid at the best of times, and the high precipitation zones that do exist (mostly confined to the north coast and the Pyrenees) attract another sort of disruptive activity: hydroelectric projects.

The mania for dams started during the 1920s and the dictatorship of Primo de Rivera and, after the disruption of the civil war years, damming was resumed with a vengeance by the Franco regime in the 1950s and 1960s, following massive American aid. The basic motivations for the projects were laudable; nobody wished for a repeat of the drought-spurred famines of the previous decades, and the turbines have also spared Spain from excessive dependence on nuclear and petrochemical power.

But lately it has become hard to dismiss the suspicion that many of the reservoirs are pork-barrels pure and simple, with benefits accruing to few except land-speculators in the suddenly irrigated plains down the hill. Battles over siting and construction are uncomfortably familiar to anyone from the western United States or south-west Tasmania in Australia. From the hiker's point of view they mar the landscape most in the Catalan Pyrenees, even in the national park there. It is only to be hoped that the civil engineers will leave at least two valleys in five alone, for the enjoyment of future generations.

A similar sort of dubious improvement involves tunnels in the Pyrenees. There's a discernible difference between valleys which have tunnel connection with France (heavily commercialised) and those which don't (considerably less so). The inhabitants of the latter valleys agitate continually for the engineers to come and bore a solution to what they see as their backwater status; they probably won't rest until their canyons, like those

of their neighbours, are a mass of ski lifts, vacation chalets, supermarkets and various après-ski excrescences.

Away from the mountains, the main threat to habitats is from breakneck agricultural development and urbanisation. Lowering of the water table and a recent pesticide poisoning have substantially reduced the birdlife in the famous Coto Doñnana bird reserve, to give the best-known example. Up to now, the environmentalist strategy has been to get vast areas declared as natural reserves or natural parks. The authorities usually acquiesce if it is seen as a matter of preserving a potential tourist attraction; however, establishment of a protected zone in no way limits or controls detrimental activities in adjacent areas.

Indeed most Spaniards see the countryside as a place where they can do as they see fit. Older men particularly resent species limits set during hunting and fishing seasons, and poaching or winking at the law is commonplace. In general, while environmental legislation may be fine on paper, the resources and political will to enforce them are generally lacking.

Nowhere is the gap between ideals and practice wider than in the matter of garbage. I never cease to be amazed by the veritable Everests of trash which accumulate in the more popular alpine areas, particularly around refuges. We can do the landscape a favour by boycotting cans as much as possible and by burning non-plastic food wrappers – taking care not to add to the dozens of wildfires which ravage the lower-altitude forests (particularly in Catalunya and Andalucía) each year. It seems, like in neighbouring Portugal and in Greece, that many of these are deliberately set, for political and economic 'reasons'.

REGIONAL ETHNICITY & LANGUAGES

It is most realistic to think of Spain as a federation of 'autonomous communities', if not necessarily full-fledged republics as in Yugoslavia. Certainly the Spaniards think this way; vis a vis the outside world everybody (except the Portuguese) on their side of the Pyrenees is Spanish, and a performing artist, athlete, etc is feted as such, but among themselves it's a different matter. They are natives and devotees of the *patria chica* (local homeland) first and of Spain in general second. But it is some measure of the country's relative political 'maturity' that the place is not coming apart at the seams as Yugoslavia seems to be doing.

This is all the more amazing because numerous appeals to nationalist instincts, some of a baser nature, were made both before and after the Franco era; Franco himself brought the hob-nailed boot down hard on the faintest whiff of decentralisation or ethnic expression, particularly in Catalunya and the Basque country where opposition to his regime was greatest. Regional languages were banned in the printed media and as a medium of education, but they were obviously kept alive by extensive clandestine use and an oral tradition, for there is no other way to explain the rapid public recovery of the regional tongues.

Within a few years of Franco's death, a new constitution provided for the establishment of several autonomous regions. Although some are fuzzily or arbitrarily drawn, their borders are usually based on an underlying historical entity, if not necessarily on the kingdoms which existed before the 'unification' of Spain in the 15th century. It is worth briefly summarising the ethnic and linguistic variety within Spain, however much that may smack of racialism, since the subject is eventually bound to come up in discussions with any group of locals you meet on the trail.

For starters, 'Spanish' is what the language is called by foreigners; more correctly it is Castellano (Castilian) and is precisely that: the tongue of Castilla (Castile), at the centre of the meseta, which over the centuries has been adopted (or imposed) as the common means of communication, nearly pushing some of the regional languages to the brink of extinction. Never commit the faux pas of referring to Catalan, Euskara (Basque) or Gallego as 'dialects' – they are all languages, with distinct vocabularies and script.

Catalunya & Catalan

The Catalans, and Catalan, will be the people and language you'll see and hear the most of in the mountains, especially as the 1992 Olympiad comes and goes. Extroverted, cultured and with a tremendous amount of communal pride, Catalunya (Cataloñia in Castellano) is a Mediterranean realm with a tradition of seafaring, commerce and artistic accomplishment. The people are a mixed bag, though the level of Jewish ancestry among them is said to be high even by the standards of the peninsula.

Along with the Basques (who established Spain's coal and steel industry in the last century), they consider themselves at the forefront of Spanish enterprise and have always, with some justification, resented giving what they see as their economic support to the relatively unproductive central regions. Indeed the Catalans have rather sourly amended the old saying 'Africa begins at the Pyrenees' to 'Africa begins at the Ebro'. Since the restoration of democracy the centre of industrial gravity has shifted perceptibly toward Madrid as new businesses move there, but the vitality of Catalunya is barely diminished. The relatively prosperous Catalans have always been eager trekkers and mountaineers, organising group outings to places as remote as Peru (where I met a party of eight more than a decade ago). Catalunya's network of marked trails and alpine refuges is the most developed on the peninsula, and you will very quickly meet large numbers of locals enjoying their 'backyard'.

Catalan is descended from medieval Provençal, and if you have a reading knowledge of either French or Spanish it's not difficult to puzzle out signs or even short texts. Understanding or speaking it is another matter, however; all Catalans speak Castellano and don't expect non-Spaniards to delve into the complexities of their language, but are overjoyed to give you on-the-spot lessons should you express an interest. Since the 1970s public and social use of Catalan has grown by leaps and bounds, and it would seem that the contrary effect of large numbers of Castilian-speaking immigrants to Barcelona has been reversed – they are in fact made to feel very uncomfortable unless they begin learning Catalan straight away.

Pays Valenciano & the Balearics

The Pays Valenciano (the coastal strip south of Catalunya) and the Balearic Islands are now classed as separate political units and constitutionally forbidden from recombining, though whether they would if allowed to do so is questionable. There is something languorous and Levantine about the people, widely assumed to be descendants of Phoenician and Saracen mariners, that distinguishes them from their Catalan neighbours. The Moors, too, left the Levante (as the peninsular coastal strip is also called) last of all Spanish territory, and a lingering North African cast to life here is occasionally as strong as or stronger than in Andalucía, where many of the present-day inhabitants are descended from resettled northerners.

The Levante itself, heavily developed agriculturally and with most facilities slanted toward domestic tourism, sees few foreign visitors outside package enclaves like Benidorm. In compensation, fiestas (particularly the *fallas* and mock battles of Moors and Christians) are some of the best in Spain. The Balearic archipelago is physically and architecturally more distinctive and unabashedly exploits this to attract foreigners, but off the beaten tourist track flashes of the graciousness which brought the international clientele in the first place still show through.

From an extreme regionalist point of view, Mallorquín and Menorquín (spoken in the Balearics) and what's spoken in the Pays Valenciano might qualify as languages, but

Spain - Autonomous Regions

most concede that these are dialects, mutually intelligible with 'standard' Catalan and written for the most part identically. You will have the opportunity to judge for yourself, since all street signs and public notices are written according to the prevailing local transcription scheme.

Abutting the Pays Valenciano to the south is the tiny, backward zone of Murcia, long dismissed as the 'Tobacco Road' of Spain but recently awakened to enormous wealth by the hothouse-produce boom. Linguistically and otherwise it constitutes a transition between the Catalan-speaking realms to the north and the vast expanse of Andalucía to the west.

Aragón

Although historically closely linked to Catalunya, underdeveloped and mountainous Aragón provides quite a contrast. The people, perhaps hardened by their environment, are proverbial in Spain for their stubbornness (or perverseness depending on how you experience it) and secretiveness. In the larger urban centres such as Zaragoza, the Aragonese are a bit more open but in the backwoods they can be dour indeed. Aragón is an autonomous region and you may hear mumblings about an Aragonese dialect, but except for a smattering of old Pyrenean topographical terms this is scarcely in evidence outside of the Valle de Gistaín.

The Basque Country & Euskara

Descending from the Aragonese highlands to the green foothills and valleys of the Basque country represents another palpable transition. Once again, as in Catalunya, you will see the effects of (by Spanish standards) early industrialisation in a notably higher standard of living, efficient public transport and a relative lack of foreign tourism. The people are sincerely helpful if not always voluble in the Catalan manner, and again there is an emphatic nationalist spirit furthered by the belief (supported by recent blood-group studies) that the Euskadi are the original inhabitants of the Iberian peninsula, and that everyone around them is a johnny-come-lately by comparison.

Basques are traditionally conservative and ultra-Catholic (Ignatius Loyola, founder of the Jesuits, for example); the leftist posture of the terrorist group ETA and its political arm *Herri Batasuna* is entirely a product of this century, when the depredations of the Falangist armies, and later Franco's regime, left many Basques, including some clerics, little apparent choice. As their aging industrial plant becomes increasingly obsolete, and the advantages of *devolución* (return of authority to the regions) are acted on, the allure and credibility of ETA and its methods diminishes steadily as the Basques see that they cannot afford to be marginalised.

One look at a sample of written Euskara (the Basque tongue), squirming with 'x's, 'r's, 'i's, 'ñ's and 't's, will convince you that this is no dialect but an horrendously complicated language, non-Indo-European in origin and perhaps the oldest in Europe. Nobody will expect you to speak it, let alone understand it, and very few of the natives are completely fluent in it. Of late there has been a conscious revival of Euskara in literature and music, but one has the impression that it has been a very strenuous resuscitation.

Cantábria & Asturias

Moving along the north coast, Cantábria is historically and linguistically an extension of Castile to the south, and as such is not even classed as an autonomous region, but the Principality of Asturias is another matter. Industrialised on a smaller scale than the Basque provinces, with mines and steel mills along the coast, it invites comparisons to Wales. It was from here that the Christian Reconquest began in the 8th century, and in token of respect the heir to the Spanish throne is still referred to as the *Príncipe* (Prince) of Asturias – slightly ironic considering the area's heritage of proletarian radicalism.

Regionalism is strong enough to engender a spate of wall slogans but if you question locals about the language most will admit that Asturiano consists largely of variant spellings (lots of final 'u's) and some unique toponymic terms – nothing you're likely to hear in the street. The people, presumed to be of mixed Visigothic, Celtic and native

Iberian descent, are still quite welcoming, a pleasant surprise considering that tourism is probably growing faster here than in any other part of the country.

Galicia & Gallego

Galicia is the most Celtic part of northern Spain, and an analogy with Ireland is not misleading. Poor, bleak, dependent on the sea and long a pool of emmigrants who fanned out over the New World, this is probably the least visited corner of the country. Its poverty, while severe, has never been quite as excruciating as Andalucía's, because of a land-use pattern whereby the moorland plots were repeatedly divided over the centuries until a minimum size barely able to support a single family was reached. Spaniards consider the local people to be eccentric, superstitious (perhaps because of the hexes on corn-cribs, a carry over from pre-Christian belief) and adept at sorcery. At the same time they are staunchly conservative and Catholic; Franco hailed from here and the festival of Santiago was instituted in that city during the 9th century.

The language, Gallego, is dubbed 'the mother of Portuguese' in some circles and indeed it's thought to be barely evolved from whatever people spoke before Spanish and Portuguese diverged during the 12th and 13th centuries. Written, it still closely resembles Portuguese, except for a preponderance of 'x's, and if you can read Portuguese you can probably stumble along in Gallego. Reports conflict as to its vigour, though most observers agree that in some remote villages it is the first language, and that almost all young people understand it while not necessarily speaking it well.

León & Castilla

It is more difficult to define the great heartland comprising the former kingdoms of León and Old/New Castile, now mostly reapportioned as the autonomous regions of León and Castilla and Extremadura and La Mancha. The finest castles and cathedrals in the country are here, way stations of the Christian armies as they edged south toward Andalucía.

Others on the peninsula disparage it as an historical exporter of *conquistadores*, inquisitors and bureaucrats, with its undeniable accomplishments in the arts and architecture parasitically derived. While there is an element of truth in these reproaches it would seem that the days when the economy was based on wine, wool, ham and taxes are long over, and that Madrid (a separate political entity) is now capital by virtue of merit rather than geographical accident and royal decree.

Here, at least among older people, you may find the stereotypical Castilian: correct and more dignified than present circumstances might inspire, often a little pompous or petty, but not at first glance the ogre of the separatist imagination or the bigot of *La Leyenda Negra*, the 'Black Legend' of fanaticism and cruelty that has long cast a shadow over Anglo-Saxon perceptions of Spain. What you may also notice is a remarkable incuriosity about you, to the point of indifference. There is an empirical self-sufficiency and insularity in the Castilian character, a lack of obsequiousness that may be either refreshing or unnerving, depending on your travel history elsewhere.

Linguistically, this is where foreigners come to learn 'Spanish'; here more than anywhere else in Spain you'll hear the *theta*, the lisped 'c' or 'z'. Among New World variants, the central Colombian dialect is probably the closest and you would be (as I was) at a very slight advantage in having learned it first, as opposed to Mexican, Chilean, etc.

Andalucía

Andalucía, the largest autonomous region, has produced the bulk of the popular cliché images – sherry, bullfights, 'white towns', *flamenco* – associated with Spain. These are indeed there but its essence is almost as difficult to define as that of the *meseta*. Most of the Castilian traits are present, but softened somewhat by wry flashes of humour, a certain genial shiftiness, and an exuberant street life prompted both by climate and innate temperament.

What this masks is a grim economic reality and dire history. After the Reconquest the intricate agricultural and industrial apparatus of the Moors was allowed to deteriorate, the conquerors preferring to turn Andalucía into a vast pasture and divide it into large estates when necessary. The consequences of this land division are still apparent: a large pool of underemployed, propertyless labour continues to exist (unemployment exceeds 20% in many places), and significant land reform is something that successive governments seem unable or disinclined to undertake.

The stopgap solution has been massive internal and external migration (mostly to Catalunya and the rest of Europe respectively) and an enlarged tourist industry which is seen as the fastest money-maker. Neither of these trends is likely to be reversed soon, though an interesting recent development has been (as in Murcia) the introduction of exotic and highly profitable fruits.

To the uninitiated, rural Andalucian Spanish seems a deluge of elided and truncated syllables, compounded by a large regional vocabulary. It can be distinctively written (there's plenty of graffiti in Granada to cut your teeth on), in the sense that American Black English can, but as yet nobody has accorded it any status other than that of a strong dialect.

LANGUAGE

Spanish is one of the easiest tongues for English-speakers to learn. Since courses and learning materials are widely available, the following phrase sections are brief, and slanted towards the special needs of walkers.

It's worth emphasising the value of learning at least some Spanish. Despite close to three decades of tourist invasion of the country, and perhaps as a corollary to the noted Castilian provinciality, very few individuals over the age of 40 speak any English – these are the people you'll most likely meet in the rural areas. Conversely, in the bigger towns English-language academies are springing up like mushrooms for an enthusiastic, young clientele, who see it as *the* way to get ahead in the post-1992 EC.

Spanish Alphabet

Spanish uses the same alphabet as English,

with the exception of 'ch', 'll' and 'ñ', which rank as separate letters and have their own dictionary entries (after 'c', 'l' and 'n' respectively). The pronunciation values of the letters listed below differ from that of English, but at least they're regular. Stress may be indicated by an accent; otherwise most words are stressed on the penultimate syllable, but those ending in -d, -l, -r, -z, and -on on the final syllable. All vowels are pure and short; there are no diphthongs or drawled vowels as in North American English.

Pronunciation

a	something between the 'a' in'rack' and 'law'
c	before 'i' or 'e', a lisped theta as in 'thin' (less marked in the north); otherwise a hard 'k' sound
d	as in English when initial, but otherwise a theta sound as in 'though'
e	as in 'bet'
g	hard 'h' sound before 'i' or 'e', otherwise ordinary 'g'
gue	pronounced 'geh'
güe	pronounced 'gweh'
h	always silent
i	as in 'police'
j	always hard 'h' sound
ll	like an English 'y'
ñ	pronounced as 'ny'
o	something between the 'o' of 'top' and 'rote'
q	almost invariably followed by 'ue'; pronounced 'keh'
r/rr	rolled/doubly so
u	as in 'kudos'
v	tends toward a soft 'b' sound
x	close to English 'x' before vowels, closer to 's' before consonants; most common in Basque, Gallego, and Catalan words, where it's 'sh' or 'zh'; when final in Catalan or Mallorquín, 'tch'
z	same rules as for 'c'

Learning Materials

The trend of late is to emphasise New World usage; thus older, 'obsolete' publications may be better for Iberian Spanish. The following inexpensive paperback items are available either in the UK or North America, and possibly Australia and New Zealand.

In the USA or Canada, try to find *The Bantam New College Spanish-English English-Spanish Dictionary*, edited by E B Williams and issued by Bantam; the *Cassells Spanish-English English-Spanish Dictionary*, issued by Collier-Macmillan, and particularly good for Iberian Spanish; or the *Langenscheidt Pocket Dictionary*, comparable in coverage to the *Collins* (see following) and good value for money in either mini or compact sizes.

For a teach-yourself course, it's worth scouring university student union bookstores for books like *Spanish for Beginners*, by Charles Duff and published by Barnes and Noble; *Spanish Grammar* by Eric Greenfield, also through Barnes and Noble; or *Teach Yourself Spanish*, an old warhorse perennially out through David MacKay.

Pickings are probably a bit better on the other side of the Atlantic. *Collins Compact* or *Collins Gem Pocket Dictionary* are attractively priced and in conjunction with the following glossaries should handle most situations.

Barring a full-scale dictionary, avail yourself of a phrasebook, of which there are several; best seem to be *Spanish Travelmate*, issued by Drew, or *Travellers' Spanish*, put out by Pan Books. For a full-tilt course, try one of two products prepared by the BBC: *¡Digame!*, with a workbook and three LPs or cassettes, or *Get By in Spanish*, consisting of a booklet and two recordings. Routledge's *Colloquial Spanish* is small and inexpensive enough to carry around with you and dog-ear.

Greetings, Partings, Basic Expressions

good morning/day	*buenas días*
good afternoon/ evening	*buenas tardes*
good night	*buenas noches*
hello, hi	*hola*
good-bye	*adios*
See you later.	*Hasta luego (logo).*

Basic Expressions

yes	*sí*
no	*no*
How are you?	*¿Cómo está(s)?* (singular-familiar/plural-formal)
What's up? (much more casual)	*¿Qúe hay?*
please	*por favor*
thank you	*gracias*
You're welcome.	*De nada.*
Don't mention it.	*No hay de qué.*
excuse me	*con permiso/perdón*
fine	*está bien*
okay, agreed (very common)	*vale*
bon voyage	*buen viaje*

Nationalities

Alternate -a forms are for women.

American	*Americano/a, estadunidense*
English	*Inglés(a)*
Australian	*Australiano/a*
Canadian	*Canadiense*
New Zealander	*Nueva Zelandés(a)*
Dutch	*Holandés(a)*
Irish	*Irlandés(a)*
German	*Alemán(a)*
French	*Francés(a)*
Belgian	*Belgo/a*

In all cases, you can form a complete sentence by preceding the adjective with *Soy ...* (I am ...).

Requests

Can I leave this here a while?
    ¿Puedo dejar esto aquí por un rato?
Can I camp around here?
    ¿Puedo acampar por acá?
How many hours from here to ...?
    ¿Cuantas horas de aquí hasta ...?
Where are the toilets?
    ¿Dónde están los servicios?
Is/are there ...?
    ¿Hay ...?
Yes, there is/are.
    Sí, hay.

No, there isn't/aren't.
No hay.

Other Useful Verbs

Those below are given in the infinitive form, as listed in dictionaries, and also in one or more persons and tenses.

to have, I have	*tener, tengo*
to go, I go, I went	*ir, voy, fui*
to be (permanent characteristic): I am, we are, you (familiar) are, you (formal) are and, he/she/it is, they are	*ser, soy, somos, es, son*
to be (location, transient condition) he/she/it is	*estar, está*
to find, I found	*encontrar, encontré*
to stay, remain; I stay	*quedar, quedo*
to cook, heat up (food, water)	*cocinar, calentar*
to want, I would like	*querer, querría*
to wait, I'll wait	*esperar, esperé*
to buy, they bought	*comprar, compraron*
to depart, he/she/it left	*salir, salió*
to understand, you understood	*entender, entendiste*

Numbers

1	*un, uno, una* (declined because also the indefinite article)
2	*dos*
3	*tres*
4	*cuatro*
5	*cinco*
6	*seis*
7	*siete*
8	*ocho*
9	*nueve*
10	*diez*
11	*once*
12	*doce*
13	*trece*
14	*catorce*
15	*quince*

16	*dieciseis* (and so on until 20)
20	*veinte*
21	*veintiuno*
22	*veintidos* (and so on)
30	*treinta*
40	*cuarenta*
50	*cinquenta*
60	*sesenta*
70	*setenta*
80	*ochenta*
90	*noventa*
100	*cien(to)*
200	*doscientos*
300	*treiscientos*
400	*cuatrocientos*
500	*quinientos*
600	*seiscientos*
700	*setecientos*
800	*ochocientos*
900	*novecientos*
1000	*mil*
15,000	*quince mil*
26,453	*veintiseis mil cuatrocientos cinquenta y tres*

Time

What time is it?	*¿Qué hora es?*
It's ... o'clock.	*Son las ...*
At what time ... ?	*¿A qué hora ...?*
When?	*Cuando?*
At ... o'clock	*A las ...*
half-hour	*media hora*
two and a half-hours	*dos horas y media*
20 minutes	*veinte minutos*
dawn	*amanecer*
sunset	*puesta del sol*
nightfall, (night is falling)	*anochecida, (cae la noche)*
morning	*mañana*
noon	*mediodía*
afternoon, evening	*tarde*
now	*ahora*
later	*más tarde*
always	*siempre*
today	*hoy*
yesterday	*ayer*
day before yesterday	*anteayer*
tomorrow (also 'morning')	*mañana*
day after tomorrow	*pasado mañana*

Weather

bad/good weather	*mal/buen tiempo*
It's sunny	*Hace sol*
It's cloudy	*Está nublado*
rain, it rains	*lluvia, llueve*
snow, it snows	*nieve*
snowstorm, blizzard	*nevasca, ventisca*
downpour, shower	*chubasco*
violent storm	*tormenta, tempestad*
mist, fog	*neblina*
white-out	*borrina, encainada*

Hiking Equipment

backpack	*mochila*
boot(s); also leather water-carrier	*bota(s)*
water canteen	*cantimplora*
crampons	*crampones*
ice axe – pronounced 'piolay'	*piolet*
gaiters	*paranieves*
small stove	*fogón*
gas cartridges	*cartuchas, bombonas*
matches	*fósforos*
tent	*tienda*
walking stick	*bastón*
sleeping bag	*saco de dormir*
down	*plumón*
fibre-fill	*fibra, sintético*
compass	*brújula*
altimeter	*altimetro*
pocketknife	*navaja*

two-way radio (in refuges)	*emisora*
backpacking store	*tienda de campaña*

Directions

All adjectives are given in the masculine; there are of course feminine forms ending in '-a'.

straight ahead	*recto, derecho*
a bit further	*un poco más adelante*
near/far	*cerca/lejos*
right/left	*derecha/izquierda*
uphill/downhill (climb)	*subida/bajada*
level/steep	*llano/escarpado*
wide/narrow	*ancho/estrecho*
good/bad	*bueno/malo*
pretty, pleasant/ugly, unpleasant	*hermoso/feo*
large/small	*grande/pequeño*
here/there	*aquí/allí*
from ... up to ...	*de ... hasta ...*
before/after	*antes de/después de*
beyond	*mas allá*
opposite from, in front of	*frente a/de*
above/below (preposition)	*encima de/debajo de*
upper/lower (adjective)	*de arriba/de abajo*
on the other side of	*al otro lado de*
adjacent	*contiguo, en seguida de*
between	*entre*
towards	*hacia*
to follow	*seguir*

Rights of Way...

These are listed in order of narrowest to widest.

trail	*senda, sendero*
path, track	*vereda, trocha*
old trade route	*camino*

same as above, but specifically intended for pack animals (literally 'horseshoe way')	camino de herradura	ditch, trench, alpine corral	tajo
		glacier	glaciar
		face (of mountain)	vertiente
cart track	carretil	incline, hillside, 'draw' in USA	coma
lane, may be sur-faced	carril	slope, hillside	ladera
		plain	planicie
jeep track	pista	'flats' in USA usage	llanos
asphalt road	carretera	stones, rocks	piedras, rocas
		boulder	canto rodado

... & Trail Science

(little) sign	cartel(ito)	blunt promontory	morro
shortcut	atajo	maritime cape	cabo
marker cairn	mojón	cliff, palisade	risco
fixed pegs to assist rock-face ascents	clavijas	crag	peña
		outcrop, pinnacle	(h)iruela
		pit, gulch	hoyo
traverse	travesía	cave	cueva
grade	pendiente	natural cave/over-hang shelter	balma
altitude difference	desnivel	chasm, sinkhole	sima, avenc

Political Units & Places

		gallery, defile	desfiladero
region; in Catalunya the smallest adminis-trative unit	comarca	gorge, river narrows	garganta
		valley	valle
		river	río
		brook	riachuelo
union of villages	mancomunidad, mancomunitat in Catalan	often seasonal stream	torrente
		waterfall	cascadas
municipality	ayuntamiento	riverbank, shore	ribera
village	aldea	ravine, gully	barranco/a
summer pasture, but also the pasto-ral hamlet associ-ated with it	majada	fountain, improved spring	fuente
		natural spring	manantial
		pond	charco/a, balsa
		well	pozo

Landmarks & Features

		cistern	(es)tanque
mountain(s)	montaña(s)	lake	lago, laguna
summit	cumbre	aqueduct	acequia
peak	pico, cima	dam	presa, barraja
trigonometric survey point	vertex	reservoir	embalse
		swimming pool	piscina
hill, knoll	loma, colina, cerro	spa resort	balneario
range	sierra, cordillera	mineral springs for bathing	baños
crest, ridge	cresta		
massif	màcizo	runoff, drainage of a body of water	desagüe
spur (especially in Gredos)	cuerda	greensward	pradera
pass, gap	cuello, collado	meadow	prado, vega
saddle	horcado(a)	grazing pasture	pasto
cirque	circo	cultivated field	campiña

moorland	*paramera*	emergency lean-to	*abrigo*
high *Festuca*-grass tundra	*cervunales*	primitive, often roofless shelter	*vivac*
broom thickets	*matorral*	a more elaborate shelter	*cabaña*
forest, woodland	*bosque*		
firebreak	*cortefuego*	bungalow	*cobertizo*
farm	*finca, cortijo*	medieval pilgrims' station	*hospital*
picnic area	*merendero*		
trout-breeding station	*piscifactoría*	old-fashioned inn	*albergue*
		barracks	*cuartel*
cable car	*teleférico*	watchtower	*atalaya*
ICONA shelter	*casa forestal*	lookout, viewpoint	*mirador*
formal refuge	*refugio*	castle	*castillo*

bridge	*puente*
wayside chapel	*ermita*
cemetery	*cementerio*
monastery	*monasterio*
convent	*convento*

Trees & Shrubs

beech	*haya*
birch	*abedul*
quaking aspen	*álamo temblón*
ash	*fresno*
black oak	*roble*
white oak	*encina*
cork oak	*alcornoque*
linden	*tilo*
poplar	*chopo*
willow	*sauce*
alder	*aliso*
elm	*olmo*
yew	*tejo*
hazelnut	*avellano*
wild cherry	*cerezo*
walnut (tree)	*nogal*
chestnut	*castaño*
almond	*almendro*
olive	*olivo*
fir	*abeto*
Pinus pinaster	*pino resinero*
Scots pine	*pino silvestre*
black pine	*pino negro*
juniper	*enebro*
box	*boj*
rhododendron	*rododendro*
Vaccinium myrtillus (bilberry)	*arándano*
cistus	*piorno*

Beasts, Birds & Bugs

bear	*oso*
wolf	*lobo*
lynx	*lince, pardelo*
wild boar	*jabalí*
bighorn sheep	*muflón*
Capra hispanica – Spanish ibex (rare)	*cabra montés*
Rupicapra rupicapra – chamois (common)	*rebeco* (Castilian) *isard* (Catalan) *sarrio* (Aragonese)
deer	*ciervo*

cow	*vaca*
sheep	*oveja*
donkey	*burro*
horse	*caballo*
fox	*zorro*
badger	*tejón*
marten	*marta garduña*
weasel	*comadreja*
feral cat	*gato montés*
otter	*nutria*
rabbit	*conejo*
hare	*liebre*
hawk, falcon	*azor, halcón*
eagle	*águila*
vulture	*buitre*
lammergeier	*quebrantahueso*
like a woodcock; no translation	*urogallo*
partridge	*perdiz*
pheasant	*faisán*
owl	*búho*
stork	*cigüeña*
frog	*rana*
salamander, newt	*salamandra*
tortoise, turtle	*tortuga*
lizard	*lagarta*
viper	*víbora*
snake	*culebra*
scorpion	*escorpión*
bee	*abeja*
wasp	*avispa*
butterfly	*mariposa*
mosquito	*mosquito*
fly	*mosca*
tick	*garrapata*
flea	*pulga*

Common Organisations & Acronyms

Guardia Civil	Civil Guard – the gendarmerie
Centro de Salud	rural health clinic
ICONA *(Instituto Nacional para la Conservación de la Naturaleza)*	National Natural Resource Conservation Institute
MOPU *(Ministerio de Obras Publicas y Urbanismo)*	Ministry of Public Works and City Development
FECSA *(Fundació Electrica de Catalunya, SA*	Catalan Electrical Power Board

Catalan Regional/Toponymic Terms

You will notice Catalan linguistic influence exerted well into 'La Franja' of Aragón, indeed up to the Gistaín valley. It's worth noting that the Catalan 'g', when medial, is pronounced like English 'j' – eg Amitges is 'Amitjes'; when final, it's like English 'tch' – eg Contraig is 'Contraitch'.

pass; same as Castilian *puerta*	*port*
saddle; same as Castilian *collado*	*coll*
diminutive of above	*colladeta*
lake	*llac, estany*
diminutive of above	*estanyet*
river	*riu*
stream	*riueta, ribera*
river valley	*noguera*
mineral/thermal springs; same as Castilian *banos*	*banys*
spring; same as Castilian *fuente*	*font*
peak	*puig, pic, tuc*
range; same as Castilian *sierra*	*serra(t)*
valley; same as Castilian *valle*	*vall*
shady spot, eg north-facing slopes	*obaga*
flat area; same as Castilian *llano*	*pla(nell)*
originally a turfy, though not necessarily flat, place where cattle would overnight usually with a herder	*pletiu*
way; same as Castilian *camino*	*camí*
cairn	*fita; fites*(plural)
mountain refuge	*refugi*
old alpine pilgrims' hostel; same as Castilian *hospital*	*opitau*
cirque; same as Castilian *circo*	*circ*
top, cape; same as Castilian *cabo*	*cap*

Mallorquín Regional/Toponymic Terms

The Catalan terms *refugi, puig, coll, camí, font* and *serra* are all in use on Mallorca, plus the following:

masculine/feminine definite articles	*es, sa*
'house of'; contraction of *casa d'en*	*c'an*
contraction meaning 'estate of'	*son*
cove, inlet	*cala*
watchtower; same as Castilian *atalaya*	*talaia*
charcoal burners' circle	*sitja*

Aragonese Regional/Toponymic Terms

As well as the Catalan contribution, Basque settlement eastwards left many linguistic traces, eg *ibón*.

mouth of subterranean river	*forau*
pond (in Catalan also)	*clot*
tarn (plural *ibons*, Castilian *ibones*)	*ibón*
same as Catalan *pletiu*	*pleta*
peak	*tuc, tozal*

Asturian Regional/Toponymic Terms

pit, cavity; same as Castilian *hoyo*	*jou*
cairn	*jito, jitu, hito*
creek, streambed	*riega*
ravine, canyon	*canal*
saddle-pass; same as Castilian *horcado*	*horcajo, jorcau*
bouldery hog-back; similar to Castilian *canto*	*cantu*

Facts for the Trekker

VISAS & IMMIGRATION

Holders of any European Community (EC) passport will experience no special formalities upon entering Spain; Americans get a 180-day stamp upon entry, Canadians 90 days. At some ports of entry, notably Málaga, customs officials are notoriously lax about actually applying the stamp.

Australians, New Zealanders and South Africans may still need visas – check with the nearest Spanish consulate. Occasionally you may be asked to present return air-tickets and a certain amount of cash; if you cannot comply with such requirements on the spot you'll have to try another consulate.

Non-EC nationals who wish to stay longer than the alotted time span are advised that it is probably easiest to exit to France or Portugal for a few days, then re-enter Spain by a different border post to get a fresh stamp. Again, be sure that you're stamped going in both directions as it's not routine.

Obtaining a *permanencia* (residence permit) at the police station (in small towns) or *Servicio de Extranjeros* (Aliens' Bureau) in larger cities is likely to be of relatively little interest to the users of this guide.

BUDGETING

Even for outsiders (let alone residents) Spain is no longer a particularly inexpensive country; it is appreciably more costly for travellers than Portugal, Yugoslavia or Greece, though not (yet) quite as draining on the wallet as France or Italy. The peseta (abbreviated ptas in the plural) has lately been relatively stable at about 110 to the US dollar, 205 to the pound sterling, and so peseta prices will be quoted throughout the book. Accommodation, still often very reasonable by European standards, will be the least of your expenses. Count on 600 to 1200ptas minimum for an acceptable single, from 1100 to 1700ptas for a bare-bones double, with showers often an extra 100 or 200ptas. A *tortilla* (omelette), coffee and croissant breakfast at a stand-up bar will cost you about 250ptas, and a set-menu lunch or dinner will run between 500 and 900ptas depending on the town. On average you'll shell out about 700ptas on transport (ie a couple of hundred for city buses one day, 1600ptas for a long second-class train trip the next).

Totting it all up, you have a daily minimum budget of about 3000ptas for a solo traveller, slightly less per person as one of a pair. At the prevailing rates of exchange this means about US$800/£500 a month to stay alive, substantially more to actually live in some comfort, take the occasional luxury conveyance or buy souvenirs. In short, bring lots of the currency of your choice.

MONEY

Handling money is the one area of tourist service where modernisation still lags slightly behind. Spanish banks are open from Monday to Friday from 9 am to 2 pm and Saturday 9 am to 12 noon, but Saturday hours are not observed in summer. Service is generally the most inefficient, and foreign exchange transaction commissions the most outrageous, in all of western Europe. Specimens for many brands of travellers' cheques are often lacking, and in their absence banks will simply refuse to change yours. If you're not careful you could spend 40 mostly unproductive minutes in various queues, and have up to 10% skimmed off the total finally delivered.

Fortunately there are a few things you can do to minimise wear and tear on yourself and your wallet. The *Banco Central* is reasonably quick, has specimens for most brands of cheques, and may even amalgamate commissions if you change cash and cheques at the same time. European readers will find that Eurocheques, widely accepted, will cut through bank bureaucracy like a hot knife through butter, with costs roughly the same as for travellers' cheques.

Outside normal banking hours you have a few options: patronising *American Express* (with full service agencies in Madrid and Barcelona) or money exchange booths in the department chain store *El Corte Inglés*, where the commission charged is a set percentage rather than a minimum as at banks (handy for small amounts); or prevailing upon a travel agent to buy your foreign currency (cash only). The latter may grumble and tell you to use the bank, but will usually give in; their rates include any commission and the result is about the same as at the two specialist agencies cited. Finally, plastic money is widely honoured and a certain number of cash-dispensing machines that work with international credit cards, or European-issued cashpoint cards, are beginning to appear here and there.

In general, try to change enough money at a time to reduce the commission to an acceptable percentage of the total (as well as the fraction of your week waiting in line), though not so much as to attract the attentions of would-be thieves.

Your pesetas come in denominations of 1, 5, 10, 25, 50, 100, and 200 (coins), and 500, 1000, 2000, 5000, and 10,000 (bills). A sum of five pesetas is often referred to as a *duro* and prices can sometimes be quoted as such. One of the most durable slang terms for peseta(s) is *pela(s)*.

BANK HOLIDAYS

Watch out for the following public holidays, when nothing is likely to be open: 1 January; 6 January (*Día de los Tres Reyes* – Epiphany); Good Friday; Easter Sunday and Monday; 1 May (May Day); Corpus Christi (usually early June); 24 June (St John's, and thus the name-saint day of King Juan Carlos); 25 July (Feast of Santiago); 15 August (Assumption of the Virgin); 12 October (*Día de la Hispanidad*); 1 November (All Saints Day); 6 December (*Día de la Constitución*); 8 December (Immaculate Conception); and 25 December (Christmas Day).

GENERAL INFORMATION
Post

Post offices (*Correos*) are usually near the middle of town and open from Monday to Friday from 9 am to 2 pm and often again from 4 to 7 pm. In the larger cities the main branches tend to be open continuously on weekdays, on Saturdays and Sunday mornings, and also slightly later in the evening.

Outgoing mail is reasonably reliable, with items taking from three to six days to get to other EC countries, from six to 10 days to North America, and slightly longer to Oceania.

You can have your inbound mail sent to the poste restante department of any Spanish

post office; have your correspondents address it to you, with your surname in capitals and underlined, care of *Lista de Correos*. You'll need a passport to collect letters, and make sure that the clerk checks under your first and middle name (the latter is often mistaken in Hispanic countries for the surname).

The *American Express* branches in Madrid and Barcelona will hold mail for one month, and have special windows for pickup; if you don't carry their cheques or card there's a fee for each enquiry.

Telephones

Spanish phones work adequately and you can make overseas calls from either a phone booth, a phone (with a meter) in a bar, or a cabin in a *Telefónica* (phone company office – look for the blue and green 'T' logo). The latter two are particularly convenient if you don't have change since in those cases you pay after completing the call.

Booths take 5, 25, or 100-peseta coins; line them up in the inclined groove at the top, and they'll drop in one by one when your party answers. You'll need a good stack of 100s for international dialling; unused coins are returned.

Spanish provincial codes, and many overseas ones, are displayed in the call boxes. Always dial 07 to get onto international circuits, then the country code (1 for the USA/Canada, 44 for Britain, 61 for Australia, etc), next the area code (without any initial zeros), and finally the subscriber number.

Within Spain, you must precede the city code by dialling 9, and all phone numbers in this book are cited in that format. If you are attempting from overseas to reach any of the numbers given, omit the initial 9.

Electricity

Electric current in Spain conforms to continental European standard, ie 220-240V AC out of a double round-pin socket. Travellers from Britain, Oceania or North America will require the appropriate plug adapter and, in the latter case, a step-down transformer.

Time

Spain (including Mallorca) is one hour ahead of Greenwich Mean Time, six hours ahead of Eastern Standard Time, and nine hours behind the most densely populated areas of eastern Australia. Daylight saving is observed from the last week in March until the last week in September. At the very beginning of April and for most of October when observance of daylight saving does not match North America's, Spain is seven and five hours respectively, ahead of the eastern US.

Business Hours

As a general rule museums, churches, shops and tradespeople observe a siesta of at least two hours during the hottest part of the day. Exact schedules vary (and logically the siesta tends to be longer in the south) but average summer working hours are from 10 am to 1.30 pm and from 4.30 to 7.30 pm. In the cooler months these hours may extend a little from 9.30 am to 2 pm and 4 to 8 pm. Private and government offices, on the other hand, tend to stay open from 9 am to about 4 pm continuously.

Urban Spain lives by night, though even in country villages people tend to be out until past midnight. Party and club-goers don't go home until the small hours, and then struggle out to face the day sometime between 9.30 and 10.30 am no matter what their line of work.

Late July and August is a bad time to see anyone or do anything in the larger cities, which are essentially ghost-towns then – this is Spain's official vacation period and everybody who's anybody is out in the country (see the warning about this in Climate and Seasons).

The stereotype of lackadaisical Latin attitudes toward appointments is only partly borne out by the facts. Transport is likely to leave on the dot at the appointed hour, so don't dawdle in that respect. Punctuality in business appointments depends to a great degree on where you are, and on things like how gung-ho professional your contact is. By and large Spaniards consider that they work to live, not vice versa, and this, with the climate, inevitably conditions not just how prompt they are, but also how many hours out of the day that they'll be open for business.

ACCOMMODATION

Spain has an occasionally bewildering variety of places to stay, ranging from the exceedingly basic to the five-star palace. The first order of business is to master the hierarchical classification system which the local tourist boards use to grade lodgings.

Ungraded/graded budget lodging

Least elaborate and expensive, and often outside the official grading scheme, are *camas* (beds) places, sometimes designated *comidas y camas* (meals and beds). These are a traditional working men's institution and are probably on the way out, but the next notches up – *fondas* (indicated by a white 'F' on a rectangular blue sign), *casas de huéspedes* ('CH'), and *pensiones* ('P') – are likely to be around for some time yet. Except at the better *pensiones*, you won't get an attached bath or free hot water.

Comfortable to expensive lodging

Hostales and *hostal-residencias*, nominally more luxurious, can often be neither more costly nor have more amenities than the preceding categories, but as you begin to see stars (any rating of 'P' or above can show them) on the blue sign, expect markedly higher prices (and hopefully facilities to match). By the time multi-starred *hoteles* ('H') and *paradores* (usually minor historical monuments refurbished as inns) are reached you're talking honeymoon havens for high-salaried individuals.

Youth hostels

As far as institutional accommodation goes, youth hostels (*albergues juveniles*) are generally not a good bet; with some outstanding exceptions, they tend to be inconveniently located and occupied en masse by student groups during school vacations. They also offer minimal savings if there are two or more of you; two bunks cost barely less than the price of a standard *fonda* double. IYHA membership is often required, as are reservations; contact your local branch before leaving home.

Alpine shelters

Conversely, in most of the higher Spanish mountain ranges, but particularly in the Pyrenees, *refugios* (alpine shelters) provide service for all comers, generally on a first-come, first-serve basis. Depending on who runs them (see Spanish Mountaineering Organisations following), they can be wonderful or just barely adequate, cheap (from 300 to 400ptas a dormitory bunk) or pricey (from 800 to 900ptas). It is advisable, especially in July/August, to arrive by midafternoon to be sure of space, though you are usually not admitted to the sleeping quarters (numerous elevated mattresses laid side by side) until evening.

As a rule, packs and boots are not allowed at any time in the sleeping areas; they're put on shelves in the *comedor* (dining room), more convenient for off-loading food anyway. The staff will generally not permit you to leave rubbish – you carry it out with you – and even if they did it would just get tossed onto the hut's private litter pile, thus aggravating the existing problem.

If you are a member of any other European alpine club you are entitled to reciprocal privileges, ie a discount on bunk rates. Passports or other ID are generally held as security against the bill, settled on the morning of departure.

Again depending on the club administration, the *comedor* may be reasonably well equipped in terms of cooking for yourself, or you may actually be forbidden from preparing meals on the premises (the staff sometimes will heat your food up for a nominal charge). If you have a choice in the matter and desire an evening meal, let the warden know when you're checking in. Served-up meals tend to be expensive (800ptas as a rule) for what they are though you would have to be pretty hard up not to avail yourself of the bar menu, particularly a litre of wine, which can be very welcome after a day on the trail. The high mark-up reflects the effort and cost of carting food and drink in – often on the warden's back (though in some cases, by helicopter).

Monasteries

More curiously, you can sometimes stay in monasteries, which are either disestablished or have cells set aside for this purpose. These are mostly found in Galicia, Catalunya and Mallorca. None are specifically covered in this guide, but since some of the walks are routed close by, they are worth mentioning. Conditions are generally spartan but they can be very good value: 300 or 400ptas for a bunk alone, 1600ptas for a bed, breakfast and evening meal.

Camping

Spain has almost 400 official camping sites, and they're even detailed in an official *Guía de Campings*, available for a few hundred pesetas at most bookstores. Like the mountain refuges these sites vary considerably: at their worst noisy, crowded dustbowls barely fit for desert rats to bathe in; at best grassy, well-appointed plots where the amenities are tasteful and unobtrusive. A per-head as well as a per-tent fee is charged, both usually around 300ptas, so if you're alone the organised grounds are relatively expensive.

Camping outside of designated areas, most obviously in the mountains, is legal but with certain conditions. You're not permitted to camp 'in urban areas, areas prohibited for military or touristic reasons, or within one km of an official campground'. This especially means camping on a frequented beach, in front of hotels – where you would have to be pretty perverse to set up a tent. The only ambiguous situation in the mountains might arise when deciding how close to camp to an operating *refugio*. Wardens are generally fairly easy-going types, and are used to people pitching tents fairly close by because they're being careful with their finances or because (not unlikely in midsummer) the hut in question is full.

LOCAL CUISINE

Most Spanish bar and restaurant food is of the hearty rather than the elegant sort, but is certainly sufficient to keep you alive and healthy during town sojourns between hikes.

You can eat *tapas* (bar snacks) or *raciones* (larger portions of the same), but this tends to be expensive as a rule. A la carte items at restaurants and *comedores* of bars and lodgings may also be relatively costly, but there is almost always a *menú del día* or *menú de la casa* offered which, for a set price, allows you a choice of selected items. A *menú* generally consists of a starter course, main course, a *postre* (dessert), and a beverage, with bread included. Occasionally a la carte can be better value, but I have subsisted well on *menús* over the years and have only been denied the most expensive seafood.

Where there is no *menú* you may often find *platos combinados* (combination plates), which feature some sort of entree – a steak, sausage, piece of fish, bacon and eggs – garnished with a salad and some bread or potatoes.

The following lists have no pretentions to completeness, but are drawn up with an eye (and a tongue) for what is most nourishing for trekkers, most appetising, most commonly encountered, of best value, and most in accord with my own prejudices. Doubtless you will find your own favourites – bon apetit!

Breakfast & Snack Food

tortilla	omelette wedge
croissant	croissant
empanadas,	turnovers (last is
empanadillas,	Mallorquín term)
ensaimadas	
rehogada	Catalan pizza, topped with anchovies, sardines, sausage, vegetables, etc

Vegetable Dishes

garbanzos	chickpeas
lentejas	lentils
guisantes	peas
coliflor	cauliflower
berenjena	aubergine, eggplant
judías negras, rojas	black, red beans
judías blancas	white haricot beans
judías verdes	green (string, French) beans
pimientos	mild peppers
acelga	chard
champiñones	mushrooms
menestra or *panache de verduras*	vegetable medley
gazpacho	Andalucian tomato, cucumber, garlic soup (cold)

Meat & Meat-Based Specialties

lengua en salsa	tongue in sauce
pollo al ajillo	chicken chunks in garlic sauce
chuleta de cerdo	pork chop
callos	tripe fricassee
riñones al jerez	kidneys in sherry
hígado	liver
criadillas	testicles
potaje castellano	rich, potato-based thick soup
caldo gallego	similar to above, but with greens and ham hock
fabada asturiana	butter beans, blood sausage and ham
habas con jamón	lima beans with ham

Seafood

gallo	rex sole (better than *lenguado*, a bonier sole)
merluza	hake
calamares	squid
raya	ray, skate
congrio	shark
paella	classic Valencian dish of saffron rice, chicken, seafood
trucha (a la Navarra)	trout (stuffed with ham chunks)

Preparation Terms

a la plancha/parilla	grilled
a la Romana, rebozado	fried in batter
cocido	stew
escalope	medallion cut of meat, usually crumbed (breaded)
rehogado	baked
bocadillo	sandwich
caserío	home-style (as in 'house' wine, private reserve cheese, etc)

Dessert & Fruit

arroz con leche	rice pudding
natillas	custard
cuajada	undefinable, but like bland yoghurt; served with honey
flan	crème caramel
nata	whipped cream
melón con jamón	melon with ham
melocotón en almíbar	canned peaches
fresas, fresones	strawberries, and giant ones – world's best
chirimoyas	cherimoyas – cheap and good in Andalucía

Drinks

zumo	juice
horchata	refreshing milky summer drink of tiger nuts
sidra	hard cider – the Asturian national drink
café con leche	cappuccino with milk
café cortado	same, but less milk
carajillo	coffee spiked with liqueur or whisky
vino	wine; comes as
blanco	white
tinto	red
rosado, clarete, claro	rosé
jerez	sherry; comes as
fino	dry
amontillado	medium
oloroso	sweet
cerveza	beer; comes as
caña	glass on tap, or
botellín	bottle, both about 300ml and same price
caña doble	500ml glass of draught

SAFETY

Spain occasionally makes the tabloid headlines with lurid tales of travellers mugged or otherwise assaulted, but these incidents are almost totally confined to the charter-package *costas*. In the big cities, precautions as you'd take in London or Chicago are generally sufficient.

In the hills, problems are virtually unheard of, though common sense (as well as common courtesy) would dictate not strewing your belongings about too freely in alpine refuges. The only documented disappearances on my treks were once, when the refuge dog ate my ham which I'd left on a table, and later when a cow chewed up all of a companion's cigarettes, which he'd carelessly left overnight in his boots outside his tent! Cows – and wilder four-footed animals – are potential nuisances, and gear should always be made beast-proof before settling in for the night.

HEALTH

Insurance A travel insurance policy to cover theft, loss and medical problems is a wise idea. There are a wide variety of policies and your travel agent will have recommendations. The international student travel policies handled by STA or other student travel organisations are usually good value. Some policies offer lower and higher medical expenses options but the higher one is chiefly for countries like the US with extremely high medical costs. Check the small print:

1 Some policies specifically exclude 'dangerous activities' which can include scuba diving, motorcycling, even trekking. If these activities are on your agenda you don't want that sort of policy.

2 You may prefer a policy which pays doctors or hospitals direct rather than you having to pay now and claim later. If you have to claim later make sure you keep all documentation. Some policies ask you to call back (reverse charges) to a centre in your home country where an immediate assessment of your problem is made.

3 Check if the policy covers ambulances or an emergency flight home. If you have to stretch out you will need two seats and somebody has to pay for it!

Medical Kit A small, straightforward medical kit is a wise thing to carry. It could include the following:

1 Aspirin or panadol – for pain or fever
2 Antihistamine (such as Benadryl) – useful as a decongestant for colds; for allergies; to ease the itch from insect bites or stings; or to help prevent motion sickness
3 Antibiotics – useful if you're travelling well off the beaten track but it must be prescribed and you should carry the prescription with you
4 Kaolin preparation (Pepto-Bismol), Imodium or Lomotil – for stomach upsets
5 Rehydration mixture – for treatment of severe diarrhoea
6 Antiseptic, mercurochrome and antibiotic powder or similar 'dry' spray – for cuts and grazes
7 Calamine lotion – to ease irritation from bites or stings
8 Bandages and band-aids – for minor injuries
9 Scissors, tweezers and a thermometer – mercury thermometers are prohibited by airlines
10 Insect repellent, sun blocker, suntan lotion, chap stick and water purification tablets

MEDICAL PROBLEMS & TREATMENT

Potential medical problems can be broken down into several areas. First there are the

climatic and geographical considerations – problems caused by extremes of temperature, altitude or motion. Then there are diseases and illnesses caused by insanitation, insect bites or stings, animal or human contact. Simple cuts, bites or scratches can also cause problems.

Climatic & Geographical Considerations
Sunburn At high altitude you can get sunburnt surprisingly quickly even through cloud. A hat provides added protection and use zinc cream or some other barrier cream for your nose and lips. Calamine lotion is good for mild sunburn.

Prickly Heat Prickly heat is an itchy rash caused by excessive perspiration trapped under the skin. It usually strikes people who have just arrived in a hot climate whose pores have not yet opened sufficiently to cope with greater sweating. Keeping cool but bathing often, using a mild talcum powder or even by resorting to air conditioning may help until you acclimatise.

Heat Exhaustion Dehydration or salt deficiency can cause heat exhaustion. Take time to acclimatise to high temperatures and make sure you get sufficient liquids. Salt deficiency is characterised by fatigue, lethargy, headaches, giddiness and muscle cramps and in this case salt tablets may help. Vomiting or diarrhoea can deplete your liquid and salt levels. Anhidrotic heat exhaustion, caused by an inability to sweat, is quite rare and unlike the other forms of heat exhaustion is likely to strike people who have been in a hot climate for some time, rather than newcomers.

Cold Too much cold is just as dangerous as too much heat, particularly if it leads to hypothermia. If you are trekking at high altitudes be prepared for cold, wet or windy conditions even if you're just out walking or hitching.

Hypothermia occurs when the body loses heat faster than it can produce it and the core temperature of the body falls. It is surprisingly easy to progress from very cold to dangerously cold due to a combination of wind, wet clothing, fatigue and hunger, even if the air temperature is above freezing. It is best to dress in layers; silk, wool and some of the new man-made fibres are all good insulating materials. A hat is important as a lot of heat is lost through the head. A strong, waterproof outer layer is essential as keeping dry is vital. Carry basic supplies, including food containing simple sugars to generate heat quickly, and lots of fluid to drink.

Symptoms of hypothermia are exhaustion, numb skin (particularly toes and fingers), shivering, slurred speech, irrational or violent behaviour, lethargy, stumbling, dizzy spells, muscle cramps and violent bursts of energy. Irrationality may take the form of sufferers claiming they are warm and trying to take off their clothes.

To treat hypothermia first get out of the wind and/or rain, remove wet clothing and replace with dry, warm clothing. Drink hot liquids, not alcohol, and eat some high calorie, easily digestible food. This should be enough for the early stages of hypothermia but, if it has gone further, it may be necessary to place the victim in a warm sleeping bag and get in too. Do not rub the patient, place them near a fire, or remove wet clothes in the wind. If possible place in a warm bath.

Intestinal Troubles
Everybody seems to get stomach troubles at least once during a visit to Spain; this is probably due to unfamiliar or slightly-past-its-prime food rather than to the water, which is safe just about everywhere (except below pastures with grazing animals).

Cuts, Bites & Stings
Cuts & Scratches Skin punctures can easily become infected in hot climates and may be difficult to heal. Treat any cut with an anti-septic solution and mercurochrome. Where possible avoid bandages and band-aids which can keep wounds wet

Venomous snakes and scorpions exist in Spain, though I have never seen either; a much more probable encounter will be with

biting and stinging insects, which assume near-tropical proportions and viciousness in the Pyrenees. Your tent must have a bug screen, and you should apply bug repellent during the day, or you'll be pretty miserable around the clock.

Snake Bite To minimise your chances of being bitten always wear boots, socks and long trousers when walking through undergrowth where snakes may be present. Don't put your hands into holes and crevices and be careful when collecting firewood.

Snakes bites do not cause instantaneous death and antivenins are usually available. Keep the victim calm and still, wrap the bitten limb tightly, as you would for a sprained ankle, and then attach a splint to immobilise it. Then seek medical help, if possible with the dead snake for identification. Don't attempt to catch the snake if there is any remote possibility of being bitten again. Tourniquets and sucking out the poison are now comprehensively discredited.

Insect & Spider Bites & Stings Bee and wasp stings are usually painful rather than dangerous. Calamine lotion will give relief or ice packs will reduce the pain and swelling. There are some spiders with dangerous bites but antivenins are usually available. Scorpions stings are notoriously painful; they often shelter in shoes or clothing.

Alpine Common Sense & Assistance

Most hazards to health and well-being, while trekking in Spain have to do with being unprepared for what the elements may dish out. Heed the recommendations in the Equipment List, and conditions will never become dangerous, though they may be less than ideal for enjoying the hike. If an accident occurs near a refuge in the Pyrenees, the Picos de Europa or the Sierra de Gredos, virtually all of the mountain huts are equipped with two-way radios (*emisoras*) to summon rescue teams as necessary. If you intend to set out under less than stable skies, or if conditions ahead are otherwise uncertain, it is fairly common practice for the departure hut to radio the destination refuge with details concerning the number and estimated speed of the party.

Especially when hiking in areas without staffed shelters, you should obviously be very conservative with route decisions, and always trek within your limits. If a mishap occurs, help is likely to be delayed at least a day.

BOOKS

'OP'here means out of print – consult a major library or second-hand book store.

Ethnology, Sociology, Anthropology

Hooper, John. *The Spaniards*. (Penguin, London/New York, 1987.) A superb portrait of post-Franco Spain and the new generation of Spaniards, by a long-time British correspondent in Madrid. It focuses on housing, education, religion and public/private mores.

Pitt-Rivers, Julian. *People of the Sierra*. (University of Chicago Press, 1971; 2nd edition.) A classic study of a village in Andalucía.

Pritchett, V S. *The Spanish Temper*. (The Hogarth Press, London, 1984; reprint of earlier edition.) A national character analysis by the famous short-story writer, based on his experiences as a journalist in Madrid some decades ago.

General History & Political Science

Carr, Raymond. *Modern Spain, 1875-1980*. (Oxford University Press, Oxford/New York, 1981.) A very densely written monograph which explores the havoc resulting when liberal – and radical – ideas are imposed on an inherently conservative culture.

Carr, Raymond and Juan Pablo Fusi Aizpura. *Spain, Dictatorship to Democracy*. (Allen & Unwin, London/Boston, 1981.) An in-depth study of the last few chapters of the previous listing – ie the period most likely to affect contemporary visitors.

Elliot, John Huxtable. *Imperial Spain, 1469-1716*. (American Library (Meridian), New York, 1977; Penguin, London, 1970.) The best single-volume account of the country in the centuries immediately after unification.

Graham, Robert. *Spain: A Nation Comes of Age*. (St Martin's Press, New York, 1984.) Study of the evolution of the current pluralistic society from the confines of the Franco dictatorship.

The Civil War & Its Aftermath

Brenan, Gerald. *The Spanish Labyrinth, An Account of the Social and Political Background of the Spanish Civil War*. (Cambridge University Press, 1950; 2nd edition.) Exactly as the subtitle says: this is *not* a history of the 1936-39 war, but one of the best layperson's studies on Spanish rural society ever produced.

Fraser, Ronald. *Blood of Spain*. (Pantheon, New York, 1986; Allen Lane, London, 1986; 2nd edition.) This voluminous account of the civil war consists entirely of oral histories collected from participants of every political stripe.

Fraser, Ronald. *In Hiding*. (Pantheon, New York, 1972; OP.) A fascinating tale of a Republican mayor, one of several such individuals, hidden by his family for 30 years until the amnesty of 1969.

Gibson, Ian. *The Assassination of Federico García Lorca*. (Penguin, New York/ Penguin, 1983.) There's meticulous background and a description of events leading up to the execution of the poet near Granada, encompassing the forces which shaped Lorca, his adversaries and Spain of that era.

Orwell, George. *Homage to Catalonia*. (Harcourt Brace Jovanovich, San Diego/ Orlando, 1980; Penguin, London, 1969.) Political reportage at its best, the author chronicles the destructive infighting between Republican forces in Barcelona, and his own increasing disillusionment.

Thomas, Hugh. *The Spanish Civil War*. (Harper & Row, New York, 1977; Hamish Hamilton/Penguin, London, 1977; 2nd edition.) The classic 'straight' study.

Belles Lettres, Travelogues, Memoirs

Borrow, George. *The Bible in Spain*. (Century, London, 1985; David &

Charles, New York, 1986; reprint of the 1842 original.) Ostensibly this is the journal of an itinerant missionary in Spain but actually is, as the subtitle puts it, 'Journeys, Impressions, & Imprisonments of an Englishman', delivered with the mixture of preciousness and drollness that marked Victorian writing.

Brenan, Gerald. *The Face of Spain*. (Penguin, London, 1987.) In the same period that spawned *A Rose for Winter* (see following), Brenan and spouse travel through central and southern Spain, witnessing the moral and material fallout of Franco's first decade. It includes a moving account of their search for Lorca's grave.

Brenan, Gerald. *South From Granada* (Cambridge University Press, 1980.) Brenan chronicles life in the small village of Yegen in the Alpujarras during the 1920s, plus visits of various literati from the Bloomsbury Group.

Kazantzakis, Nikos. *Spain*. (Creative Arts, Berkeley, 1983.) Kazantzakis the journalist is always more accessible to non-Greeks than Kazantzakis the novelist; people were amazingly frank with him as he toured the country during the civil war.

Lee, Laurie. *As I Walked Out One Summer Morning*. (Penguin, London/New York, 1971; reprinted regularly.) A short but bittersweet account of a young man busking and walking his way from Vigo to Malaga, and of his gradual realisation of the forces moving the country toward civil war. Of the same genre as Patrick Leigh Fermor's better known trans-European rambles.

Lee, Laurie. *A Rose for Winter*. (Penguin, New York/London, 1971; reprinted regularly.) The author with his wife return to Andalucía 15 years later, and find the country still in an abject limbo just before the advent of massive American aid.

Lewis, Norman. *Voices of the Old Sea*. (Penguin, London/New York, 1985.) In the same period as Lee's second visit, two Catalonian fishing villages are insidiously but inexorably transformed into tourist playpens, as recounted semi-novelistically by Lewis' sly pen. It's just possibly the best book on this phenomenon which has irrevocably altered the Mediterranean.

Luard, Nicholas. *Andalucía*. (Century, London, 1985.) A good general survey of southern Spain, covering folklore and wildlife.

Macaulay, Rose. *The Fabled Shore*. (Oxford University Press, 1986; 2nd edition.) The Spanish littoral from Provence to the Portuguese Algarve is described. This was also written during the same era as the Lee and Lewis works.

Myhill, Henry. *The Spanish Pyrenees*. (Faber & Faber, London, 1966; OP.) This cultural, archaeological and geographical survey of the area provides good background, but isn't of much practical use to today's hiker.

Spanish Literature in Recent Translations

Barea, Arturo. *The Forging of a Rebel* (Trilogy: *The Forge, The Track, The Clash.*) (Fontana-Flamingo, London, 1984.) This absorbing autobiography begins with childhood, then chronicles a youth spent in the disastrous Spanish Moroccan war and culminates in the author's part in the civil war.

Pérez Galdós, Benito. *Torquemada*. (Columbia University Press, New York, 1986; André Deutsch, London, 1988.) A brilliant chronicle of a social-climbing moneylender in 19th-century Madrid, who resembles the notorious inquisitor in more than just surname.

Villalonga, Llorenç. *The Doll's Room*. (André Deutsch, London, 1988.) Like di Lampedusa's *The Leopard*, this is a masterful portrait of backwater nobility (in this case Mallorca's) in decline during the 1890s. The family chaplain is confessor and friend to free-thinking, free-loving Don Toni and witness to his foibles. Originally in Mallorquín by Mallorca's greatest novelist.

Natural History Field Guides

Grunfeld, Frederic V and Teresa Farino. *Wild Spain*. (Sheldrake Press, London, 1988.) Provides a fairly thorough cataloguing of

Spain's more isolated regions, with good descriptions of most salient wildlife to be seen, but beware of the spotty practical details and walking instructions.

Peterson, Roger T, et al. *Field Guide to the Birds of Britain and Europe*. (Collins, London, 1983.)

Polunin, Oleg and Anthony Huxley. *Flowers of the Mediterranean*. (Hogarth, London, 1987; Salem House, Boston, 1987.) This good all-round guide is by no means exhaustive, covering only the most common low-altitude species.

Polunin, Oleg, and B E Smythies. *Flowers of South-West Europe, A Field Guide*. (Oxford University Press, 1988.)

Taylor, A W. *Wild Flowers of Spain and Portugal*. (Chatto & Windus, London, 1972.) OP, but probably worth the effort to find.

Taylor, A W. *Wild Flowers of the Pyrenees*. (Chatto & Windus, London, 1972; OP.)

General Guidebooks

Ellingham, Mark, et al *The Rough/Real Guide to Spain*. (Harrap-Columbus, London, 1989; Prentice Hall, New York, 1989; 3rd edition.) Despite the British title, a guide for independent travellers to all but luxury budget levels.

Regional Hiking Guides

While the author feels that this book provides the best single-volume coverage of mainland Spain and Mallorca available, there is no doubt that certain narrowly focused guides are more detailed for their backyards.

Collomb, Robin. *Gredos Mountains and Sierra Nevada*. (West Col, Reading, 1987.) This starkly produced guide for trekkers and climbers has very good coverage of Gredos, but a very poor write-up on the Sierra – nothing on the Alpujarras and is rather desperately fleshed out with accounts of Granada city.

Crespi-Green, Valerie. *Landscapes of Mallorca*. (Sunflower Books, London, 1987; Hunter, Edison (NJ), 1987; 2nd edition.) One of the series of 'car tours/walks/picnic' volumes aimed at the charter-package market. It's meticulously produced, but the walking routes are decidedly on the timid side.

Guía de Sóller. A quadrilingual guide produced by Sóller tourist office and sold there and in the bookstore, gives dead accurate and sensible directions for a dozen popular hikes.

Heinrich, Herbert. *Twelve Classic Hikes Through Mallorca*. (Editorial Moll, Palma, 1987.) There's good taste in the walk selection, and a thorough glossary of Mallorquín sure to endear you to the country folk – but the bizarre prose perhaps lost something in translation from the German.

Palmer, June. *Walking in Mallorca*. (Cicerone, Milnthorpe, 1987.) This includes much more hard-core mountaineering and ridge-walking than the preceding volumes – occasionally directing you up razor-sharp hogbacks and through gorse; not everyone's thing.

Reynolds, Kev. *Walks and Climbs in the Pyrenees*. (Cicerone, Milnthorpe, 1987; 2nd edition.) The uneven, confusingly organised text hops back and forth across the Franco-Spanish frontier. Decent maps and reliable information perhaps cater more for climbers than for trekkers.

Somoano, Juan Luis and Erik Perez. *50 Excursiones Selectes de la Montaña Asturiana*. (The authors, Cangas de Onís, 1989; 3rd edition.) A good choice of walks short and long, in easy-to-read Spanish; less than half the book is devoted to the Picos de Europa, so there's scope for a lot more hiking in Asturias.

SPANISH MOUNTAINEERING ORGANISATIONS & INFORMATION SOURCES

The largest alpine interest club in the country is the *Federación Español de Montañismo* (FEM) which has a loose affiliate in Catalunya, the *Federació de Entitats Excursionistes de Catalunya* (FEEC). There are in addition the *Unió Excursionista de Catalunya* (UEC) and the *Centre Excursionista de Catalunya* (CEC). These abbreviations will be used throughout the text.

The main branch of the FEM is at Calle Apodaca 16, Madrid (metro Tribunal; tel (91) 448-0724). Though open between 8 and 10 pm most days, they are basically a climbing school and organise outings for locals. The office does, however, have a notice board listing used mountaineering equipment for sale. Other branches of the FEM are found in Granada, Valencia, Zaragoza, Palencia, León, Torrelavega (near Santander), Oviedo, Vigo and Beasaín (Guipúzcoa).

The FEEC's headquarters are at Ramblas 61, 1st floor, Barcelona (tel (93) 302-6416); the UEC have an office at Gran Via de les Corts Catalans 580, Barcelona 08011 (no phone); and the CEC can be reached at Paradís 10, Barcelona 08002 (tel (93) 315 2311).

In all cases your most likely contact with the various clubs will be through the mountain refuges which they administer, but it's also well worth keeping an eye out for the different mountaineering journals which they publish. *Desnivel*, the FEM publication, appears in Spanish, but the FEEC bimonthly *Vertex* and the CEC monthly *Muntanya* are, not surprisingly, in Catalan. Still, as discussed previously in Regional Ethnicity & Languages, it's not hard to pick up the gist of Catalan texts with a reading knowledge of Spanish or French.

In any given issue there are likely to be one or two foreign destination reports and a piece each on nordic skiing and rock-climbing, but many local walks will be detailed (especially in the Catalan magazines). New Spanish, French and Catalan walkers' and climbers' guidebooks are periodically reviewed, and the advertisements for new lines of Spanish mountaineering equipment, as well as their retail outlets, are also of interest.

Most staffed refuges in Catalunya have stacks of current and back issues for both *Vertex* and *Muntanya*; copies of *Desnivel* are most easily picked up in Madrid at *Librería Deportiva*, Calle de la Paz 4 (near Plaza Mayor; tel (91) 521-3868), or at *Tienda Verde* (see address in Maps for Hiking following).

MAPS FOR HIKING

Cartographic riches await the hiker in Spain.

Any area worth walking in has at least two coverages: one by a private publisher, one by the military mapping service. Often there are two non-governmental endeavours, sometimes as many as three.

Private Publications

The most widely distributed of the popular press publications, though not always the best, are the 50-plus *Guías Cartográficas* issued by Editorial Alpina. These are slender (around 32 pages), red or brown covered pamphlets sold for from 275 to 400ptas, with fold-out, four-colour topographical maps with scales varying from 1:25,000 to 1:50,000. There are mistakes on each one, about which everybody grumbles continually: routes tend to be on the wrong side of watercourses, suggesting a consistent problem with overlay registry, and hut locations are schematic rather than exact. But contours and villages – the most vital points – are shown adequately and these products are certainly a vast improvement over nothing at all. The guidelet texts vary from the commendable to the inane, but in any case fourth-year proficiency in Spanish is required to read them. The series offers reasonably thorough coverage of the Spanish Pyrenees, the Catalan coasts, the Picos de Europa, and the *sierras* of Gredos and Guadarrama. Unfortunately their list of titles has not yet been extended to massifs or areas in southern Spain such as the Sierra Nevada, and occasionally there are better alternatives.

Governmental Mapping

Where no Editorial Alpina or other private offerings exist, you must rely on topographical maps prepared by the *Servicio Geográfico del Ejército* (SGE), referred to on different sheets as the *Mapa Militar de España* or the *Cartografía Militar de España*. A complete series for the entire country exists at 1:50,000; as yet very little of the new 1:25,000 project is available. The SGE publications have, incidentally, almost totally superseded the older and now obsolete IGN (*Instituto Geográfico Nacional*) quads.

While some sheets are recent and excellent, many others are from 10 to 50 years old (as in most other countries with a geological survey program), fail to show all trails or recently built roads or dams, and are often of indifferent legibility. The maps also tend to be frustratingly aligned, necessitating purchase of many quads to gazette a single hike; with a per item price (though fortunately not weight) similar to the Editorial Alpina products, this adds up quickly. Accordingly, the pertinent SGE pages will only be listed under the map recommendations for each hike if there are no alternatives. A new grid numbering system for SGE maps was recently introduced; the new number is cited first, with the old figure in brackets, just as they appear on the maps (eg 38-25 (643)).

Small-Scale Overview Maps

For a general, journey-planning map of Spain, the best are either that published by Editorial Almax in Madrid, at a scale of 1:600,000 (available only in Spain but with a comprehensive index for every village of more than a few dozen people), or the 1:800,000 fold-out produced by RV (*Reise und Verkehrsverlag*) in Germany. These are packaged and distributed by Roger Lascelles in the UK (red cover) and by Plaza and Janés in Spain (in a grey cover with blue trim). RV also issues a half-dozen regional maps – north-western Spain, Pyrenees and Costa Brava including Mallorca, central Spain, the Levante, Andalucía, and Galicia with Portugal – at a scale of 1:300,000.

Map Retailers

Some or all of the SGE, Editorial Alpina and RV/Plaza and Janés publications are available at each of the following stores. It will, of course, be less expensive to pick up the Spanish products in Madrid or Barcelona, but if you're travelling directly to your chosen walking region, thus avoiding the big cities, it's wise to pick up what you need beforehand as you cannot always rely on finding maps in the provinces. In or near major mountain resorts many book, stationery or outdoor shops do tend to carry the Editorial Alpina line for neighbouring areas, and often the SGE quads as well; away from these communities, however, you may find yourself in for a long trudge out to the nearest office of the military mapping service.

La Tienda Verde, Calle Maudes 38, Madrid 28003 (tel (91)233-6454) carries everything discussed above and much more; also compasses and altimeters (see note following). It has 10 years of experience.

Llibreria Quera, Petritxol 2, Barcelona 08003 (tel (93) 318-0743) is the oldest map and walking-guide store in the country, with similar stock to that of *Tienda Verde*.

Libros Años Luz, Francisco de Ricci 8, Madrid 28015 (tel (91) 243-0192) has no hiking maps but certainly carries the small-scale ones and is the best general travel-guide store in Spain. If you're browsing through someone else's copy of this book, for instance, and want your own, they will very likely stock it.

Stanford's Map Centre, 12-14 Long Acre, London WC2E 9LP, UK (tel 01-836 1321) is the largest map and guide store in the world, with the pick of the SGE, Alpina and other publications. They also prepare a series of leaflets numbered from one to six describing exactly which maps and books they sell for each region of Spain.

McCarta Ltd., 122 King's Cross Rd, London WC1X 9DS, UK (tel 01-278 8278) is useful for filling any gaps in *Stanford's* holdings, but is unlikely to have anything unique.

Pacific Travellers Supply, 529 State St, Santa Barbara, CA 93101, USA (tel (805) 963-4438) carries the small-scale general maps, some of the Almax line, and 1:200,000 SGE quads only.

All of these establishments conduct mail-order business.

A Note on Nomenclature

Some maps from the Franco era, or those published by right-wing entities, are still in circulation and these invariably will give Castilian renditions and terminology for toponyms. In the course of the regional autonomy movement since the dissolution of the dictatorship, most place names have reverted to their vernacular version, both in spoken use and printed material. So do not be alarmed if you see variant spellings, eg Astos/Estos,Mulleres/Moliers, Urdiceta/Ordiceta, etc; they refer to the same spot. My policy has been to use the most prevalent term (almost always the regional language or dialect), with the alias in brackets immedi-

ately following. A geographical terms glossary for several languages/dialects, helpful for interpreting maps, is included in the language section of Facts About the Country.

ORIENTATION & TRAIL CONVENTIONS

Spanish trails, at least the ones I have chosen to focus on, are usually quite distinct, or marked, or occasionally both. Thus agonising over a choice of routes, a common experience in other countries, is not as a rule necessary, especially not in Catalunya.

With a large-scale map, compass, and altimeter (see Locally Available Hiking Equipment), it should be possible to pinpoint your location to within a few hundred horizontal metres. The magnetic declination in Spain varies from 3° to 5° west of sidereal (true) north and is given exactly on the margin of all of the SGE maps (but not on the Alpina products). For the purposes of this book, magnetic north will be treated as true north.

While many Spanish trails are indeed marked, perversely, they may not be on the rare occasions when they are actually needed! Blazes and waymarks used vary

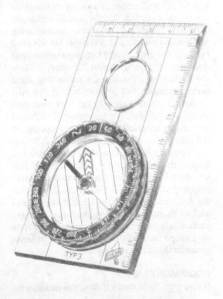

from simple paint splashes on rocks or trees to the elaborate red and white stripes or rectangles indicating long-distance trails (*gran recorrido* in Castilian, *gran recurrgat* in Catalan) in the Pyrenees and Catalunya. You will also occasionally see yellow and white stripes in Catalunya, which indicate *petit recurrgat* (short-haul) paths, meant for completion in a single day, as opposed to the overnight treks along the red and white routes.

The stripe blazes have some variations with special meanings. Bent into an L-shape, they indicate a turn left or right; a pair of them crisscrossed signals a wrong turn — do not enter.

A couple of other devices are common. At the base of passes and other strategic locales in the Pyrenees, you will probably notice four-metre-high, multicoloured 'barber's poles'. These are probably intended for nordic skiers, since they're found where winter snow pack is likely to be heaviest, but because of their high visibility summer hikers should also find them extremely useful.

Another marker found throughout Spain, and which will drive you crazy unless you know its meaning, is the small rectangle divided equally and lengthwise into a black and a white triangle. This is a symbol for *coto privado de caza* (private hunting reserve) but does not necessarily mean 'no entry'. They are indirectly helpful in the sense that their presence means that people, hunting or otherwise, do come this way on foot, and that you're probably still on some sort of path and not lost in an utterly godforsaken corner of the hills.

Cairns are built and widely understood in Spain, though more so in the north. The standard Castilian for one is *mojón* (plural *mojones*), the Catalan is *fita* (plural *fites*), and the Asturian is *jito* or *hito*. Cherish them, and add to them if you can spare the energy; particularly in the misty Pyrenees and Picos de Europa they might save a life or at least considerable unpleasantness.

EQUIPMENT LIST

If you were to do every trek in this guide, you would find it advisable to carry all of the following items. Most of them will come in handy even for short hikes on Mallorca. If you need to acquire, or replace, certain articles while in Spain, you'll find a discussion of Spanish solutions in the next section, Locally Available Hiking Equipment, and a glossary of their names in the language section.

Clothing

2 pairs lightweight, loose cotton pants
1 pair heavier-duty pants for high-altitude use (corduroy, wool, part synthetic, etc)
1 pair shorts or cut-offs
1 warm-weather hat/cap, brimmed all around, reflective colour
1 long-sleeved cotton turtleneck top, sweatshirt, or similar
1 shell windbreaker, warm-up jacket, wool-lined water-resistant coat, or Gore Tex product

The last four items, used in layers as you choose, should protect you in most conditions encountered from late June to early

September below 2700 metres. However, outside these months and/or at higher elevations, add the next five articles:

1 down or fibre-fill parka
1 pair gloves, lined and waterproof
1 pair long underwear
1 pair gaiters
1 hat/cap, wool or otherwise, to extend down over ears

Footwear

socks – assortment of cotton/synthetic (85%/15% – obtainable in North America at most backpacking or sporting goods stores (difficult to find in the UK), polypropylene/natural fibre (various formulas), and wool (90 to 100%) pairs to handle all conditions

hiking boots – 1 pair medium-duty or better, leather upper, over-the-ankle, Vibram or equivalent sole. Do NOT be seduced into buying newfangled synthetic-upper boots – they provide poor ankle support, are steamy in hot weather, and let in water like a sieve in wet conditions. If you are North American and don't already own a pair, wait until arriving in Britain or Spain, where choices and prices of quality leather boots are far better.

kick-around shoes – these can be anything you want – trainers, Rockports, Hush-puppies, lightweight 'walking' shoes – for evenings at camp and strolling through town

leather conditioner – natural oil or wax-based preferable to silicone formulas

Camping Gear

Backpack Your backpack should have a minimum capacity of 60 litres (3750 cubic inches), and be designed to effectively carry up to 18 kg on long treks.

I threw away my external frame pack in favour of internal frame models some years ago. While I intend to stick with my choice, with its numerous advantages (easier loading on buses, convertibility to 'suitcase' guise, lack of metal parts to break/bend), I readily admit that I could carry heavy loads more efficiently with the old-style designs, and that I sometimes miss the convenience of rigid struts on which to hang daypack, etc. Any pack purchased must have slit-sockets from which to suspend foam pad, tent, sleeping bag, etc.

Tent Because of the unpredictability of the weather and popularity of the alpine refuges

in the Spanish mountains, a tent is mandatory for all treks in Spain except on Mallorca and in low-altitude Andalucía. This is one item not to scrimp on; as a minimum bring a free-standing (ie dome design) of rip-stop nylon with a securely mounting rainfly. Cheapo models from military surplus or similar outlets which must be tied to trees (usually absent at trekking altitudes) are not going to cut it. Bear in mind that your tent will possibly have to endure a howling storm or two; after one such episode at Vega Urriello in the Picos de Europa, it was very obvious from the number of collapsed tents who had paid attention to quality and who hadn't.

Other recommended camping gear includes:

daypack – sufficient to carry snacks, map, extra clothes, water container, toilet paper, sunglasses, etc

camera belt pack – several companies make serviceable carriers for up to two bodies and most lenses; will pay for itself within a month in terms of falls cushioned and repairs thus avoided

long-handled ice axe or walking stick – The former is suggested for many passes and dicey sections in the hike write-ups. To a certain extent a 'real' walking stick is more versatile, preventing many a fall on slippery scree slopes, and can effectively substitute for an axe. Some folks use ski poles, some high-tech items from speciality stores, but you can improvise in the Pyrenees, where below treeline (particularly in the Cardós/Ferrera valleys) there is usually suitable birch, poplar, or beech deadfall.

ground pad – medium density, blue foam, or Therma-Rest types seem to work best

sleeping bag – three-season, down or fibre-fill according to taste

poncho/cagoule – large enough (eg 250 cm x 150 cm) to fit over you *and* your pack, and perhaps double as a groundcloth

campstove – should be a butane-burning one; see discussion in next section

mess kit – steel sets are non-toxic, as opposed to aluminium ones, but food, especially eggs, sticks badly; in either case carry cooking oil with you in a small (around 50ml) plastic bottle

cutlery – in addition to the obvious, wide wooden tongue depressors make excellent impromptu spatulas

egg case – for six eggs

water container – see extensive discussion in the Locally Available Hiking Equipment section following for more details

Odds & Ends

nylon stuffsacks – assorted sizes with drawstrings

plastic bags – especially flat ones large enough to protect maps

sunglasses – again, don't scrimp

compass – essential, even if you weren't trying to follow this book's directions

altimeter – another near-essential; see the discussion in the next section

compact flashlight – AA batteries are common, bulbs perhaps less so; Tekna spares will be easier to find, say, than Mini Maglite items, and something like an Eveready Durabeam will be easiest to maintain

candle lantern – great morale booster after dark, saves flashlight batteries. Buy a model that takes standard candles.

camp mirror – for looking like the folks in the campstove catalogues, and possibly signalling

portable clothesline – these can be bought as such, or improvise with parachute cord and clips

Nalgene or polyurethane bottles – assorted sizes: large for storing laundry powder, medium for mixing dry milk

tape – strong, lightweight, translucent product such as Micropore, in addition to securing gauze pads, is unsurpassed for mending maps, book bindings and torn paper money

first-aid kit – at a minimum, should contain an elastic bandage to wrap sprains; band-aids and gauze for minor abrasions; topical antibiotic/antiseptic; itch-suppressant ointment/lotion to keep you from scratching bug bites

insect repellent – a preventative for the last-mentioned problem

lip balm – good for low-humidity areas

sunblock – sunscreen; 'Bullfrog', zinc oxide, or similar is an absolute necessity with factor 15 as a minimum

moleskin – old boots, not to mention new ones, will find fresh spots to irritate at unpredictable moments

cuticle scissors, curved blade – used in tandem with the blunt end of a sewing needle, deals effectively with ingrown big toenails

dental floss – for Spanish *chorizo* stuck between molars, if you're not already a regular user

sewing kit – assorted needle sizes, thread gauges and patching materials, for emergency repair to luggage or clothes

Swiss Army or similar pocketknife – invaluable; I have used every attachment on mine, several times

timepiece with alarm (loud) – if not a wrist watch, then a little quartz clock running on an AA battery

pocket or wallet calendar – very easy to lose track of days in the hills (unless that's intended ...)

moneybelt – in the mountains at least, more for convenience than safety; mine stays in my pack unless I'm overnighting in a hut

photo film – E-6 type is widely available in Spain, but somewhat expensive. Processing, however, is good and reasonably priced.

waterproof broad-tipped marker – for labelling rolls of film and addressing large envelopes at the post office

Last, but not least, bring spares and replacements for everything that could conceivably be impossible or tedious to find overseas and doesn't take up much pack space. Examples which come to mind: eyeglasses (or prescription anyway), contact lenses, bootlaces, widgets for backpack, photocopy of front page of your passport, special medications or cosmetics, oddball watch batteries, spring for scissors on a pocketknife, flashlight bulbs, etc.

LOCALLY AVAILABLE HIKING EQUIPMENT

Were you to decide in the middle of a conventional vacation in Spain that you wanted to go trekking, or (God forbid) should you lose or have stolen any or all of your hiking gear, you could be in far worse countries from the point of view of (re)outfitting yourself. The Spanish mountaineering equipment industry is alive and growing, and the quality available for the price is occasionally unbeatable in the rest of Europe.

Backpacks

You would be at some disadvantage only concerning backpacks; the primary brands seem to be *Altus* and *Serval*, whose design and standard of manufacturing are not quite up to the state of the art in the USA and Britain.

Boots

Footwear, on the other hand, is excellent; the main firms manufacture semi-rigid, general-purpose, all-leather boots suitable for crampons are *Kamet* (Madrid) and *Boreal* (Valencia). You can score a more than adequate pair for something between 7000 and 11,000ptas, which compares very well with British and especially North American prices. *Kelme* makes good replacement insole pads for about 300ptas.

Crampons & Axes

Speaking of crampons, you can get serviceable strap-around models manufactured by the Catalan outfit *Faders* for somewhere between 6000 and 8000ptas; the same people make ice axes at roughly the same price. Alternatively you can shell out up to 10,000ptas for fancy Italian models of either. If you're short of cash, a fair quantity of off-brand or second-hand crampons and axes sell for a third less than the above figures.

Fluid Containers

Water and beverage carriers are even better. After many years spent in Turkey and Greece on what has amounted to a pilgrimage in search of this secular grail, I think I've found the ideal combination here.

For water I use porcelain-lined aluminium bottles with a spring-loaded, leak-proof cap; the most common brand is *Laken*, and one-litre models (there are also half, one and a half, and two-litre specimens) can be found for as little as 1000ptas. Their only drawback seems to be that they're fairly fragile – avoid banging them against rocks, as the resulting dents can harm the porcelain lining and defeat its purpose.

For wine (yes) I have found that genuine, non-plastic *bota* flasks manufactured in the Basque country are ideal. These come in a wide range of capacities, cured or uncured, from one-half to two litres, in quarter-litre steps. One good workshop in Vitoria is at Calle Pintorería 18, though there are certainly others. Whatever you do, avoid the silly ones with plastic lining, tassels, and 'Pamplona' logos – generally junk. For a decent one-litre *bota* expect to pay about 1700ptas.

If you look after your *bota* properly, they will last long enough to make the initial expense seem trivial, so some words on their care and feeding seem in order. When full or nearly so, their storage position is immaterial (though upright seems logical). Between uses, however, they should be stored on their side but rotated from time to time, with enough wine inside to keep it moist. When the time comes to refill it, massage your *bota* to insure the proper redistribution of the resin which is applied on the inner surfaces at 'birth' to make it impermeable. If you don't, and/or if you leave it upright and empty, the resin will collect in one spot (ie the bottom) and the seams will begin to leak.

Stoves

Butane-burning stoves are widely sold in Spain, as this is the only fuel readily available. The *Bleuet 206* is the most common portable model, and the 190-ml cartridges for them (*cartuchas*, '*bombonas*', or just plain '*Camping Gaz*', almost always *Cointra* brand) are sold in hardware stores (*ferreterías*) and household appliance outlets as well as at outdoor and camping retailers. Butane refills are not, unfortunately, as widespread as they might be; often only one store

for dozens of km around stocks them, and invariably they have 'just run out' or 'the shipment was supposed to come yesterday'. Moral: always carry at least a spare more than you think you'll need. In the hike descriptions I have made an effort to note verified outlets for the cartridges.

Altimeters

If you've ever wanted an altimeter, especially a metric one, then this is your chance – Spain is one of the best countries in the world to find one. For obscure reasons they, along with compasses, are often sold in *ópticas* (opticians) as well as outdoor shops. Prices range from 5000 to 14,000ptas; at the lower end of the scale you can expect something perfectly adequate, perhaps imported from the Far East by way of Italy, with 50-metre altitude increments. If money is no object, you can buy a very nice toy indeed, super-sensitive and calibrated to five or ten-metre gauge intervals. Being miniature barometers, they also double as weather-prediction devices and you will have some advance warning before all hell breaks loose in a storm. I honestly don't know how I've coped without one for all these years.

Pocketknives

Spain is also a good place to purchase a pocketknife. There's a local brand, *Aitor*, which is modelled on the *Victorinox/Swiss*

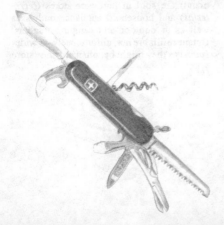

Army line and costs about two-thirds as much. Both makes are commonly available in novelty/leather/briefcase shops, as well as at the more obvious *cuchillerías* (knife and scissor stores). Those are also where you'd go to have blades sharpened or scissor springs (the most commonly failing part) replaced.

Backpackers' Stores

In an emergency you could always try your luck at replacing gear at a *tienda de deportes* (sporting goods store) or at an *armería* (hunter's supply), the latter stocking water bottles and knives, but if you have the choice head for a proper backpacking/skiing store (*tienda de campaña*). The directory below is confined to Madrid and Barcelona; worthy establishments in the provinces are detailed under the hike write-ups closest to them. All listings are meant to be suggestions only, and are not necessarily exhaustive nor do they constitute an endorsement. I would appreciate hearing of any new finds for future editions.

Madrid

Legazpi, Ribera de Curtidores 8, the Rastro (tel (91) 227-0437)

Gonza Sport, Ribera de Curtidores 10, the Rastro (tel (91) 227-5748)

(metro Tirso de Molina for both these)

Koala, Amor de Dios 11, metro Antón Martín (tel (91) 429-9189)

La Tienda, Corredera Baja de San Pablo 10, metro Callao, north of the Gran Vía

Mont Camp Sport, António López 156, across the Manzanares River from metro Legazpi

Barcelona

Pedra-Neu, Brasil 48 (Cinturó de Ronda/Avenguda Madrid), metro Badal (tel (93) 330-2774)

Sanjust, Canuda 6 (tel (93) 302-3695)

Campamá, Urgel 95 bis (tel (93) 253-5001)

Esports Lluch, Hipolit Lázaro 34

Entensa, SA, on Calle Entensa

La Tenda, corner Pau Claris and Conseil de Cent (off Via Laetana)

FOOD FOR THE TRAIL

Unfortunately the availability of lightweight, non-perishable trail food in Spain is limited, and the quality of what exists is not up to that of the Spanish landscape, maps or trails themselves. Spaniards rely heavily on fresh and canned items when out in the woods, the cans becoming all too evident after the fact (see An Unnatural History of the Countryside).

Given the interest in the outdoors and trekking, it seems incredible that no local entrepreneurs have introduced a line of dehydrated or concentrated foodstuffs; anyone who does will not only find a ready, captive market, but will earn my undying gratitude and possibly reduce the enormous wilderness trash-heaps.

In the meantime, with a little imagination much is still possible; for example, a small can of clams and some instant mashed potato as thickener/extender added to a pot of cream of mushroom envelope-soup results in chowder.

Grocery shopping hours are nominally from 10 am to 2 pm and from 6 to 9 pm, with most stores shut Saturday afternoon and all day Sunday. However '10' effectively means '10.30', so if you want a reasonable start on the day, always get your supplies the night before!

As a rule, food suitable for walkers is easier to obtain in the more industrialised part of Spain (ie from Madrid north), where mountaineering as a leisure activity is more established. Wherever you're off to in Spain it's worth stuffing your pack in Madrid or Barcelona, to save time and frustration in trailhead towns, particularly in Andalucía. You are well advised to hoard items like powdered milk, dried vegetables, muesli, or whole-grain bread whenever you see them, carrying them about cheerfully until needed. In Madrid a good one-stop, ordinary grocery with a large stock of foodstuffs suitable for hikers is at the corner of Calle de la Palma and Corredera Alta de San Pablo in the Malasaña district (metro Tribunal).

If you're in despair about the prevailing fetish for cans and canned goods, ask to be directed to an *almacén de alimentos naturales/regimen* (health/diet food store) where you will always be able to find at least muesli, oat flakes, dark bread, and dry fruits and nuts, in bulk or lightly wrapped. Many such shops have a tell-tale sign out in front promoting *Santiveri* products, herbal and health supplements packaged by a Catalan company.

In the following lists, a brand may be given if the product is unique in some respect or if it will help the shopkeeper identify it; this does not imply an endorsement.

Dehydrated/Powdered Items

té – tea; imported English, also *de hierbas* (herbal)

café – instant coffee tends to be Nescafé, in small cans or more convenient individual sachets for about 11ptas each

chocolate a la taza or *tazón* – drinking cocoa, which in Spain resembles molten pudding since it's mixed with sweetened flour

azúcar – sugar, sold almost always by the kilo; very difficult to find little packets – when available these tend to be displayed next to the Nescafe sachets

leche en polvo – powdered milk, almost all of it manufactured in Asturias and Cantábria; *El Buen Pastor* (in a cardboard box) and one other foil-wrapped brand are the most effectively packaged, in a variety of sizes. *La Lechera* (Nestle) comes in big, heavy round tins making 2½ litres. The same people make a 170 gm tube of condensed, oversweetened stuff, which is expensive and only mixes up to half a litre.

papillas – baby pablum; if you're desperate, *Riera Marsa* makes 170 gm boxes of *crema de arroz*, 6 *cereales*, *harina tostada*, *trigo con miel*, and other scrumptious flavors to bring out the infantile in you if you can't get oatmeal (see following).

puré de patatas – instant mashed potatoes

sopa en sobres – envelope soup; useful flavours include (*Knorr* brand) *guisantes con jamón* (peas and ham), *de verduras* (vegetable), *pollo con pasta* (chicken noodle), *bullabesa* (bouillabaisse), and '*casera*' packs ('homestyle' – heartier but more expensive); or (*Maggi* brand) *de once verduras* (11-vegetable) and *champiñones* (cream of mushroom)

juliana de verduras – dried, grated vegetables, found only in fancy delis; *Trevijano*, based in Logroño, is one brand.

Flanin (trademark) – instant pudding mix in small, 32 gm envelopes

natillas – quick-setting custard, *Royal* brand; read label carefully to make sure that only milk, and no egg is required, and that no cooking ('*sin cocción*') is necessary

Staples

copos de avena – oat flakes, meant to be cooked but in an emergency could be eaten raw; besides the health-food lines, *Kellogs* makes a 350 gm pack *muesli* – granola to North Americans; available in boxes or plastic bags at both health stores and some ordinary groceries

muesli crujiente – puffed wheat, super-lightweight

arroz – available only in one kg and 500 gm packages; the smaller may be *SOS* brand, a roundish, short-grain variety that's quick-cooking (5 to 10 minutes)

pasta – noodles in various shapes and flavours, including spinach-egg (in delis) and tortellini (expensive, but worth it)

lentejas – lentils, in plastic wrap or cardboard box

judías, garbanzos – white beans and chickpeas are available but need to be soaked, and still take forever to cook, sucking up valuable fuel

Semi-Perishable Items

pan integral – whole-grain bread; rare except in Catalunya, but keeps well

embutido – generic term for any cured sausage

salchichón – salami; tends to be greasy

longaniza – less fatty than above, better value

Any of the above designated *caserío*, *de montaña*, or *cuadrada* tend to be very dry, long-keeping, and a better deal.

jamón serrano – cured ham; lowest fat content, most appetising, and best value (despite a per-kilo price of between 1200 and 1800ptas) of the 'room temperature' meats

lomo – smoked pork loin; also a good sandwich filler

huevos – eggs

queso – cheese: comes as *fundido* (processed spread wedges); imported, wax-sealed balls (eg gouda with black pepper or *fines herbes*), good keepers at a good price at about 350ptas for a half-kilo; *manchego*, a hard cheese of mixed (sheep/goat) milk; and (best if you can find it) *ovejuno*, pure sheep cheese from León and Palencia

Canned Goods

guisantes – peas

pimientos – peppers

pulpo en salsa – octopus in sauce

mejillones – mussels

berberechones – cockles

calamares – squid

navajas – razor clams

atun – tuna; get the more expensive brands, as the cheap cans tend to contain at least half oil

The above are best considered as flavouring accents like in Chinese cooking, since the cans are small and cumulative weight prohibitive.

Liquids

zumos – juices; available in various flavours as 160 ml cans, 200 ml cartons, and (best) 250 ml *Don Simón* brand cartons

vino – wine, *clarete/rosado* always better than *blanco*; available in litre cartons, bottles, and in bulk, the latter two for transfer to your own container (see the Locally Available Hiking Equipment section).

Snacks

Frutos secos is the generic terms for nuts and dried fruit. Much of it is imported from the USA; *Borges* is one of the biggest brands. In some towns there are small stores specialising in bulk *frutos secos*. A dry roast medley, heavy on the peanuts, is known as *panchita* and sold as such.

avellanas – hazelnuts

cacahuetes – peanuts

almendras – almonds

albaricoques – apricots

higos – figs

pasas – raisins; imported and expensive

pasas muscatelas – flavoursome but very seedy

ciruelas pasas – prunes

ciruelas sin pipita – pitted prunes; bland

datiles – dates

orejones de melocotón – peach slices

casadielles – Asturian honey/almond nougat

crema de melocotón – peach paste; packaged in wedge-wheels

galletas – cookies; best are either the petit-beurre type or *Molino Blanco* brand

Pyrenees/Ordesa – descending from Refugio de Góriz to Circo de Soaso

Top: Pyrenees/Benasque to Viadós – Granjas de Viadós, Posets peak from Refugio
de Viadós
Left: Pyrenees/Panticosa to Sallent – Ibón de Tebarray
Right: Cazorla Town – La Yedra Castle

Getting There

As well as flying to Spain you can reach the country overland by train or bus, as well as by driving or sailing from Britain.

AIR

Madrid is the capital, and most centrally placed for all regions, but it's by no means the busiest or least expensive destination. That award probably goes to Málaga in Andalucía, followed closely by Almería, Alicante and Palma (Mallorca). Bilbao is a useful airport if your main interest focuses on the Picos de Europa, and Barcelona or Girona would be an obvious choice if you were mostly intent on visiting the Pyrenees.

From Northern Europe

The package holiday, pioneered in the postwar decades when European currency export restrictions spawned a host of (chiefly British) dodges for getting around the law, still reigns supreme in coastal Spain; if you shop around carefully you can benefit handsomely from the still-thriving industry without necessarily being tied down by it.

A late winter or early spring charter departure for Andalucía or Mallorca need not cost more than £80 return from Britain, often with a night's lodging thrown in at the beginning and end of your visit. You will of course pay more for a scheduled airline, but often not much more, and this sometimes nets additional flexibility. Except in midsummer you can even find scheduled flights to Madrid from Britain for about £120 return, from the Netherlands and Scandinavia for slightly more, and from Germany for slightly less.

For up-to-the-minute prices and agents, consult (in Britain) the classified pages of such listings magazines as *Time Out* or the travel sections of the *Evening Standard*, the *Sunday Times* and *The Observer*. One agency in London worth trying for flights to northern Spain is Pilgrim Air (227 Shepherds Bush Rd, London W6 7AS, or 44 Goodge St;

tel (01) 748 1333 and 637 5311/5333). Another, little-publicised outfit is Springways Travel (71 Oxford St, London W1; tel (01) 439 8714) which caters principally to the large Spanish expat community in Britain, so you'll have to be quick or lucky to get a seat at a good price.

If you're a student or under 26, you might contact specialist youth/university agencies who will be able to knock another 10 or 15% off of the fares cited; even if you don't meet their age/status criteria such outlets can still be a very good source of deals. Flights offered tend to be slanted toward Spanish university towns (ie Madrid and Barcelona), but both are convenient jumping-off points for trekking. Two long-standing agencies in the UK are STA (head office 86 Old Brompton Rd, London SW7; tel (01) 581 8233 – and many other locations) and USIT (52 Grosvenor Gardens, London SW1; tel (01) 730 6525 – with many franchises including some in Dublin).

From the USA

In recent years direct fares to Spain have become increasingly competitive, mostly eliminating the necessity of detouring through Britain to get a good deal. Scheduled flights, as well as 'consolidator' seats (see following) on scheduled flights, tend to outnumber charter services.

When beginning to hunt for a ticket, it's wise to scan the Sunday travel supplements to get an idea of what you should end up paying; major ones in the USA include those of the *Los Angeles Times*, *San Francisco Chronicle*, *Miami Herald*, *Chicago Tribune*, *Washington Post*, *Boston Globe* and the *New York Times*.

You'll probably find that minimum single/return fares out of east-coast cities weigh in at about $200/$400 out of New York and $250/$450 from Washington DC. Chicago/Madrid is roughly the same, with charter/consolidator service out of California setting you back at least $300/$600 single/return.

Reliable and consistent consolidator agents – outfits which buy up and re-sell seats which the airline reckons it can't unload for full price – include Access International, 250 W 57th St, Suite 511, New York, NY 10107 (tel (212) 333-7280 or (800) 825-3633) and 55 E Washington St, Suite 220, Chicago, IL 60602 (tel (312) 977-4800); *TFI* (tel (800) 223-6363); or Airkit, 16 California St, San Francisco, CA 94111 (tel (415) 362-1106) or 1125 W 6th St, Los Angeles, CA 90017 (tel (213) 482-8778).

If you buy directly from the three airlines – Iberia, KLM or Pan Am – offering the most frequent and competitive flights to Spain, you may find a wider range of destinations at each end, but of course you'll pay more. Iberia flies nonstop to Madrid out of Miami, New York and Los Angeles; KLM offers services from Atlanta, Chicago and Houston (via Amsterdam, and on to a range of Spanish cities); and Pan Am serves Dallas, Chicago, San Francisco, Los Angeles, and Seattle (via New York). In general APEX fares with the scheduled airlines will run a good 35 to 50% more than the average cheapo flight, but in compensation you get (especially with Pan Am) far more frequent connections and, with Iberia, one Spanish domestic flight thrown in.

Student and youth fares are handled through three reputable agencies – Nouvelles Frontières, STA and CIEE – and usually run about the same as those advertised through the consolidators' newspaper adverts. There are certain differences in style and emphasis of the three outfits. Nouvelles Frontières is the most flexible if not always the cheapest, welcoming non-student/non-youth clients; STA isn't obsessed with your student status but is more wary about booking over-32s; CIEE offices often refuse point-blank to deal with older, non-student customers.

Nouvelles Frontières' head office is at 19 W 44th St, Suite 1702, New York, NY 10036 (tel (212) 764-6494), with other branches in California; STA has 11 outlets nationwide, with the largest concentration in California (eg 920 Westwood Blvd, Los Angeles, CA 90024 (tel (213) 824-1574); and CIEE's headquarters are at 205 E 42nd St, New York, NY 10017 (tel (800) 223-7401), with 22 branches around the country, primarily in California, New York and Massachusetts.

From Canada

Unfortunately Canadians have relatively little choice in the matter of reasonable flights to Spain and are probably best off getting to London as cheaply as possible (count on CDN$500 return from Toronto) and arranging onward transport there. Generally, the best direct service going is a seasonal charter from Toronto/Montreal to Madrid for about CDN$750 return, which usually makes a stop in London anyway.

The student/youth outfit Travel CUTS (Voyages CUTS in Québec) may be worth a call (head office: 187 College St, Toronto, Ontario M5T 1P7; tel (416) 979-2406, with 19 other branches across Canada). Try also Iberia in Montreal (1224 Peel St, 2nd Floor; tel (514) 861-7211) to see if they have any seasonal deals.

From Australia

STA offers flights from Melbourne to Madrid flying with Thai International. Return fares range from A$1895 (low-season in January, February, October and November) to $2355 (peak May, June, July and from 11 to 23 December). From Sydney to Madrid costs low-season/peak A$1910/2365 return.

From Melbourne or Sydney to Barcelona you can fly Melbourne/Los Angeles (with Continental) and Los Angeles/Barcelona (with Iberia) for A$2063 return in December, June, July and August. During the rest of the year, the return fare costs A$1953.

TRAIN

There are three surviving rail links, through or around the Pyrenees, between Spain and the rest of Europe: via Hendaye-Irún on the Atlantic, Cérbère-Port Bou on the Mediterranean, or Toulouse-Puigcerdà in the Catalan foothills (change trains at the border). The previously convenient and central service from French Pau to Spanish Jaca has been suspended; the French were annoyed by the booming success of the cheaper Spanish ski resorts, and you can now only go as far as Oloron by train, changing to a bus for the trip over to Spain.

All major international routes from Italy, the south of France, Switzerland and Germany go through Port Bou; if you're coming from further north in Europe or Britain, you can choose between the two more or less identically timed and priced coastal alternatives. From London Victoria to San Sebastián (handy for the Picos de Europa and central Spain) or Barcelona (appropriate for Mallorca and the Pyrenees) each takes just under 24 hours, with a change of trains and stations in Paris.

If you're under 26, consider an InterRail pass currently £155), good for a month of travel, and a good deal if you plan to walk in several regions of Spain (though supplements are payable within the country). If you plan to stay more than a month, and/or stay in one area, get a Eurotrain ticket instead. To, for example, either San Sebastián or Barcelona will set you back single/return £60/115; to Granada in the south, £70/140. Because such tickets are valid for two months, and useable in each direction along any 'reasonable' route, you just might be able to fit in stopovers near several Spanish mountain ranges (though, as with InterRail, you'll be liable for the odd supplement).

If you for any reason don't qualify for the above special tickets, you'd better consider flying – a standard rail fare to Barcelona from London will run at least £85 a single. North Americans holding a standard (non-youth) Eurail pass will find themselves at a similar disadvantage unless they plan to virtually live on Spanish trains for the term of its validity (hardly the point of this book...)

BUS

If for some reason you can't get a reasonable flight or train ticket, then your last resort will be the bus. From Britain there are two basic routes: from London to Algeciras (48 hours) via Paris, San Sebastián (26 hours), Vitoria, Burgos, Madrid (33 hours), Córdoba and Málaga; and from London to Alicante (35 hours) via Figueras, Girona, Barcelona (27 hours) and Valencia. Both services are operated by Eurolines (a subsidiary of National Express – tel (01) 730 0202 in London) out of Britain and Iberbus in Spain (tel (91) 467-2565 in Madrid). Also in England, Miracle Bus (408 The Strand, London WC2; tel (01) 379 6055) is a spin-off of the now defunct Magic Bus and occasionally undercuts Eurolines.

Depending on the season, there are departures two to four times weekly. In winter, the eastern line stops at Barcelona. Single fares average around £50 to San Sebastián, £60 to Madrid, and £55 to Barcelona, with return fares just under double these figures (unless you're under 26, in which case you can take advantage of a £99 return special to most points in Spain).

A more attractive alternative might be a combination plane/bus round-trip scheme available from Pegasus Holidays (24a Earls Court Gardens, London SWS; tel (01) 370 6986). For £60 to £95 depending on the time of the year, you fly to Madrid, stay the night in a hotel and then you return by bus to the UK on specified days.

CAR & FERRY

For trekkers in particular who generally construct point-to-point itineraries, this is unlikely to be worth it except in the Picos de Europa where loop hikes are more than feasible. In the Pyrenees you would have to double back, hopefully over a different route (quite possible), to reach a car that may have been left parked for a couple of weeks...

Still for the record, the shortest ferry links between Britain and the continent (Dover-Calais and Folkestone-Boulogne) will be best en route to Barcelona; for the Spanish north coast and Madrid crossings from Le Havre (from Portsmouth), Cherbourg (from Portsmouth and Weymouth), St Malo (from Portsmouth), or even Roscoff (from Plymouth) are convenient. You bypass Paris and can see some of the French Atlantic coast along the way. Of course driving will become a considerably more attractive and cheaper option once the channel tunnel opens in 1992 or 1993.

Unlikely to be affected by the tunnel

opening, and most useful for lazy drivers wishing to sleep their way to Spain, is the Plymouth-Santander ferry, the last surviving direct passenger link between Spain and Britain. Run by Brittany Ferries (tel (0705) 827701), this takes 24 hours with twice weekly sailings except between mid-December and mid-January. Fares are seasonal, but never exceptionally cheap, ranging from £57 to £84 per car plus £48 to £55 per person (admittedly in a cabin). Book well in advance for this popular crossing – it might very well turn out cost-effective for someone from the south-west of England with a special interest in, say, the Picos de Europa.

Getting Around

Spanish public transportation is usually adequate to get you to the trailheads, though as the country gets wealthier and more people own cars, departure frequencies are beginning to drop. Most visitors will prefer to reach the general vicinity of their hike(s) by train, covering the final necessary distance by bus. Taxis and hitching are useful for emergency short hops; you probably wouldn't want to treat yourself to internal plane flights too often as they are fairly expensive, as are the Mallorca-bound ferry services.

AIR

Internal plane flights are handled by Iberia and the marginally cheaper charter subsidiary Aviaco. While more or less in line with commuter fares in the USA and Britain, they are mostly worth considering if you have lots of money and little time. Two exceptions to this caveat exist. If you purchase an APEX flight on Iberia from North America to Spain, the airline will often throw in a domestic round-trip for free; allowable destinations include Palma, Santiago, Bilbao and Malaga, and this can make it very worthwhile.

TRAIN

RENFE, the state railway corporation, links all of the major towns with at least twice-daily departures – more often on the popular lines. Before setting out, visit the station or (preferably) the downtown RENFE office, if there's a separate one, to pick up schedule leaflets for mainline and spur-line services.

For most daytime trips anything rated *rápido* or *expresso* is fine; during summer many cars are air-conditioned. (Food, even of the sandwich-and-soda variety, is always expensive so bring your own.) Short stretches are also covered by *semidirectos* and *tranvías*, running on electrified track with overhead pantographs (wires) and these are the sorts of departures most likely to serve the smaller communities.

TER, *Talgo* and *Pendular* are all expensive categories of train crossing large stretches of the peninsula, often at night with couchette cars, though *literas* (bunks) can be also be found on the cheaper *electrotrenes* and some *expressos*.

An average, one-way second-class ticket on a *rápido* will set you back about 5.5ptas per km, not including the frequent supplements. If you buy a round-trip ticket at the outset, and do both legs of your journey on a so-called *Día Azul* ('Blue Day'), the cost drops to about 3.5ptas per km. There is also a domestic rail pass scheme called *Chequetren*, the cheapest of which currently sells for 25,000ptas and nets you 29,500ptas worth of train travel. They're not really worth it unless there are two or three of you (they can be shared) and you plan to spend a lot of time barnstorming around the country.

Eurail and InterRail passes are honoured, except on the FEVE systems near Valencia and along the north coast which have their own pass (in summer at least), and the Nuria line in the Catalan Pyrenees. Supplements and seat reservation fees, however, are always payable by Eurail or InterRail holders.

Ticket-window queues are often enormous, so buy your fare as far in advance as possible, particularly for the long-distance services which are now computerised. You can usually change the day of a departure and seat reservation without penalty, but an actual refund entails a service charge of 10% of the original ticket price.

BOAT

The domestic ferry network to Mallorca (Valencia-Palma and Barcelona-Palma) is grossly overpriced, and Aviaco charters purchased in those two cities can work out (round-trip anyway) the same as the boat, though still not much less than a one-way ticket, from Britain!

BUS

Buses serve almost every village, with networks hubbing through the capital of the province and sometimes through secondary towns if warranted. They cost about the same per km as trains and can be up to 20% faster or slower, depending on the state of the roads and traffic. One typical pattern is *from* the hill village *to* the market/school town in the early morning, returning in the afternoon, but this is by no means a hard and fast rule; Spanish buses may complete their out-and-back within a couple of hours at midday or even at sunset. Sunday services, however, are invariably reduced or non-existent except between major cities.

TAXI

Taxis are about eight to 10 times more expensive than the bus for the same trip. You are charged per ride, not per passenger, so if you can travel with several other people they are useful for rural drop-offs. Country taxis have no meter – you just have to know the distance to be covered and agree on the price accordingly.

HITCH-HIKING & RIDE-SHARING

Many guides have written disparaging things about hitching in Spain but I (admittedly a single male) have always found it fairly easy to get a ride when necessary; of course, the more isolated the road and the smaller your pack, the better your chances of success. It is also distinctly easier to hitch in northern Spain and Catalunya than in the south, where cars are fewer and, frankly, the locals are a little jaded about tourists.

If thumbing is too daunting, there is a ride-sharing centre in Madrid (A Dedo, Calle Estudios 9, tel (91) 265-6565) who for a one-shot; quarterly; or yearly membership fee will fix you up with a private driver. If you use the scheme often enough, costs drop to a bit over half that of train or bus travel.

Andalucía

Although the quality of trekking available in Andalucía frankly doesn't compare with that further north in Spain, there are compensations: a stunning range of wildflowers and birdlife, easy combination with a seaside holiday, and relatively settled weather conditions. Trekking as a leisure activity is still in its infancy in the south, with rudimentary trail markings (if any) and few other walkers.

The Sierra de Cazorla

This range at the eastern edge of Andalucía is unusual in several respects. It is one of the few important ones in Spain to have a north-south axis, its limestone formations overlie sedimentary strata, and the whole is riven with numerous gorges. The Río Guadal-

quivir, quickly added to by various tributaries, rises here, flowing north until being deflected by the neighbouring Sierra de Segura in a hairpin turn to the south-west.

With this orientation, the mountains act as an efficient barrier to warm, moist air masses moving west from the Levante. As a result the climate is far rainier and cooler than you would imagine for this latitude. Vegetation is thus on the temperate side of Mediterranean, especially on the valley floors where deciduous trees outnumber the thick pines and oaks of higher elevations.

The upper slopes provided a haven for now-relict alpine species at the end of the last Ice Age. Among the rare endemic species, with close relatives (if any) only in the Balkans, are a viola, a columbine, a butterwort and two types each of daffodils and narcissi. A *reserva natural* has been established to protect these treasures, whose reputation has begun to attract growing numbers of tourists interested in botany.

Lost in the promotion of the wildflowers, however, is the truth that the fauna are equally if not more spectacular, and more consistently on view. Over a brief period of walking I was privileged to sight 15 *muflón* (bighorn sheep – including two rams I got within seven metres of), five *cabra montés* (Spanish mountain goat – *Capra hispanica*), four deer, five wild boars, and more colourful birds and butterflies than my poor skills could identify. Also underrated is the town of Cazorla, an architectural gem and starting/ending point for a very worthwhile loop-walk in the south-western corner of the reserve.

Walking and wildlife in the heart of the park, by contrast, is not so exceptional, since trails are short, few and literally far between, with a conscious emphasis on private-car and hired-jeep tourism. Still, you can fill a few days nicely in this worthwhile stopover place for warm-up hikes en route to the Alpujarras and the Sierra Nevada.

Getting to the Trailhead

A train departing at around 7.30 or 8 am from Madrid will arrive at Linares/Baeza station by 12 noon, allowing quick connection with one of four daily buses (outside the station door to the left) bound for Úbeda, a few km east. From Úbeda three daily buses (10 am, 1.30 pm and 6.15 pm) continue the final distance to Cazorla town, arriving about 45 minutes later. Most trains bound for Córdoba or Granada make a stop in Linares/Baeza, but you cannot always catch a sufficiently timely bus to Úbeda to connect with one of the three daily onward services.

From Cazorla into the nature reserve there are only twice daily bus departures: one at 6.30 am (the only feasible service unless you plan to overnight in the reserve) and another at 2 pm, which returns, conveniently for day-hikers, at 5.30 pm. The turn-around point is Coto Ríos, one of the few still-functioning camping sites in the Guadalquivir valley, and just downstream from the trailhead to one of the walks described.

Supplies

The biggest selection is at Cazorla's central market, just below the Plaza de la Constitución (follow the signs).

CAZORLA TOWN & PARK

With its homogeneous, elegant architecture and incomparable setting at the base of towering cliffs, Cazorla town is worth a visit whether you intend to walk or not. Tourism is beginning to pick up in a modest way, and expatriates of a fairly benign variety are beginning to settle here, but for the moment the place is relatively unspoiled.

The bus from Úbeda leaves you just below the privately-run tourist office in the Plaza de la Constitución, the first of three squares connected by the main street. All are surrounded by food and accommodation establishments of every category, but the innermost plaza of Santa María is the most interesting. The shell of a Renaissance-vintage cathedral, gutted by Napoleonic troops in the early 1800s, stands to one side, overlooked by the keep of La Yedra castle, built by the Moors and later appropriated and

Carzola town, La Yedra castle

modified by the Christian conquerors as they moved south.

The 'tourist office' is actually a private operation dedicated to promoting nature tours, jeep excursions and photo safaris. The staff is friendly enough, but offers minimal walking information. The best use an independent rambler can make of them is to buy one or most of the recommended maps and/or an altimeter – all priced at a slight premium.

Cazorla makes the best base for staying in the area, particularly if you don't have a car. The *zonas de acampada* (free camping sites) of Los Rasos, Puente de las Herrerías, Narejos and Torre del Vinagre shown on the two 1:100,000 maps were closed in 1988, and you can only camp at three privately-run and rather grubby grounds at Coto Ríos or at a handful of ICONA (Instituto Nacional para la Conservación de la Naturaleza) sites on the far shore of the Tranco de Beas dam. The latter are not particularly handy for the

Borosa gorge, and are often restricted to youth/school groups. The general trend seems to be to discourage long stays in the wilderness areas and to cluster people in developments (including several *hostales*) on the main road between Vadillo junction and Segura village.

Even away from this asphalt link, much of the park is crisscrossed by forest roads, and two signposted trails near Vadillo are pitifully inadequate for serious walkers. So the message seems clear: hikers not particularly welcome. The two following itineraries, the latter incorporating a third officially prepared trail in the park, are the best I have found.

GILILLO-LOMA DE LOS CASTELLONES LOOP

This circuit, mostly on excellent old trails, represents the Cazorla country well, taking in a monastery, fine ridge and gorge scenery, the upper valley of the Guadalquivir and pastoral meadows along the way.

Rating
Moderate to strenuous, owing to the distance involved and a nett altitude gain/loss of over 2200 metres.

Duration
Allow seven-plus hours of walking for the entire loop.

Season
It's best in the long, cool days of late spring from late April to early June when it's not likely to rain. You will appreciate 10 hours of daylight for the loop.

Map
SGE sheet 21-37 (928), *Cazorla*, 1:50,000.

Route Directions
From the Plaza de Santa María in town, turn right onto the street beginning between the fountain and the *Mesón La Cueva*. Heading west initially, clear the outskirts of Cazorla, and after 10 minutes reach another fountain on the left. Turn left, at about '10 o'clock', onto a gravel drive, then bear left again at a

third, smaller fountain onto a dirt mule track. Skirt several farms, and then curl south onto the ascending option at the next fork, pausing for a final view of the town.

There's a final left to take just before passing under the abandoned castle of Cinco Esquinas, so re-named by the Christians for its five-sided keep. Here the route levels out for a while until a brook crosses the path some 45 minutes out of town. Complete the first hour of walking by switchbacking up to a small pass in the ridge ahead, and immediately veer left to keep to the ridgeline. The trail has deteriorated slightly but, with the aid of occasional white blazes, can still be followed.

You should reach the Ermita (monastery) de Monte Sion some 75 minutes along. This 16th-century cloister was recently restored, and barking dogs will usually bring one of the two remaining Dominican brothers to the gate. Padre Juan is a bit 'odd' but genial enough; he may or may not invite you in to the fenced community with its orchard and spring.

The trail improves again as it continues south, climbing to allow a final view of Monte Sion and Cinco Esquinas behind, and then curves east into the forest. The town of Quesada comes into view, and you can also begin to contemplate the sea of olive groves which extends virtually uninterrupted to Jaén. The greenery gives a deceptive picture of generalised wealth; most of the acreage is in fact owned by a half-dozen families.

Half an hour above the monastery, you'll hit a new forest road; cross it, continuing uphill and east to the resumption of the path (look for masoned edging). Tread quietly and you may, as I did, surprise groups of *Capra hispanica* or *muflón* here or slightly beyond.

About an hour beyond Monte Sion, you reach a fork in the trail – a paint-splashed rock marks it but other blazes and signs on the boulder behind are worn to the point of illegibility. To the right (south) there's a sheer drop-off into the Arroyo del Chorro, where an irrigation tank sparkles in the sun. It may be tempting to bear left onto a trail which leads back to Cazorla, via Ríogazas farms, but the path proper ends within an hour and

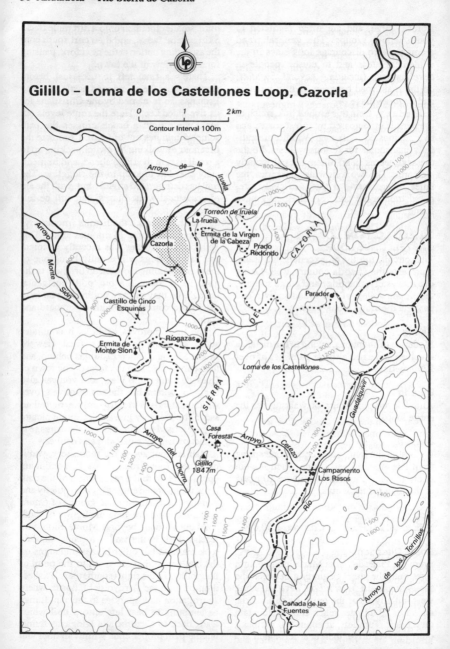

Gilillo – Loma de los Castellones Loop, Cazorla

0   1   2 km

Contour Interval 100m

most of the 2½-hour descent will be spent on a rather confusing and not particularly alluring maze of tractor tracks.

Far better to continue straight, then right, for the 40-minute climb, along a well-engineered trail, to a pass in the rocky ridge just north of Gilillo (1847 metres), highest point in this corner of the reserve. Just below the saddle sits the dilapidated casa forestal of El Chorro, suitable only for sheltering from thunderstorms.

Ignore a hairpin left 20 minutes below the hut, then take the next left you meet (the right-hand turning leads toward Cañada de la Fuente and the sources of the Guadalquivir but entails six extra km of road-walking thereafter). The camino has widened now, reflected on the SGE map as a solid black line supplanting the dotted one. A final left turn is required to stay with the main route on the subsequent 20-minute descent to the bed of Arroyo Cerezo and the first water since Monte Sion.

Adopt a steady east-south-east course, past an abandoned farm and giant cairns in the watercourse, which the way briefly merges with. A poplar grove makes a good place for a lunch stop – often water has surfaced in the stream here. Shortly after, take a right; the camino narrows again before halting (1 hour 20 minutes beyond El Chorro shelter) at a fountain (often dry) and a 'Km 9' marker on the main road, across from the now-abandoned campsite of Los Rasos. Water is always available from the infant Guadalquivir, 100 metres ahead.

Barely 200 metres north along the valley bottom road, the ruined edge of a camino (or the more circuitous jeep drive just before) beckons you for the 60 or 90-minute climb up through forest to the meadows of Loma de los Castellones, a beautiful, deer-frequented spot.

Beyond the grassy area lies a windswept pass and a fork in the route; turning right leads down to the local parador (red roof visible), while the left option (signalled with a red blaze on a rock) goes toward Cazorla. You can get spring water 10 minutes down this trail which loops around various crags, affording views of the Ríogazas valley and

Cinco Esquinas; a half-hour beyond the pass the descent into the Iruela valley begins in earnest.

The landscape here, with tree-studded meadows in the foreground and the wonderfully mottled green and orange terrain of Andalucía beyond, is seductive and it's tempting to continue another 30 minutes on the obvious trail to the abandoned farm and rushing water (and at dusk, wild pigs) of Prado Redondo. This path, however, opens out onto the national park access road just outside La Iruela hamlet – a considerable distance out of your way if you're staying in Cazorla, and it's likely to be late in the day.

Instead, 45 to 50 minutes below the pass, bear left onto a fainter trail toward the Ermita de la Virgen de la Cabeza; do not pass the power lines, and follow them when in doubt as to the exact route. The Torreón de Iruela, the most intricate yet of the castles seen, rears up on your right some 25 minutes down this turning. You will probably have a front-row view of an Andalucian sunset for the whole way (40 minutes) to the monastery, a big white compound with a splendid view over Cazorla. If you're even luckier the bar/mirador here will be open. Otherwise, you've another half-hour down various tracks and short cuts to town.

TRAVERSE OF THE BOROSA GORGE

This walk is the most popular in Cazorla, but is no less worthwhile for that; as it flows from two small lakes below Empanada (2106 metres), the reserve's highest point, the Río Borosa has carved a picturesque canyon on its way to join the Guadalquivir.

Rating

It's moderate.

Duration

Allow 3½ hours one-way from the visitor's centre to the lakes, slightly less back; you should have plenty of time to catch the Cazorla-bound bus, which passes Torre del Vinagre at 5 pm.

Season

Again, it's best during the long days of

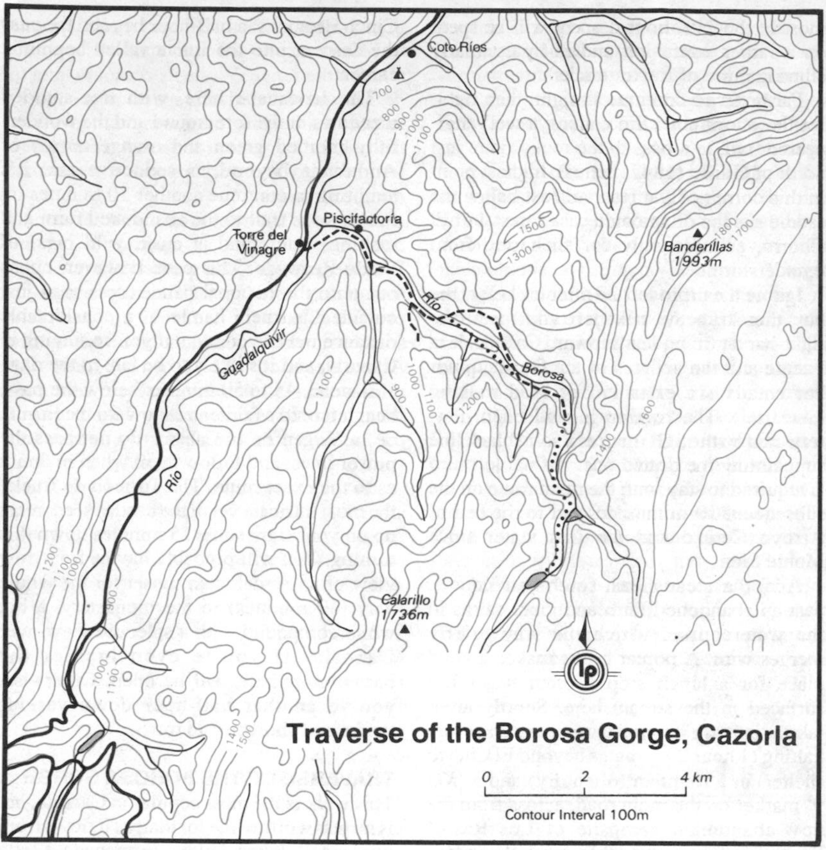

Traverse of the Borosa Gorge, Cazorla

0   2   4 km

Contour Interval 100m

spring, but not so early in the year that water levels in the gorge are a problem.

Map

SGE sheet 22-36 (908), *Santiago de la Espada* (1:50,000), provides the best coverage. *Parque Natural de las Sierras de Cazorla y Segura* (1:100,000), published by Editorial Everest, and *Sierras de Cazorla y Segura* (1:100,000), issued by ICONA, are barely adequate.

Route Directions

The morning bus from Cazorla will leave you at the Torre del Vinagre visitor information centre at about 7.45 am. Backtrack very slightly south to cross the Guadalquivir on a low causeway (which can be awash after snowmelt), and walk for two km (30 minutes) to a parking lot on the far side of a *piscifactoría* (trout farm). Vehicles are prohibited beyond this point; continue on the jeep track parallel to the north-east (true right, as you face the direction of flow) bank of the Río Borosa.

Shortly a signposted footpath diverges, going right, for 1800 marked metres along the river; this is crossed and re-crossed by several wooden bridges, and the narrowest part of the gorge is negotiated by catwalks bolted into the rock. Air temperature permitting, a dip in a calmer pool of the swift, cold river is conceivable, and you may see a water snake or two.

The path soon rejoins the jeep track, which heads determinedly up towards what appears to be the head of the valley hemmed in by impressive limestone walls. Some two hours beyond Torre del Vinagre, you should clear the last of the narrows and after crossing the river a final time, you'll arrive after another half-hour at a power turbine, with pipes plunging down to it. Go through a gate nearby, with a sharply inclined ravine behind. Cross a footbridge and begin the steep climb through the rocks at the base of the palisade overhead.

At one point the route narrows to a natural ledge at the foot of the cliff, and then appears to reach a dead end part way up in a natural amphitheatre, but look carefully at several holes in the rock ahead. One is actually a tunnel leading up to the pair of lakes, a natural one and a small reservoir. Allow a full hour's ascent from near the turbine.

Las Alpujarras & the Sierra Nevada

A casual visitor to the Alhambra in Granada will see, except perhaps from July until October, a vast wall of snow-fringed peaks closing off the rich *vega* (fertile lowland) of Granada to the south. This is the Sierra Nevada, containing continental Spain's two highest points, plus a dozen other peaks over 3000 metres. The main crest extends for 80 km, from the Guadix-Almería rail line in the east to the Puerto del Suspiro del Moro in the west, with a maximum breadth of about 30 km in the environs of the high peaks.

However, height and extent are not always reliable indicators of quality trekking, and this is arguably the case here. Even before the advent of various roads, ski resorts, *paradores*, radio telescopes and other such

impedimenta, Victorian and *belle epoque* travellers expressed universal disappointment in the range. While its contours tend to be dull and rounded, and spectacular summit landscapes fleeting, there *is* enough to justify the trekker's attention for a few days before returning to the perhaps more rewarding middle altitudes.

Although snowpack and weather conditions are not quite as rigorous as in the Pyrenees, owing to the southerly latitude, the mountains here are sufficiently alpine to provide a home for numerous bird and plant species normally found much further north. Above elevations of 1700 or 1800 metres the mica-schist slopes are largely denuded, though the limestone, shale and sandstone of the foothills are more supportive of trees and shrubs.

This is especially true on the Sierra's less sheer south flank, where a half-dozen roughly parallel ravines plunge into the complicated, semi-tropical valley system of Las Alpujarras. This is sheltered in turn from the Mediterranean (40 km distant) by the low, arid ranges of Lujar and Contraviesa.

Las Alpujarras have been an oasis and a redoubt since earliest times, as borne out by Ibero-Celtic archaeological finds near Capileira. Most of the ongoing human ecology, however, dates from 12th-century settlement of the 70-plus villages by Berbers. This heritage is reflected in the traditional architecture of low, match-box houses, arranged in stepped tiers with flat roofs used as workspace – design features found nowhere else in Spain but strongly related to High Atlas building styles. As the years go by, however, the Berber flavour diminishes and most communities have assumed a more generalised Mediterranean aspect. Pigs, goats, chickens and rabbits, or draft animals live on the ground floor, with the humans above, though increasingly one finds the livestock replaced by a bar or a store.

Another carry over from Moorish times is the intricate system of *acequias* or irrigation canals, which enabled the cultivation (on the rich alluvial debris washed down from the Sierra Nevada) of a wide range of crops and fruits, including citrus and avocado orchards in the warmest spots. Though scholarly opinion is by no means unanimous, it is thought that 'Alpujarras' is a corruption of the Hispano-Arabic *Al-Busherat*, 'grassy hills'. Meadowland certainly abounds, but more common are woods of (in order of ascending altitude) olive, almond, oak, poplar, willow, pine, chestnut, walnut, and cherry.

After the conquest of Granada by the 'Catholic Kings' in 1492, the population of Las Alpujarras swelled as numerous Spanish Muslim refugees, guaranteed freedom of worship by treaty, withdrew here. The victors, however, quickly reneged on these promises and instituted a policy of forced conversion. Following the last and most severe of several unsuccessful rebellions against these persecutions, in 1570, the new rulers of Granada finally deported their opponents to Asturias and Galicia, replacing them with Christian settlers relocated from the same corner of Spain. Two Moorish families in each village, however, were required to stay behind and show the newcomers how to breed silkworms – sericulture was the main cash-earning industry here until this century – and manage the complex irrigation systems.

Thereafter the Alpujarras lapsed into backwater status, a process accelerated around 1800 when many of the original land grants to those resettled were snapped up by large landlords. The forests of the lower hills were destroyed for the sake of their charcoal during the 19th century by mining companies; immigration to the New World acted as a social safety valve when conditions became too dire (as they did in the 1880s when phylloxera destroyed the native grapevines).

Today, foreigners are beginning to patronise various up-market establishments (horseback-riding ranches, yoga farms, etc) and also to buy, rent, or merely squat when they find property they consider a veritable Shangri-La. Three of the highest, most dramatic, but most road-accessible villages, Pampaneira, Bubión and Capileira, are beginning to get positively busy in season.

Reality for most locals, though, remains less than rosy; the more isolated hamlets possess neither shop nor bar, and just subsist. Generally, the region still lags far behind most of Spain in literacy, erosion control, income and health; the effects of polio, for instance, or mental deficiency brought on by either malnutrition or inbreeding, will be evident even to transient visitors.

The following circuit includes most of the highlights of the so-called 'High Alpujarras', the western, upper valleys north of the Río Guadalfeo which drains them, rather than the 'Low' villages on the south bank or to the east in the Río Grande's watershed. Also appended is a three-day traverse of the highest peaks of the Sierra Nevada, which can easily be omitted or bypassed by those unequipped for mountain travel.

Regrettably, I have in certain instances had to compromise my high standards for trail surfaces. The bulldozer and the asphalt cauldrons have been busy around here; the days are past when the walk from Órgiva to Yegen could rate as an 'unpredictable adventure', as Gerald Brenan asserts it was before the civil war. Promotional brochures issued by certain trekking holiday companies operating in the area portray Las Alpujarras as a hikers' paradise, which borders on an irresponsible exaggeration. Rewarding the terrain certainly is, but one can't just wander off in any direction and expect success. Grades are punishing, and what one moment may be a delightful riverside trail, may in the next have expired in a mess of brambles and nettles.

Rating

For the Alpujarras alone, moderate if you include the Sierra, whether approached from north or south, it's difficult, owing to the 1600 to 1800-metre altitude difference over a short run and the necessity of carrying substantial extra equipment.

Duration

Allow at least 10 days to cover all of the points described, with at least a day of leeway – both in terms of scheduling and supplies – for weather-related contingencies.

Season

Unfortunately combining excursions in the Alpujarras and the Sierra Nevada is a bit difficult, since the optimal months for each are almost opposite. The High Alpujarras are at their best from late March to early June, and again from October to early November. From mid-June until September the muggy heat, except in the immediate environs of Capileira and Trevélez, will be debilitating.

The Sierra Nevada is likely to be snowed under completely from late October until mid-May, with considerable pack above 3000 metres and/or on shaded slopes until July. Weather in the mountains is always fickle, with gusting winds and snow flurries not unheard of even in July; in June blinding mists and thunderstorms are liable to occur on any given day, though this is the month (owing to an abundance of running water at high altitudes which tends to disappear later in the summer) when you could schedule a visit to both regions at once.

Supplies

It's best to get these in Granada, particularly on Calle Calderrería Nueva at the base of the Albaicín quarter; *Panadero Loco*, at No 8, is a good health food store, but the whole street provides a bonanza of natural/Moroccan/traditional Spanish groceries, some of which will do very well for the trail. Stores in each of the villages are commented on in the account.

Map

Use *Sierra Nevada Granada (Estación Invernal & Alpujarras)*, 1:50,000, co-produced by the IGN and the FEM in 1981. This is a composite of sections of nine separate IGN sheets, incorporated in whole or in part; owing to its age numerous small errors have crept in, though it is perfectly adequate for the locations of villages, refuges and the most important features of the landscape.

The map can sometimes be purchased in Granada at the *Librería Dauro*, on Calle Zacatín 3 (a shopping mall) between the cathedral and Calle Reyes Católicos. They often run out so, if at all possible, get the map in Madrid or Barcelona.

Getting to/from the Trailhead

Four times daily (currently at 8.30 am, 10.30 am, 1 pm and 1.30 pm) there is a bus from Granada to Órgiva, the start of the hiking itinerary. The trip will take at least two hours, so with either of the later departures it's wisest to plan on overnighting in Orgiva and getting an early, cool start on the morrow.

The last afternoon bus continues to most of the villages of the High Alpujarras, including Trevélez and Bérchules, turning around at Murtas; coming back the other way, it passes through Bérchules at 7.15 am, Trevélez at 8 am, Capileira at 9 am, and Órgiva at 9.45 am, arriving in Granada around 12 noon.

To or from Cadiar there is a separate service, via Órgiva, Torvizcón, and then parts of the Low Alpujarras along the bank of the Guadalfeo, once a day, which takes over three hours in each direction.

LAS ALPUJARRAS
Stage 1: Órgiva (Órjiva) to Capileira

Órgiva, the county seat and main centre of the High Alpujarras, is actually rather low (456 metres) but is still the logical jumping-off point for the suggested trek. There are several places to stay, including (from the most luxurious to the simplest) *Mirasol* by the bridge, the *Fonda Simón* and *Pensión Nemesis* facing each other further into town, a *fonda* above the *Bar Ortega* and a *comidas/camas* next to the *Alsina Graells* bus terminal. Prepared meals are limited to *Mirasol* and the *Simon*.

To begin, leave Órgiva on the track going north from beside the CAMPSA gas pump, between the bridge and the *Mirasol*. Once clear of the built-up area, keep to the east (true left) bank of the Río Chico ravine (dry because all the water is confined to the hillside aqueduct) for about an hour, until you see Bayacas hamlet and a large junction, to the left. Head straight for now, without angling up or sharply right, staying instead with the watercourse to pass under the bridge on the asphalt road.

Once past this, cross over immediately to the west bank, where the trail surmounts a cement weir and becomes more obvious. It threads through low-altitude forest before attaining the top of a second, more natural 25-metre waterfall some two hours out of Órgiva. Standing on the edge of the cascade, facing downstream, point left to the continuation of the route, a well-engineered and stone-revetted path. This climbs in zig zags through conifers; when you meet another

ditch, cross it to keep switchbacking east over open hillside rather than continuing north up the Chico gorge.

As you emerge onto meadowland, the path becomes grassily overgrown but is still hemmed in by defining walls. Just over three hours from Órgiva, you enter Soportújar (945 metres); as the accents multiply, it is worth noting that they are critical when asking for information or just conversing, as the locals may fail to understand a wrongly stressed toponym.

Soportújar is a sleepy place with two bars (one with *camas*), and a single store with a

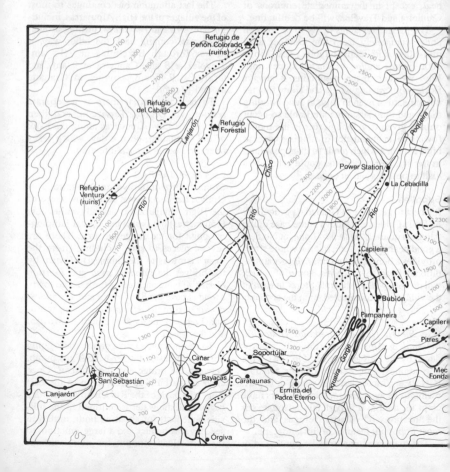

limited stock of interest (sardines, juice, canned fruit). Best to fill up on water from the fountain and enjoy the view over the Órgiva valley and Carataunas village below.

Leave the village on the auto-access road (alas, no alternative) and join up with the main Alpujarran highway. Some 30 minutes out of Soportújar, you arrive at the tiny Ermita del Padre Eterno. A signposted forest road heads off to the left; follow it for 200 metres until you see power lines and a path marching away to the right (east).

This is a parallel spur of the old 'Camino Real' which the asphalt has largely replaced.

It's unpromising terrain initially, but at least it's a path, and matters quickly improve as water, vegetation, and small *fincas* (farms) appear. There's a good picnic spot about 20 minutes beyond the forest track, by a shady pool where a small waterfall crosses the path, sporadically marked now with red blazes.

Round the hillside to head north along the west flank of the Poqueira gorge, a vast gash in the landscape leading down more or less directly from the Sierra Nevada summits. Pampaneira village is visible almost immediately; vegetation is lush, courtesy of the many runnels, along this route ambling past

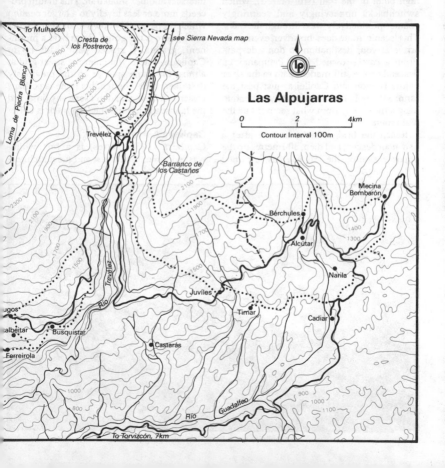

semi or totally abandoned farms and fields. Cuckoos call out intermittently in the woods; our era is represented by the power pylons and road glimpsed far below.

Some two hours from the *ermita*, the path as such disappears, and the blazed way, often overgrown, continues along the edge of the *acequia*. A half-hour later, the aqueduct is confined to a pipe where a prominent downward right turn (waymarked) leads to Pampaneira; instead bear up and left, to find another blaze signalling the way for Capileira.

Another hour's walking brings you to the high point of the trail (still blazed), which switchbacks unnervingly and seemingly counter-productively west through the oaks. This 'scenic' route does, however, eventually arrive at your destination so don't despair. From a *cortijo* owned by a Pampaneiran, descend on the still-marked path to the river below Bubión and Capileira; just past the farm, 3½ hours from the *ermita* you need to hang a right away from what seems to be the main route.

Reach the bridge at the bottom after a half-hour descent and then, 300 metres up the opposite side on the left just past a ruined farmhouse, take an exceedingly faint path. This is almost totally blocked at times but is in fact the shortest direct way up to Capileira. If you stay with what appears to be the main *camino* you will end up in Bubión. From the stream it's a full 30 minutes up to Capileira's lowest houses, making for nearly five hours of walking from Padre Eterno and a good eight-hour total from Órgiva.

Alternatively, you can continue straight, rather than right, from the noted *cortijo*, but this trail soon ends near some ruined farmhouses. Near them you must pick up an ugly logging/jeep track, which snakes down to intersect another small trail. This in turn proceeds more or less levelly to a larger *camino* which drops quickly down to another, higher bridge across the gorge. From here a prominent, gradually graded path leads up to Capileira, where you enter the street grid at almost the same spot as on the previously described trail. Though this route is perhaps easier to follow, you don't save any time, and the landscape around the jeep track is ugly.

Capileira & Around

Capileira (1436 metres) is a fine white-washed town, the largest and most architec-

Capileira town from Poqueira gorge

turally uniform of the three in this valley. It's been tangibly polished up for tourism, but is still countrified enough for rabbits and chickens to be kept under stairwells. For supplies there are two good groceries – *Udaco*, and another next to the *farmacía* between the *Fonda Tilo* and the excellent *Mesón/Hostal Poqueiro* – two of the three places to stay/eat.

You probably won't need much encouragement to linger an extra day in Capileira, as the first day's hike is admittedly a killer. If you're up to it, use the rest day for an enjoyable, short walk in the gorge.

Leave the village at its north end, passing the *Pueblo Alpujarreño* vacation villas (yes), and descend the path to the highest of the three bridges over the river. The trail, always clear at this stage, climbs on the far bank to a succession of small farms devoted to growing cereals, corn, peas and potatoes. In the spring these are back-breakingly worked with short-handled hoes, a necessity since no machinery can get to most of the plots.

At the one-hour mark the route occasionally becomes vague, with only a few blazes to help out, but as a you draw abreast of homely La Cebadilla hamlet (some 75 minutes out) the trail widens to a dirt driveway, the landscape becomes noticeably bleaker and you see a power station ahead. You could vary the return by taking the visible jeep track from La Cebadilla to Capileira, but it's far more worthwhile to retrace your steps, not least for the sake of the wonderful pools inviting you to plunge in back by the bridge.

Stage 2: Capileira/Bubión to Busquistar

It's a 45-minute road walk to Bubión, with a brief initial trail short cut, or you can take the 9 am bus. Once in Bubión, turn left (just past *Artesanía Troquel*) when you see a side street and a *'No 15'* legend on the wall. Follow the subsequent dirt track up for about 15 minutes, at which point you should take a faint trail beginning on the right. This works its way up through scrub to a 'double-horned' hill and some water-storage works, surrounded by a square of fencing which disrupts the path. Manoeuvre around this to the right until you find where the trail

resumes; you then emerge on the ridgetop about an hour above Bubión.

Ignore minor jeep tracks scattering in all directions, and instead cross the top of the Barranco de la Sangre at your feet, intersecting the main dirt road and then taking an instant fork left. You should soon see an initially wide trail descending down and right through the maquis; choose it, following red dots when necessary. The villages of Portugos, Pitres and (closest) Capilerilla lie in plain sight. At the point where the waymarks counsel a turn up and left, disregard them and continue along the path aiming obviously for the belfry of the Pitres church, going to the left of a *piscina* (swimming pool).

About two hours after quitting Bubión, you should arrive in the central plaza of Pitres, with its *fonda* and a couple of *bar/restaurantes*. Pitres (1250 metres) is a representative enough Alpujarran village, neither so 'quaint' nor so touristed as the communities of the Poqueira canyon. As for the day's route thus far, I'm no fan of maquis, and the only points to recommend the hike (rather than the afternoon bus from Capileira) are an early start and the views (from the ridge crossed) back to the Sierra and forward to the valley of the lower Río Trevélez, its terraces speckled with white villages.

Fortunately the rest of the trekking day is considerably more rewarding. From the right side (as you face it) of the *Bar La Carretera*, out on the main road as the name implies, take the old walled trail which dips sharply in 20 minutes to Mecina Fondales (1029 metres, with no facilities). There you're forced to follow the road 25 minutes east to Ferreirola (1005 metres), a beautiful hamlet clinging to the north bank of the river. Fill water containers at the central fountain, which if you have supplies and can hold out this long, makes a better lunch stop than Pitres.

Clear the settlement on the obvious *camino* ambling through apple and orchard groves, with an unshaded stretch menacingly visible on the slope ahead. An artesian well to the left gushes effervescent, soda-tasting water. A few minutes beyond this curiosity, veer left at a junction in a bare area; as you climb, turn around for a simultaneous view of Mecina Fondales, Ferreirola, Pitres and Atalbeitar.

Your path, now high above the bed of the river, levels off somewhat as it rounds the bend and aims for Busquistar, perched appealingly above the fields ahead. From Ferreirola it's a total of 75 minutes to the latter village, pretty and unspoiled despite being just below the road.

At Busquistar there's a very simple inn, without a sign and run by a woman named Lola, in the building to the left of the church as you face its facade. You enter by a back door; the front ground floor is taken up by a bar which by night becomes the hottest one in town – you are willy-nilly privy to many a discussion and/or domino game. There is no restaurant; you ask for two stores, one run by 'Josefina', then cook in the fully-equipped kitchen of the inn.

Should you require greater luxury, or have any energy left after over five hours traversing from Bubión, you can walk 30 minutes west along the asphalt back toward Portugos, where there are more conventional facilities (though the village is considerably more modernised). At the very eastern outskirts, and shown approximately correctly on the recommended map, a wide trail descends to the vicinity of sombre and half-deserted Atalbeitar.

Stage 3: Busquistar/Portugos to Juvíles via Trevélez

A path at the east end of Busquistar begins promisingly, but after an hour of threading along above the river, it expires on the asphalt, with 2½ hours of road-walking still separating you from Trevélez. Alternatively, from Portugos you can take a path for 90 minutes through the oak woods, but this again opens out onto the main road at the Barranco de los Alisos, far short (two hours) of Trevélez. It is wisest to accept that the old 'Camino Real' has been irretrievably destroyed around here and take a taxi, or afternoon bus, over the 12 kilometres in question.

Trevélez is fully described at the end of this walk; for the moment most walkers will want to get to the large, walled cemetery on the opposite slope of the Río Trevélez from the village. Just past it (along the road toward the eastern Alpujarras) a large, prominent path appears suddenly on the left. Following this, it's a 90-minute climb through a mixture of maquis, broom and oak to a firebreak; an *acequia* crossed early on has the only water. The trail barrels down the middle of the firebreak (less objectionable than it sounds, as the pines on either side are decidedly like a park) and rounds the hill gently at about the 1700-metre contour, tending gradually from a southerly to an easterly bearing.

The firebreak ends about two hours out, at a jeep track running down the spine of the ridge, and you cross to a narrow path winding off through the sort of clumpy grass that perhaps gave the region its name. From here a vast panorama unfolds, taking in the almond and olive (both in colour and vegetation) hills in the distance; this is also a good place to see partridge. Once past the high point of today's leg of the route, you've an hour-plus descent, with no ambiguities, to Juvíles, for a total of just over three hours out of Trevélez.

Straddling the road, Juvíles (1255 metres) is an attractive linear village three streets wide. Only the buildings fronting the 'main drag' (by now carrying a considerably reduced volume of traffic) are whitewashed. The church and many other buildings remain in their natural masoned state, so you can appreciate the appearance of the Alpujarras 50 years ago before changing fashion, and tourism prompted the use of the lime bucket.

In the evening people rather confidently take their *paseo* (stroll) in the road, ignoring the perfectly good plaza by the church. There's a single all-in-one *fonda/restaurante* bar/store; in the *comedor* the video-pinball games which have afflicted Spain like a plague in the last decade are thankfully absent. Instead the local kids indulge more social instincts with hand-operated table soccer – five balls cost 25 ptas.

Stage 4: Juvíles to Cadiar

At the north end of the village, *before* reaching the bridge over the Barranco de la Umbria, take the *camino* which descends north-east through a cluster of cottages and then winds around the monolith of Fuerte (1301 metres) dominating the locale. Within an hour you should arrive at Timar (1076 metres), an intriguing village at the eastern foot of Fuerte. The name *'Timar'* is probably derived from Hispano-Arabic for 'feudal estate'; there is one bar and a shady plaza by the church where you can rest.

Leave Timar on its asphalt access drive, and after 10 minutes veer left onto a dirt track. Continue through low, bare hills and over a poplar gully, forsaking two successive left forks as first Narila, then Cadiar, come into view. There's an obvious trail shortcut to Cadiar, which sprawls just across the upper reaches of the Río Guadalfeo.

Cadiar, reached an hour out of Timar, is more attractive than it appears from above and hosts a street market on the 3rd and 18th of each month. Tacky clothing and cassette tapes threaten to eclipse the produce sales and very low-key livestock trading, but the fresh fruit and vegetables, ironically something of a miracle in the contemporary Alpujarras, could be reason enough to detour

here. You can stay, if necessary or desired, in one of a handful or *hostales* and *camas*; midday *platos combinados* are served at various 'downtown' bars.

Stage 5: Cadiar to Bérchules

To continue the day's walk, head for the north end of what is actually a fairly substantial town, past the *cuartel* of the *Guardia Civil*, to a landscaped zone by the *Centro de Salud*. There's a big four-way junction here; the northerly option goes to Narila, but instead proceed 150 metres east and turn left onto a cement apron. This quickly becomes a *camino* through olive and almond trees, with a north-easterly bearing. Beyond the cultivated area you come to a neck of land with whitewashed stones; the main trail loops back down toward a poplar-choked valley and the Cadiar-Narila track.

Instead, charge straight up onto the fainter continuation of the route, reaching the asphalt road after 30 minutes. Turn left, walk along the highway about 400 metres, and then scramble right onto another faint path leading past an almond orchard to a low saddle. Change there to an old, overgrown *camino* which negotiates another minor pass

Riverside plaza, market day, Cadiar

within view of a pine plantation. The right of way improves as you descend briefly through blue-grey-tinted badlands, then climb again along a draw to connect with a tractor drive one hour beyond Cadiar.

After 15 minutes along this, ignore a right fork descending to Yator and keep bearing north-east. On reaching another, bigger junction, charge straight across the road to find the re-emergence of the walled-in camino among young olive trees. As you climb to a gentle saddle, the walking surface and landscape becomes more hospitable; there's cobbling, ample greenery, and water for the first time since before Timar. As you veer up toward visible Mecina Bombarón though, this interlude ends as the all-too-brief trail hits the asphalt again near the cemetery. You enter the village itself some two hours after quitting Cadiar. Head for its upper plaza via the cement drive, and fill up on water.

The cement track toward Bérchules takes off from the left side of the fountain; it soon becomes dirt and winds for 40 minutes between farms to a pine-tufted pass. First you'll see Alcútar, then Bérchules apparently close below. At a fork 50 minutes above Mecina, bear left; after rounding the hillside to face north, leave the track, heading down cross-country through semi-abandoned farms, toward an outcrop painted with 'coto privado de caza' in white. From behind the bluff a legitimate trail snakes down into a severe ravine; this is the only way off the otherwise sheer cliffs looming over the headwaters of the Guadalfeo, reached 40 minutes after the fork at the pass. Cross the canyon on the bridge, to face a final 25 minutes uphill to the centre of Bérchules.

Stage 6: Bérchules to Trévelez

Bérchules (1322 metres) is only five road-km from Juvíles (you've gone the long way around!), but with its deciduous woods and precipitous setting has an entirely different feel. While also three streets wide, these are pitched sharply and end abruptly at the edge of the slope plunging to the lowlands around Cadiar. There's one, fortunately good fonda/ restaurante (the Carvol) and next door, one of the better grocery stores around – a godsend in this region where most shops are still fairly basic.

Leave Bérchules at its highest, westernmost point (ask to be pointed to the Plaza Zapata); from there an old cobbled camino climbs sensibly with a west-south-westerly bearing. After 45 minutes, cross the first jeep track of the day and approach a lone cortijo; take a left fork here, and cross a gully (with the last water for a while) to emerge on the high bunchgrass upland similar to that directly above Juvíles.

Cross another driveway – autos and their owners are often around to confirm directions – and head up to a notch in the ridge ahead, reached 75 minutes out of Bérchules. Within another 15 minutes, intersect a third and very substantial road, shown as a white line on the suggested map. Head west-north-west, keeping the pine grove of the last few minutes on your left. By now the camino is virtually nonexistent; some 400 metres past the road, hang a left onto a distinct track beginning here and winding through the last of the pines onto open moorland.

Luckily the track is too narrow to be useful to vehicles, and two hours along you slip around a gate preventing their theoretical passage. Avoid a downturn to the left. You will probably be alone except for the birds, butterflies, cows and spring flowers; the Sierra de Contraviesa spreads along the horizon to the left.

The track ends at the ridgeline and a fire break (the same one that crosses the Juvíle trail lower down) after 2 hours and 1: minutes. Descend cross-country into the pin plantation on the west-facing incline moving perpendicular to various terraces you won't encounter a proper trail until you're about 300 metres down the slope Trévelez quickly pops into view, so there' no question of getting badly lost – just pic your route without getting stuck too far dow the hill and not finding the trail.

Descend 45 minutes from the ridge, ami the sweet smells of pine and broom, to cur around the top of the Barranco de lo Castaños some 200 to 300 metres above th Juvíles trail. Within another 15 minutes yo reach a rock painted 'R1', where you fork le to clamber down through several farms to a bend in the road, just below Trevélez and four hours out of Bérchules. Allow another 15 minutes to close the distance between the very edge of the lower quarter and the square of the upper *barrio*.

Trevélez

Trevélez (1476 metres) is the most famous of the high villages because of its hams, which is how the pigs fattened on the surrounding *cortijos* and slaughtered around Christmas time end up. Assuming you have lots of money (the hams are not cheap) and lots of room in your pack, you can haul one away, but in all honesty good ham, sliced or whole, is available in any of the neighbouring communities.

As a supposed architectural showcase, Trevélez is a bit of a washout; while it is still divided into the traditional Alpujarran upper and lower districts, many of the structures are modern concrete blocks. Even its (self-bestowed?) title of 'highest permanently inhabited community in Spain' would seem to be fraudulent, since a random glance at a map reveals that Taüll in the Catalan Pyrenees, a sizeable village with a winter sports area nearby, is 20 metres higher; there are also some claimants in the Maestrazgo area of Aragón.

Be all that as it may, you will probably want or have to spend a night here no matter what your further walking plans are. This is one village, though, where even in May or June you'll probably have to trudge around for a while before finding a bed. Owing to the ham-and-height hype, the place is popular with Spaniards and prices are a bit above normal for the region. There are two clusters of *hostales* and *camas*: three near the square of the upper quarter, and four in a row down on the road just before the bridge. Some of the best meals are at *Río Grande*, just before the bridge, and hiker's food can be bought at a handful of stores (including the next to the lower places to stay).

THE SIERRA NEVADA

Stage 1: Trevélez to Cañada de Siete Lagunas

With the return to Trevélez, the High Alpujarran village itinerary comes to an end and you must ponder the choice of onward, upward routes. As the settlement closest to the Sierra Nevada summits, Trevélez is the traditional jumping-off point for their ascent. There is even a midnight *romería* (religious procession) departing from here on 5/6 August (Christ's Transfiguration) up the mountain.

Trevélez is also the terminus of an ancient, and still regularly used, trade route across the Sierra via the single pass viable for pack animals. This begins in lower Trevélez on the street passing (logically enough) *Bar Camino de la Sierra*; the *camino* in question promptly appears. Contrary to what the FEM/IGN map indicates, this pleasant though muddy route stays on the west (true right) bank of the river for the first hour or so before switching to the opposite side. There follows the more severe, 900-metre climb up to the Puerto de Trevélez (2800 metres), and the long descent through beautiful forest to Jeres del Marquesado (1234 metres), from where there is a bus service to Guadix. Judging from the section I have done myself and the accounts of other travellers, the entire traverse would be a long, occasionally bleak haul of at least eight hours.

The most usual thing to do from Trevélez, however, is the hike up to the summit area. For this you'll need the trail which leaves the upper village, heading almost due north and (after leaving the last farms) meets up with *acequias* at the Cresta de los Postreros just over two hours further along. Here the route curves north-west, then west, taking you high above the valley of the aptly named Río Culo Perro (Dog's Arse River), an impenetrable quagmire to be shunned at all costs.

Once around the bend, angle gradually up the slope to your left (south), crossing two aqueducts within the next hour. Soon you're in the alpine zone, and after another hour of walking, the river on your right feeds the last, highest *acequia* shown on the FEM/IGN map. Pick up a clearer path paralleling the

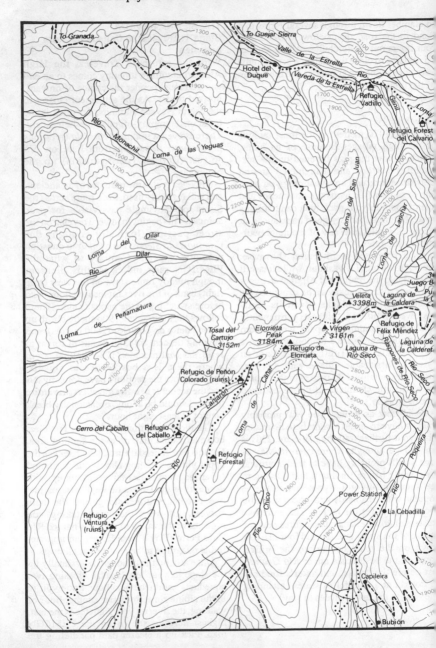

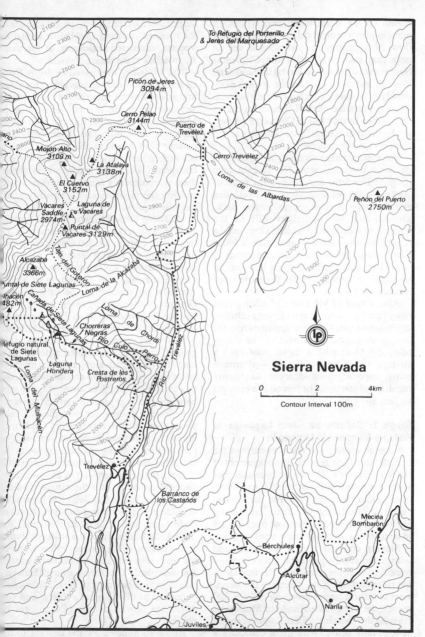

Sierra Nevada

Contour Interval 100m

0   2   4km

stream on the south bank, and within 15 minutes pass a cement culvert funnelling the flow. Mist permitting, you should see an imposing rock wall with the Chorreras Negras cascading off on the right-hand side. You can and should follow the stream more closely now, through high turf spangled with flowers. From the cement 'funnel' continue 75 minutes further to the Chorreras proper; get by them to their left, tracking back and forth up a stable rock pile.

You emerge rather suddenly at the Cañada de Siete Lagunas, with the largest lake (Laguna Hondera) immediately in front of you; with cooperative weather, Mulhacén and Alcazaba should appear in the background. Just to your right will be the augmented rock lean-to which is the famous *refugio natural*. Some sources say it holds five persons, but a more realistic figure is two. There's plenty of tent space however, in the meadow beyond – really the more comfortable option.

After a total of 5½ hours of hiking time from Trevélez, without even having climbed any summits yet, it's fairly apparent that the trek up should not be considered as a day-hike, and even with a dawn start such a strategy would be inadvisable – afternoon mists, impeding your descent, are pretty regular, and you could be forced to overnight up here anyway.

Stage 2: Cañada de Siete Lagunas to Refugio Méndez via Mulhacén

Nineteenth-century travellers exempted the Cañada from their general disparagement of the Sierra Nevada. The cirque here still provides a worthwhile morning's (or afternoon's) tour. With patience you can indeed count seven lakes or tarns, including Hondera, though the uppermost ones are apt to be frozen up or under snow until summer.

Moving onwards with a full pack, and without technical equipment, your choice of routes is somewhat restricted. The far side of the ridge closing off the cirque to the north-west is a sheer arrête dropping off for 300 metres; the north-east palisade of Mulhacén, flanking the Cañada de Siete Lagunas to one side, is little better. With great difficulty a laden hiker can find a way past Alcazaba to the standard camping spot below Puntal de Vacares, discussed following in Northern Approaches to the Sierra Nevada.

The classical continuation from Siete Lagunas involves either angling up the ridge immediately to the south of the cave-refuge and then following this all the way up to Mulhacén, or ascending directly west up its flank via a couloir. The latter method is quicker (2½ hours to the summit) but is snowed up until July, requiring ice axe and crampons. When the snowpack is absent there is reportedly a faint trail up this route and you can probably knock a half-hour off the time required.

Mulhacén (at 3482 metres) is the highest point in continental Spain, but arrival at the top, where there is a small shrine (probably the focus of the August festival), is liable to be an anticlimax unless conditions allow a view. The name is an adaptation of Muley Abul Hassan, penultimate Moorish king of Granada, who according to legend is entombed in a cairn near the peak. This is patently unlikely, since Muslims are generally reluctant to bury someone in unconsecrated ground, especially so exalted a person as a king. There is a path along the summit ridge to the triangulation point and the chapel, but this is useful mainly to cover the distance between wherever you emerge and the top.

Following it south, for example, will take you way out of your way (toward Capileira) it's advisable to head down and west, with no path, before reaching the parking lot at the end of the new driveway which has been built to facilitate jeep ascents (!) of the mountain. Descend carefully into the cirque cradling both the dirt road to Capileira and Laguna de la Caldera with its various satellites. North of these tarns, and a bend in the road, the Collado de Mulhacén or the adjacent Punta de la Caldera (3226 metres) offers some of the best views into the chasms north-east of the watershed. The Juego Bolos (Bowling Alley) incline lies at your feet, Mulhacén' pyramidal profile is most evident, and you might see how Alcazaba (Castle) got its name.

Allow 90 minutes for the descent to the

road, and then another 75 minutes to the Félix Méndez hut (visible below and to the left), reached by a short side-drive. You must follow the track the entire way; there is no feasible ridge route. Some amusement may be provided by the spectacle of cars attempting to cross to Capileira too early in the season, encountering a snowbank, and having to retreat in reverse for several km of rough surface.

The refuge (3054 metres), when you arrive, is a welcome sight at the end of a six-hour walking day, much of that over difficult surface. There is space for 60 inside, with very simple meal service and provision for self-catering, but the toilet is some distance away – in a very bizarre and obvious tower – and water must be fetched from rivulets down the hill. Between October and July, when the hut will be closed, an annexe (with four bunks) immediately adjacent is kept permanently unlocked.

The Laguna del Río Seco and various other tarns surround the shelter, and the Raspones de Río Seco form a forbidding backdrop to the west. The view down and south encompasses the Río Seco valley, which runs into the Poqueira canyon. Capileira itself is out of sight, and more than 20 km away in any case; should there be a need for assistance it will be much more efficient to use the two-way radio at Félix Méndez (if it's open) or to summon help from the *parador* or ski resort to the north of Veleta (see following).

Stage 3: Refugio Méndez to Refugio del Caballo or Refugio Forestal

It is again mandatory to stick with the dirt road for the hour and a quarter to an important breach in the watershed, the so-called Veleta pass', where the track descends sharply north to meet the asphalt coming up from the *parador* and the ski centre. On the way the Collado del Ciervo provides something of a consolation-prize vantage for those who were whited out at Puntal de la Caldera the previous day.

The FEM/IGN map shows, and other sources report, a trail from the saddle (noted previously) to Elorrieta hut, skirting the base of Virgen (3161 metres) and Elorrieta peak (3184 metres). I was unable, however, to find or reach it, owing to inadequate equipment and thick June snow cover – the ridge itself, studded with icy gaps and pinnacles, requires technical skills. Accordingly the route description to the Refugio del Caballo is second-hand and cannot be relied on absolutely.

You will probably require 90 minutes to traverse the base of the impassable section and climb back onto the ridge near point 3157 shown on the FEM/IGN map. Just to the left perches the small Elorrieta shelter (3160 metres), a spartan affair with places for 20 persons. A clear path descends 30 minutes more and west into the head of the Río Lanjarón valley, just south of the Tosal de Cartujo (3152 metres); bear right at a junction to stay on the west (true right) side of the canyon, passing the ruins of the Peñón Colorado hut. With very little altitude change, proceed for another two hours, just in the lee of the ridge to your right, to the primitive, 'eight-person' (ie four-person) hut (Refugio del Caballo) at 2830 metres, with water available from a nearby tarn.

If you are forced by snowpack and bad weather, as I was, to detour south from Veleta pass, you will need 3½ hours to traverse the base of Virgen and Elorrieta on its south-east flank and reach the saddle just north of point 3064 on the Loma de Cañar as shown on the recommended map. This involves a descent into, and a climb out of, three consecutive high ravines, with the barest traces of trail most of the time; in compensation you are likely to spot many animals – particularly fox and wild goat – since hardly anyone comes here. Water and good picnic spots are also not a problem, especially in the second hollow you reach. Once over the 3064-metre saddle you descend slightly into the Lanjarón drainage to pick up a clear trail, actually the rejected left-hand option between Elorrieta and Peñón Colorado, and head another 90 minutes south, without losing altitude, to the Refugio Forestal (2800 metres).

This is right on the path (thus impossible to miss even in poor weather), with fine views across the river valley to the Cerro del

Caballo. It sleeps three in comfort, five in an emergency; water comes from seeps nearby and recently the hut was in reasonable condition. It takes five hours to walk from the Veleta gap (as opposed to the four hours reported for the Caballo route), reflecting the unavoidable up-and-down just south of Virgen.

Stage 4: Refugio del Caballo or Refugio Forestal to Lanjarón

From Caballo the onward path, which is in good condition, descends in five hours – through forest once you're below 2300 metres, and past the ruined Ventura shelter – to Lanjarón. Two-thirds of the drop in elevation occurs in the last half of the horizontal distance; keep to the crest as much as possible.

From the Refugio Forestal, continue south for 45 minutes until the trail dwindles in the midst of an alpine tundra of spiny, miniaturised vegetation. The path does an S-bend, as shown on the FEM/IGN map, then proceeds steadily south-south-west along the edge of a precipice. Genuine grasses appear as you approach a firebreak and the first trees, 1 hour and 45 minutes along.

A trail does continue through the pine grove ahead, but it's very overgrown and not worth following. It's better to descend to the right, using the firebreak, and link up with the end of the forest road coming up from the Ermita del Padre Eterno. Follow this track until you see several *cortijos* on the right, and a grove of mixed deciduous and conifers on top of a bluff on the far bank of the river. Take a twisty driveway down past the lowest farm to (1½ hours from the firebreak) meet a trail which begins following the Río Lanjarón downstream.

This path is often exquisitely engineered as it drops sharply, through terraced orchards, to the bridge over the river just east of Lanjarón (660 metres). The town is in sight much of the way, and you should reach the bridge some two hours after leaving the highest farms, for a total on the day of six hours.

Spurred by reports of a direct Lanjarón-Cañar trail, I tried to find the same by exploring various paths heading east from just above the bridge. All such attempts ended in miserable failure – I ended up in Órgiva after three hours – and I later learned that I had aimed too low, and that the path which exists veers away from the Lanjarón canyon a considerable distance before the bridge so as to avoid the numerous *barrancas* (gullies) which slash the landscape west of Cañar.

Similarly there are no attractive direct walking routes from Lanjarón to Órgiva; if you don't plan to stay in Lanjarón, see if you can flag down the last Lanjarón-Órgiva bus, which passes by shortly before 5 pm.

For a bit of luxury after your trek, Lanjarón, an old established spa resort, would be a good bet. The town is strung out along the main road, with a good deal of modern building but also some elegant old hotels and restaurants. Bus service is identical to that for Órgiva.

Northern Approaches to the Sierra Nevada

For those who do not wish to tour the High Alpujarras on foot, particularly in midsummer, there exists a pair of useful access points to the Cañada de Siete Lagunas from the north. Either of these itineraries can be appended onto the courses already described to make up what the Spanish call the *Ruta Integral de los Tres Mil*, the complete traverse of all the Sierra Nevada peaks over 3000 metres in elevation.

Starting from Jeres del Marquesado, you can reach the open ICONA refuge (1480 metres, with eight places) at Porterillo within 90 minutes. The next stage would be, once clear of a hairpin turn above the hut, to pick up the old caravan path up to the Puerto de Trevélez, which (unlike on the south side of this pass) does not follow a river valley but mounts a mostly forested spur.

From the *puerto* you would head west-north-west, up an initially gentle grade along the major watershed ridge until arriving at Cerro Pelao (3144 metres). This is actually the second peak over 3000 metres high; Picón de Jeres (3094 metres), just to the north, would be omitted following this strategy. Count on a six-hour climb from Porterillo to this point. There is water in tiny tarns nearby and if daylight was running out you could pitch a tent in a flat lee of Cerro Pelao.

If they can, however, climbers usually camp a bit further on. From Pelao the route curls south to follow the main ridge, passing La Atalaya (3138 metres) and El Cuervo (3152 metres), separated by a prominent pass (just under 2900 metres, 1½ hours past Pelao) where again one might erect a tent. The third and most usual camping site is another hour-plus south, at the Vacares saddle (2974 metres) where there is a final seasonal tarn (shown as the Laguna de Vacares on the FEM/IGN map). However it is unlikely that you will arrive here in a single walking day from Porterillo. You can reach this point from the valley described following.

From Granada, *Autocares Bonal* (Avenida Calvo Sotelo 19) run a bus service up to the village of Guejar Sierra, in the valley of the Río Genil. Follow the road paralleling the river and an abandoned ore tramway 6 km further east to a river-crossing, the *Hotel del Duque*, and the start of an old trail, the 'Vereda de la Estrella'. This leads, initially gradually, for 90 minutes up to the Vadillo hut (1350 metres), another eight-person

ICONA special, in the appealingly forested Valle de la Estrella.

Here you should leave the river valley and begin climbing in earnest up the Loma del Calvario; within 2½ hours a path leads you to the last hut on the north side (Refugio Forestal del Calvario) at the relatively low altitude of 1900 metres. The trail continues south-east out of the forest until petering out at the base of the ridge formed by Mojón Alto (3109 metres) and El Cuervo, with the last stretch up to the Vacares saddle being cross-country. The climb from the Calvario hut to the 'ridge of the 3000' takes four hours, which when added to the distance of the lower legs on the Vereda de la Estrella makes a long, seven-hour day. Unless you've been able to make a very early start, it's advisable to overnight at Calvario.

Whichever way you arrive at Vacares, the next step is infinitely more difficult than anything before it. Beyond the Puntal de Vacares (3129 metres), most trekkers will have to fall off to the east to skirt Goterón and its nasty spur, slipping around it and the outriders of Alcazaba with appreciable loss of altitude before arriving in the Cañada de Siete Lagunas. Sticking as close to the summit ridge as possible, someone with a good head for heights could take four hours to reach the Cañada from the Laguna de Vacares.

Castilla

Mountains or other wilderness areas are not the first thing that comes to mind when pondering Spain's vast and at times bleak centre, but many minor ranges and valleys furrow the landscape. To the north-east are the Montes Universales above Cuenca, with their strange rock formations and traces of prehistoric occupation, attract some attention. The Sierra de Urbión and its Laguna Negra, north of Madrid on the border with the Basque provinces, are popular with local hunters and weekenders. And the Sierra de Guadarrama functions year round as the capital's closest 'hill station', chock full of ski runs, villas, institutional hostels, etc – but with precious few walking trails. For a rewarding alpine trekking experience in the heart of Spain, the peaks described following have no serious competition.

The Sierra de Gredos

The Gredos range forms an abrupt alpine barrier between León and Old Castile to the north and Extremadura and New Castile to the south and south-east. Though technically speaking, the sierra begins almost immediately west of Madrid and merges to the east-north-east with the lower Sierra de Guadarrama, the most visited area (and the one of most interest to hikers) consists of a relatively compact zone of about 150 square km around the ridgeline's centre.

The north and south flanks of the Gredos display a marked dissimilarity. On the Ávila side the terrain drops away in rolling *paramera* (moorland) to the Tormes river valley and an average elevation of 1300 metres, with a handful of villages scattered a hundred metres higher or lower. This cold upland has big horizons and ample pasture for the numerous cows, source of the region's famous cheese and sausages. Above about 1500 metres grazing land often alternates

with stands of broom, gorse, dwarf juniper and inedible alpine grasses.

The Gredos crest is composed almost entirely of granite, and for much of its length is well suited to ridge-walking. Partly owing to this strata, numerous springs well up relatively close to the summits, so that finding water is rarely a problem. The granite has been sculpted into weird and improbably shaped pinnacles, most notably (moving from east to west) at Peña del Mediodía, Los Galayos/La Mira, and to either side of 2592-metre Almanzor, the highest point in the sierra. Glacial action has resulted in two chains of appealing tarns (one at the Laguna Grande cirque below Almanzor and the other at the nearby Circo de las Cinco Lagunas) which provide most of the pleasure in visiting these mountains and attract the greatest number of walkers.

Further enjoyment comes from the near certainty of sighting *Capra pyrenaica gloriae*, the native Gredos ibex, discussed fully later. Several species of birds of prey, particularly eagles and vultures, also patrol the high peaks.

South of the watershed, the landscape falls away far more sharply from minimum altitudes at several passes of about 2000 metres to the valley of the Río Tiétar, with a vertical interval of up to 1500 metres. This somewhat exaggerates the strenuousness of an approach from this direction, since most of the trails begin at elevations of around 1000 metres, but still don't underestimate the difficulty of this task.

The effort is certainly worthwhile, since this is the most dramatic and attractive face of the range. Sheltered by the alpine wall, citrus, olives and vineyards flourish below 600 metres near the river; just above, certain picturesque villages nestle amid fruit orchards, with pine and oak forests extending in some places up to 1400 metres.

While the Gredos might be scorned by aficionados of the Pyrenees and the Picos de

Europa as minor-league, it has undeniable advantages – principally the relative accessibility of the alpine area and the good condition of the most important trails. The following itinerary has been designed as the most representative and practicable to trekkers, with minimised unnecessary altitude gain. However hundreds of Spaniards from the nearby metropolises of Madrid, Valldolid, Ávila and Toledo agree that this is a great way to spend a weekend and you won't exactly have the place to yourself.

Rating

This is moderate for the central Gredos if done in the recommended direction, though be prepared for long trekking days. It's more difficult in reverse. Conditions in the western group are unverified, but unlikely to be easier.

Duration

Starting from Madrid, Toledo or Cáceres,

you can be in or around Guisando by the first night, at Prado de las Pozas the second and third nights (with a day excursion to the two lake-cirques), and down to Candeleda on the fourth afternoon in time to catch outward transportation if desired. Bus connections (eg the impossibility of getting anything *from* Guisando to Arenas in time for any reasonably prompt bus to Talavera or Madrid), as well as the net altitude changes, make reversing this order inadvisable.

For the gung-ho, the fourth night could be spent in Madrigal de la Vera or Jarandilla, bases for traverse or ascent respectively; the fifth day in the western sierra; and another traverse or descent on the sixth and final trekking day.

Season

Most stationary facilities and bus schedules are geared toward July-August visitors, but this coincides with infernal heat which plagues ascents from the south. If at all pos-

sible, visit in late June or early July (when long days provide some assurance of completing lengthy traverses), or in early September. Summer weather is quite stable, though storms can start at any time after the autumnal equinox. Snow is a potential obstacle above 2000 metres until the end of May, or well into June after a bad winter.

Supplies
It's best to get these in Madrid or some other large town, as your time in Arenas will probably be limited and there is little available in Guisando, El Hornillo or El Arenal. Candeleda, Madrigal de la Vera and Jarandilla are adequate for provisioning an extra stint in the western sierra.

Map
For the central Gredos, use Editorial Alpina's No 302 *Sierra de Gredos* (1:40,000), plus *Mapas de la Sierra de Gredos* (1:50,000 on one side, 1:200,000 on the other) by Miguel A Adrados et al, extracted and sold separately from a Spanish-language guide by the same authors. You need both: the Alpina for detailed coverage, the Adrados for route-planning and the range's relationship to surrounding villages.

If you plan to do any exploring in the western Gredos, SGE sheets 14-23 (577) *Bohoyo* and 14-24 (600) *Villanueva de la Vera* (both 1:50,000) are mandatory investments.

Getting to/from the Trailheads
Although the range (except for its extreme western end) lies entirely within Ávila province, the standard approach for those relying on public transport is from towns of New Castile to the south.

Starting in Madrid, the first step is to take a train from Atocha station to Talavera de la Reina. You must leave by 12 noon to be assured of a significant choice in onward buses from Talavera to the Gredos foothills. Other well-travelled routes include from Toledo to Talavera (by bus) and from Cáceres to Talavera (by train). On arrival, the bus terminal is an easy 400-metre walk south of RENFE.

The ideal connection will be with the 3 pm *Gredos Auto* bus (not on Sunday) to Arenas de San Pedro, a large town astride a tributary of the Río Tiétar. The same company also runs buses directly from Madrid to Arenas, but this is a bumpy and squalid (especially in summer) ride and cannot be recommended over a comfortable, air-conditioned train as long as you pay attention to schedules.

In Arenas there are extremely elusive (ie possibly non-existent) minibus services up to Guisando, El Hornillo and El Arenal, but these are only six, 5½ and nine road km distant respectively, so either taxi hire or hitching will be relatively easy.

If you miss the 3 pm bus, one alternative is to take the 5 pm bus (company *Rubio*) to Parillas, about halfway to Arenas, and hitch or take a taxi from there – both tough propositions due to lack of appropriate vehicles.

Your other choice is to take a direct bus to Candeleda and do the hiking itinerary in reverse – not recommended as this causes unnecessary hardship. If you must, both *Sepulvedana* (daily, 7 pm) and *Rubio* (5 pm, not Sundays) serve this route; from July to September *Sepulvedana* lays on an extra departure out of Talavera at 1.15 pm.

More worthy of knowing about are the return departures from Jarandilla (4.30 pm year-round, also 7.45 am summer only) passing through Madrigal de la Vera and Candeleda (30 and 45 minutes later respectively) en route back to Talavera. Timing the hike's end to coincide with the passage of the afternoon bus will minimise problems involved with staying in Candeleda (see following).

Coming from the north, it is best to start fresh from Ávila, the theoretical base of an infrequent bus service along the C-500 road which threads the Tormes valley. You would get off at Hoyos del Espino and then face a further 11-km road-walk, taxi ride, or thumbing job up to the Prado de las Pozas. Should you miss, or there not be, a direct service to the villages along the Tormes, your fallback would be to take an Ávila-Plasencia bus as far as Barco de Ávila and then hitch or take a taxi for the necessary distance up the Tormes valley to Hoyos. In all frankness

Top: Las Alpujarras – Capileira from the Poqueira gorge
Left: Cazorla – Borosa gorge
Right: Cazorla – Ermita de Monte Sion

Top: Sierra de Gredos – Gredos goat at Circo Lagunas
Left: Sierra de Gredos – middle lake of Circo Lagunas
Right: Sierra de Gredos – Puente Puerto

approach or exit from/to the north cannot be recommended unless you have your own vehicle.

CENTRAL GREDOS
Stage 1: Guisando to Prado de las Pozas

You can stay in Arenas de San Pedro, but (despite its foundation in Roman times, and a castle, bridge and church all dating from the 15th century) the town itself is nothing out of the ordinary and you are better off using the rest of the day by proceeding to Guisando.

This proves to be an attractive hamlet (766 metres up) tiered on a slope just above the Río Pelayo. There is one *hostal* in Guisando, *El Galayar* (tel (918) 370914), and another (*Pepe*) about one km uphill, just beyond the official camping site *Los Galayos* which is well equipped and even has a small indoor dormitory – reassuring in the very possible event of the two *hostales* being full.

A surfaced but narrow road leads, via the camping site and within four km, to the Nogal del Barranco trailhead, at the margin of the forest 1160 metres up. Here is a spring, a picnic ground and (most important for those wanting an early start on the next day) an ICONA refuge a few minutes up the trail which begins at the parking lot. The hut has bunks for a dozen or so persons, and basic meal service in a separate building. At times other than from July to September you will need to fetch the keys from the ICONA warden in Guisando.

Once past the shelter, the trail – initially quite distinct – soon begins climbing in earnest to the headwaters of the Pelayo, entering a defile known fittingly as 'La Apretura' (The Squeeze). The grade stiffens considerably, but unless you have an elephantine load this is still the quickest and most straightforward approach to the high country. It is obviously best to make this ascent in the early morning before the sun has a chance to roast you alive in the confines of the gorge.

After a couple of switchback series over talus piles and passing two springs, you'll arrive after three hours at the 'Victory' hut,

elevation 1950 metres, on the true right (west) bank of the nascent Pelayo. With places for a dozen, but in poor condition, this hut is better for a lunch stop than an overnight stay.

For the next hour-plus the trail, marked by cairns, worms its way up the cliff to emerge (just below 2300 metres) at the edge of Los Pelaos, the relatively flat incline tilting up from the north-east to La Mira (2343 metres). Around the altimeter, there is a curious round tower-base (reached by a short flight of steps), the remnant of what was once an optical telegraph station. Visually the site's characteristics haven't changed – this is the best simultaneous vantage in the Gredos, with views south over the Tiétar basin, immediately east to the spires of Los Galayos, and just south of west to the Almanzor group.

Continuing involves a two-hour, gradually descending and uncomplicated ridge walk to the Puerto de Candeleda (2016 metres). When necessary you dip to the right (north-west) side of the watershed to circumvent various boulder piles, slabs and sharp drops. The path is passably clear much of the way, with cairns appearing when necessary. As you look north from the pass, a giant cairn marks the onward route; there are other occasional markers on the final hour down through cow pastures to the Prado de las Pozas, but as long as you eventually go along the west (true left) of the stream here, you'll have no problems.

In any case, the Refugio de Reguero Llano (1890 metres) is in plain sight during the final minutes of the walking day; it's unlikely that you'll get much further. The hut is permanently staffed from June to September, weekends and holidays at other times of the year. Up to 40 people can sleep on the wooden platforms downstairs (150ptas a head); when the hut is not attended an adjacent auxiliary building may be open. There is a fountain at the back of the building, and an expensive bar/cantina on the upper floor.

However, the atmosphere can be a bit on the unsavoury side because of proximity (20 minutes) to the so-called 'Plataforma' roadhead just down the hill, where half the urban population of the *meseta* appears to be parked on a Saturday. You can enjoy a little more privacy by camping, in mostly bug-free surroundings, down by the Río Pozas, just a few minutes to the west.

Stage 2: Prado de las Pozas to Laguna Grande & Circo de Cinco Lagunas

On a summer day the path to these beauty spots resembles an expressway at rush hour. Grooved in as it is, it shouldn't be too hard to find the trail at any time. From the cement pedestrian bridge over the Pozas, with some popular camping sites just upstream, it's a 45-minute climb to the *cuerda* (spur) and

spring of Los Barrerones (2200 metres). After a like period of descent, passing two more springs and with continual panoramas of the main Gredos cirque, you reach a signposted junction.

You can proceed straight ahead for 15 minutes more (1 hour 45 minutes in total, two hours with a full pack, as accurate signs at Pozas explicitly state) to the far shore of the attractive Laguna Grande. The refuge of José Antonio Elola (2000 metres) seems to have been officially renamed Laguna de Gredos, but this has neither affected its schedule (the same as Reguero Llano's), its capacity (over 100 bunks, plus a permanently open wing

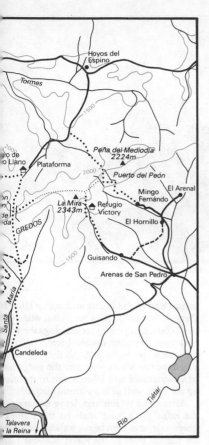

Laguna Grande, the well-engineered trail zigzags up for 45 minutes around the 2000 metre Risco Negro, then drops into the valley of Gargantón (one hour out) – a sign gives accurate walking times. The Gargantón area offers the last water before the climb up to the Portilla del Rey (2374 metres), plus some relatively private camping.

The made trail ends two hours beyond the Laguna Grande junction, just below the *portilla* (small pass) itself. Next comes a 45-minute, 300-metre descent to the shore of the largest lake in the Cinco Lagunas cirque. This is without doubt the most secluded camping site in central Spain, but it'll cost you heavily to get a full pack in from Laguna Grande – there is no path down the final, sharp grade, only cairns on a semi-stable boulder slide between the gap and the water.

Most people arrive via a path along the Garganta del Pinar, past the small, open Refugio de la Barranca, 90 minutes below the northernmost tarn, and 2½ hours above the village of Navalperal de Tormes on the C-500 road; this would seem to be a reasonable trekkers' route out. With a daypack, the drop into the cirque presents few problems to the fit and is eminently worthwhile, not least because the tarns do not show themselves until you are part way down the hill.

Another excellent reason to cover the full distance is for the opportunity to sight the Gredos ibex, though these also frequent the Gargantón canyon in large numbers. Protected since the 1930s, the population has risen from a nadir of 100-odd to several thousand. They are quite tame (almost cheeky, since they're not hunted), and you'll all but stumble upon them, perched nonchalantly on flat rocks with their legs tucked under. The males, with metre-long scimitars of horn, are particularly beautiful. During the summer months the 'ibexes' (more properly a mountain goat, *Capra pyrenaica gloriae*) are found almost exclusively on the shadier north-facing slopes of the Gredos.

The return to the Portilla del Rey, owing to the care necessary on the way down, takes about the same time – 45 minutes. From up top the deforestation of the sierra's north slope is obvious; you also catch glimpses of

with space for 20) nor its provision of meal service (expensive as usual) and two-way radio connection. Not to worry if it is full, there are numerous excellent camping spots on the shore of the large lake and also beside the several small tarns near its drainage.

Most people, especially if they are based at Prado de las Pozas, will want to use the balance of the day to continue to the Circo de las Cinco Lagunas, easily done by bearing right at the signposted junction noted previously and following the *trocha real* (king's way), a hunting path constructed by order of Alfonso XIII in the 1920s. Beginning from the tarns where you can camp just below

Gredos ibex at Gargantón

various villages on the Tormes plateau, but among the summits of eastern Gredos only Los Galayos are at all pronounced.

Continuing to retrace your steps, you've an hour down to Gargantón, again 45 minutes over Risco Negro to the signposted junction, and 1 hour 45 minutes back to the Prado de las Pozas. The elapsed time for the return-leg is virtually identical to that for the outbound trip; this is not too surprising since the altitude changes involved are symmetrical, as the recommended maps (and an altimeter) will confirm.

Stage 3: Prado de las Pozas to Candeleda

From your camping site or from near the Reguero Llano refuge it's simple to reverse your arrival route up to the Puerto de Candeleda; this should take no more than 75 minutes with an average load.

Descend from the saddle for just over half an hour to where the Fuente de Vaciazurrones (1760 metres) spills across the trail; fill up, as there will be no other water source for a few hours. This spring is shown vaguely on the suggested Editorial Alpina map, as is the *camino*, which actually runs a few milli-

metres east of the points making up Hiruela Cimera. Sporadic cairns are useful when this year's (and last year's) broom clogs the way trail traces are often double-barrelled, so it's difficult to get badly lost. All the way down you have fine views west into the *garganta* of Casqueruela and Blanca, not to mention up the back wall of the summit cirque.

After about 90 minutes, leave the spine of the ridge for a brief spell on the Lóbrega gorge side, and then begin walking amongst the highest trees of the forest at about 1200 metres, less than two hours below the spring. Drop more steeply now, grateful for the shade, for slightly less than an hour to a forest road at just under 900 metres; this is shown or listed incorrectly in both the Alpina and the Collomb (see Books in the Facts for the Trekker chapter) guides as being over 1000 metres up.

In season a few cars are often parked by the debouchement of the path; turn left onto the *pista* and walk 300 metres to the downward-and-right continuation of the *camino* which since the edge of the forest has been descending in wide swings rather than the highly schematic straight course shown on all maps. It continues to zig-zag lazily for the final half-hour down to the Garganta de Santa María and its famous bridge, reached a total of five walking hours from Prado de las Pozas.

The Puente Puerto (known locally as the 'Romano' – Roman (bridge) – which it may well be) makes an excellent lunch stop, with the chance to take a dip in the inviting pools to either side. Beyond the bridge (650 metres) you parallel the river briefly and then actually climb slightly to the Fuente del Sauce, again shown inexactly on the Alpina, 1 hour 40 minutes after quitting the Puente Puerto.

You are now in the thick of the oak forest; over the next half-hour you should pass the Fuente del Roble and see a few farms downhill and to the right before linking up with the wider track coming up from these. (If ascending it's better to bear right at this fork for the least complicated course to Fuente del Sauce).

Within another half-hour you will walk off the Alpina map's coverage, no cause for concern as the now-wide *camino* swerves westward and drops steadily down to Candeleda, which has been in sight intermittently since the spring up by the pass. The trail merges with a street descending past a convent (easily distinguished by a large belfry) to a junction by a *Mahou* beer depot, giving a total of just under 2½ hours of walking from the bridge, and just under 7½ hours for the day.

Candeleda (430 metres) as a town is no great shakes despite a 15th-century church, though it is certainly easier to find your way around than Arenas de San Pedro. There are a couple of banks and *supermercados*, and the possibility of finding *Cointra* gas. Somewhat inexplicably it's an extremely popular resort for Spaniards in the warm months and the *hostal* and *fonda* at the east edge of Candeleda, on the road to Arenas, are reserved weeks in advance during the summer. Ditto for the *Hostal Pastora*, reached by turning right at the beer warehouse and following signs toward it and 'Piscina Carrera', though the *Pastora* also does table d'hôte suppers for all comers. If you deliberately or otherwise miss the 5.15

pm bus back to Talavera, you'll probably find yourself camping with literally hundreds of others along the river Santa María, between the two *piscinas* (natural pools) of which 'Carrera' is the upper one.

Alternate Route to La Mira

There exists a slightly gentler approach to La Mira, but it is about an hour longer and initially fraught with some organisational problems.

From Arenas de San Pedro you can get yourself up to El Hornillo (5½ km) or El Arenal (9 km), the next villages north-east from Guisando – again by rumoured shuttle minibus, taxi or hitching. El Hornillo (750 metres), a pretty enough village, is the jumping-off point for this alternate hike, but unfortunately has no facilities whatsoever for casual tourists. All of these – in the form of a pair of *fondas* and restaurants – are in El Arenal (900 metres), which is reached by a direct road from El Hornillo (despite what the Alpina map says).

Local map errors are not entirely Editorial Alpina's fault, since the bulldozers have been recently busy hereabouts and most of the lower stretches of the 'Camino del Peón' up to the Peón pass have been badly chewed up. To begin hiking it's best to get a taxi the six km (nine from El Arenal) of narrow asphalt road up the Cantos river valley to the Mingo Fernándo trailhead. At the final turnaround you'll see the refuge (supposedly open from July to September, but usually locked), with a couple of barns and a tiny open hut a few minutes past the road's end.

For the start of the usual walking route, backtrack 300 metres to picnic tables and a fountain beside the road. An initially wide cairned trail leads sharply up (north-north-east) into the trees and through some fernbrakes, until after a few minutes you meet the remnant of the old *camino* coming up on the right from El Hornillo. Bear left and soon meet a new forestry road not shown on any maps; follow it for only 300 metres before turning sharply right onto a faint path, then left at a junction just up the slope. Matters improve quickly though, as you wend your way through pine woods to the

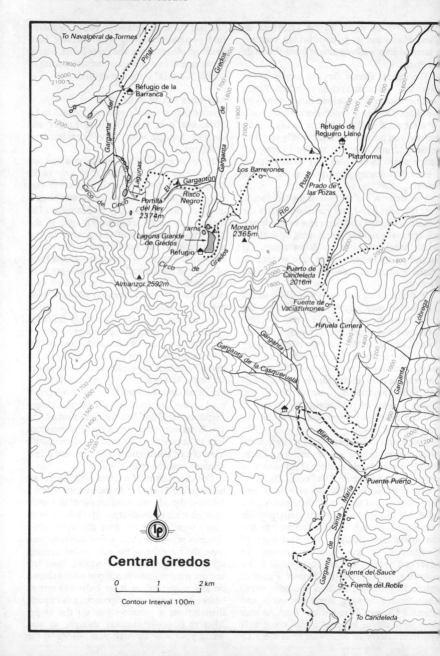

To Navalperal de Tormes

Refugio de la Barranca

Garganta del Pinar

Garganta de Gredos

Refugio de Reguero Llano

Plataforma

Los Barrerones

El Gargantón

Risco Negro

Portilla del Rey 2374m

Circo del Cinco

Lagunas

tarns

Laguna Grande de Gredos

Refugio

Morezón 2365m

Circo de Gredos

Almanzor 2592m

Prado de las Pozas

Río Pozas

Puerto de Candeleda 2016m

Fuente de Vaciazurrones

Hiruela Cimera

Garganta de la Casqueruela

Garganta Lóbrega

Garganta Blanca

Puente Puerto

Garganta de Santa María

Fuente del Sauce

Fuente del Roble

To Candeleda

Central Gredos

0   1   2 km

Contour Interval 100m

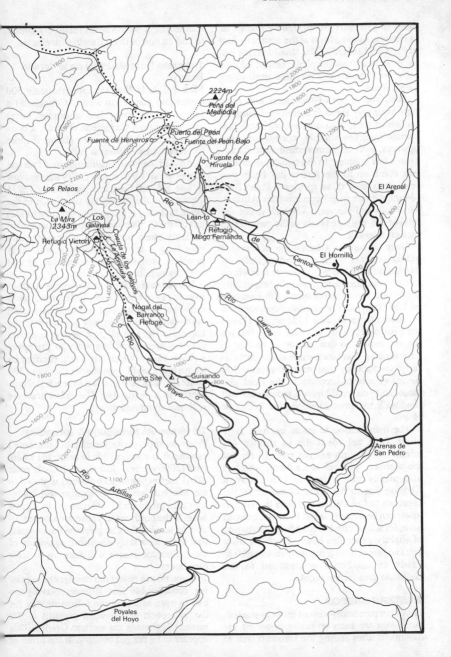

banks of a stream (1400m) fed by Fuente de la Hiruela, surging forth at the southern foot of Peña del Mediodía. You should arrive just under an hour from the picnic tables; take on some water as there is no more until about 1800 metres.

Soon you're out of the forest and must fight your way through a *matorral*-clogged section of trail; after another half-hour the *camino* swerves sharply northwards and upwards, with an improvement in surface – even a few cobbles! In the two-hour, shadeless climb up to the Puerto del Peón you fortunately pass three springs – Peón Bajo (on the Adrado map but not on the Alpina), Tío Feolo and Herveros – which make the total of 3½ walking hours to the pass (2013 metres) tolerable.

Once up top, in a landscape of hoodoo granite courtesy of the outriders of Peña del Mediodía (2224 metres), there are fine views north toward the Tormes basin but especially south-west to the seldom seen north-east face of Los Galayos. The *camino* continues for two hours down to point 1551 on the Hoyos del Espino-Prado de las Pozas road, but it's not recommended that you use it except in emergencies. The countryside is not particularly spectacular, you must traverse 500 metres of private property in the final distance, and you would have a tedious six-km road-walk to either Prado de las Pozas or Hoyos.

The main reason to come up here is to climb Peña del Mediodía (a simple 45-minute detour north-east) or, more likely, for the alternate approach to La Mira, which is also plainly visible beyond Los Galayos. Keeping just to the north of the crest, the approach to Los Pelaos and then the watchtower can be accomplished in a little over an hour, for a total climb from Mingo Fernando of slightly under five hours. From La Mira you can proceed (as previously discussed) to Prado de las Pozas or descend to the Guisando area for the night.

WESTERN GREDOS

I have not personally visited this sub-massif, but if you are keen on seeing more of the mountains after ending the standard trek at Candeleda, it would seem relatively simple to add on one of the following itineraries.

Traverses from Madrigal de la Vera to Bohoyo

Madrigal de la Vera (at approximately 500 metres and just 12 km west of Candeleda) is served by the same late afternoon buses passing through Candeleda. There's a bona fide camping site for overnighting if more formal accommodation is full.

An old *camino* beginning in Madrigal proper winds up to a pass (2179 metres) just to one side of Casquero de Peones (2271 metres) and then down the north side of the range to Bohoyo, a small hamlet (one *fonda*) just off the C-500 road. Though not an excruciatingly steep traverse, it is consequently very long – up to 12 hours – and fairly pointless unless adapted somewhat to add some mountaineering interest.

Instead take a taxi nine km up the Alardos river valley to Magazales (700 metres), cross the upper Alardos, and continue east (then north-east) up the Garganta del Sauce to the Lagunillo del Corral. Just above is a pass (2179 metres) providing entry to the upper Bohoyo valley, which has a trail running its length and a small open shelter (Seca at 1300 metres) available if you fail to reach Bohoyo hamlet in a single day. The entire traverse will take about nine hours.

Traverses via Navalguijo & Jarandilla

From an appropriate turning off the noted *camino*, it is also possible to reach the Lucia pass (2096 metres), just west of Lucia peak (2161 metres), with a continuation down to the two hamlets of Navalguijo and Navalonguilla (at around 1200 metres) in a great basin to the north-west. These are also reachable by leaving the Casquero de Peones pass trail in the necessary direction; again any of these alternate routes will take up at least nine hours.

If you do not object too strongly to regaining considerable lost altitude, Navalguijo can be used as a base the following day for the approach to Covacha summit (2390 metres), highest in the western Gredos. This appears to be rugged country, in the order of

that surrounding the Circo de Cinco Lagunas; three small lakes – Barco, Nava and Caballeros – are divided by various steep *cuerdas* radiating from Covacha. Fully laden trekkers may be forced to exit the area to the south via a pass (1995 metres) on the main Gredos crest between Covacha and El Cancho (2274 metres).

Assuming that a way can be found up to and around the summit to its west, one can descend via a saddle (2034 metres), where a clear trail leads down within 90 minutes to the Nuestra Señora de las Nieves refuge – at 1700 metres and usually locked. The route continues down another two hours to Guijo de Santa Bárbara (876 metres), which is just a few road km above Jarandilla (585 metres), terminus for the *Rubio* and *Sepulvedana* bus routes and blessed with two *hostales*, a camping site and (should you be feeling like treating yourself) a *parador* housed in the old castle.

It might be more practicable to start a traverse in Jarandilla and finish in Navalguijo, losing no unnecessary altitude and covering the steepest terrain going downhill rather than up. From Navalguijo or Navalonguilla you should be able to arrange a taxi or hitch to El Barco de Ávila, which has good bus connections.

The Spanish Pyrenees

The Pyrenees form the most majestic mountain system in Spain – indeed one of the finest in Western Europe – and no discussion of Spanish trekking opportunities would be complete without them. The range is actually shared between France and Spain, and the frontier follows the major watershed most of the way, but Spain comes out the luckier in the bargain, with the three highest summits and arguably the more impressive scenery on its side.

A few sources measure the Pyrenees' extent as 400-plus km by 50 to 200 km, but this is only true if you count every bump and knoll between the Bay of Biscay and the Gulf of Marseilles; a more realistic estimate, encompassing the rough rectangle of the High Pyrenees (territory from 2500 to 3500 metres in altitude), would be 170 km in length – from the Somport pass to Andorra – and 25 to 70 km in breadth. It is this relatively compact area that is described in the following sections.

Contrary to what many might imagine, the Pyrenees (*Pirineo* in Castilian, *Pirineu* in Catalan) do not form a single unbroken crest but are actually two chains, which overlap for 12 km to create the Vall d'Aran, the widest area, near the centre of the range. Except for this one, most valleys on the Spanish side run along a roughly north-south axis; communication between them is not easy until well down into the Ebro basin, though their heads often curl to one side and nearly meet. Thus there are (for the trekker anyway) usually negotiable passes between neighbouring valleys, and between corresponding French and Spanish ones (nowadays increasingly joined by automobile tunnels as well).

The Spanish Pyrenees are generally divided into three regions: Catalan, Aragonese, and Navarran, moving from east to west.

The high Catalan Pyrenees, falling almost entirely in the province of Lleida (Lérida), form a wonderland with hundreds of glacial lakes, showcased in the Parc Nacional de Aigües Tortes i de Sant Maurici. Regrettably many of the natural lakes have been altered by hydro-electric dams which together with the never-cleared construction debris, tram lines and continual tinkering with the water levels detract considerably from their grandeur.

However, this should not be allowed to overshadow the additional reality of idyllic high river valleys where old stone villages cluster around historic Romanesque churches, monasteries, and towers, surrounded in turn by orchards and hay meadows. Surprisingly, not all of these have been abandoned, or ruined by the tourist trade, and there are many such settlements past La Franja (the transition zone between Catalunya and Aragón) and well into Aragón proper.

Thick forests of ash, alder, birch, beech and aspen clog the valley bottoms, with black and Scots pine and silver fir dominating the higher elevations up to 2000 metres. Shrubbery features rhododendron, box and *Vaccinium*, with festuca grasses underfoot at the alpine levels. Such vegetation graces not only the Catalan mountains but continues a goodly distance into Aragón, cloaking the feet of Aneto, Maladeta (3404 metres) and Posets (3367 metres), the two highest summits. Beyond this pair of peaks the grandeur of massed trees is largely replaced by that of the forbidding U-shaped glacial canyons and rock walls of western Aragón.

Leaving the Aragonese peaks and the province of Huesca to which they belong, there's another transition to the rolling green, low mountains of Navarra, west of the Somport pass. While certainly pleasant for those who have them as their own backyard, they can scarcely rank as world-class mountains. But including these, and the low Mediterranean-flavoured sierras of the 'Prepireno' in Girona province, results in a totality of rich contrasts, with the bucolic and the unearthly often juxtaposed.

Hikewise, there is a bit of everything, and something for everyone, in the Pyrenees: wide lanes and well-marked long-distance trails (in particular GR11), less known paths, cairned cross-country routes, and just plain scrambling. For distraction (as if the general scenery isn't enough) the smallest flora make a botanist's paradise, with hundreds of native plants bearing witness to the meeting of Mediterranean and alpine species. Animal life is equally widespread, particularly chamois (*rebeco* in Castilian, *sarrio* in Aragonés, *isard* in Catalan) on land and birds of prey (including lammergeiers) in the air. Strangest of all is the shy desman, an aquatic, mole-like creature whose closest relatives live in the Caucasus.

In terms of other amenities and conditions, mountain refuges are common and often well positioned, though variable in terms of standard. They will be much appreciated, though, even if you carry a tent, since setting one up in a downpour is no fun. And weather, even in midsummer, can be fickle – take the equipment recommendations in the list in the Facts for the Trekker chapter seriously. On the bright side, precipitation and the absorbent granite and slate core of the mountains (though there is also abundant limestone), are responsible for a surfeit of water almost everywhere in the form of seeps, torrents, springs and lakes – this is the one Spanish range where you can probably get away with just a one-litre bottle. Unfortunately, the humidity is ideal for insects, including ferociously biting ones.

The greater part (in all senses of the word) of the Catalan and Aragonese Pyrenees has been linked by the east-to-west itinerary which follows. Some sections, such as the initial Cardós-Ferrera area, are necessarily self-contained, while other legs of the route can be done in isolation by consulting the organisational details provided. The treks described stay exclusively on the Spanish side, partly to avoid any potential embarrassments for visa-less North Americans and Australians, and a conscious effort was undertaken to avoid unnecessary duplication of existing English-language material (see the Books section), opting instead to dovetail with it by covering routes not previously

documented. The result, hopefully, is a challenging and rewarding traverse through often little-visited country.

Rating/Duration

Obviously if you were to accomplish all of the treks as described back-to-back, you would be both very fit, and fortunate to have the month of leisure to do so.

Season

In general, the best time is from early July to early September. Come before, and you face intimidating snowbanks; come later, and the weather is unreliable (though its reliability is only relative in the Pyrenees).

Maps

Most of the Pyrenees are gazetted by Editorial Alpina products and are prone to the usual defects as specified in Maps for Hiking. When the pertinent Alpina is badly mistaken, the correct details are furnished both in the text and the accompanying maps.

Equipment

Bring as much as you can from the list in Facts for the Trekker – I used everything several times. The Pyrenees are not mountains for the unprepared.

Difficulty ratings for individual legs of the trip, supply points, and organisational details on how to approach or leave various trailheads, are given at appropriate points during the description of the traverse.

The Catalan Pyrenees

VALL DE CARDÓS-VALL FERRERA

These two relatively isolated and unspoiled river valleys lie just west of Andorra and the Pica d'Estats (3143 metres), easternmost of the 3000-metre-plus summits and the 'roof' of Catalunya. The route outlined links them, via a pair of even higher tributaries (the Sellente and the Sotllo) and the wonderland of lakes in between. Approaching, you get a good idea of the traditional architecture and way of life in the half-dozen villages lining the two main rivers.

The basic circuit offers ample opportunity for side trips and variations: to Pic d'Estats, onward to (or entry from) Andorra via the Port de Boet, a loop around the Certascan/Noarre area, or a reverse itinerary with exit to Vall d'Aran past Mont Roig, along the classic 'High Route'.

Getting to the Trailheads

From Lleida (direct trains from Barcelona, usually with a change at Tarragona if starting from Madrid) you should take the 8.04 am train to Pobla de Segur. The 2½-hour ride, through tunnels and past reservoirs of the Pyrenean foothills, is a good introduction to what lies ahead. The rail journey connects well with the daily 11.40 am departure (also late afternoon on Sundays) of the *Alsina Graells* bus up the Noguera Pallaresa valley; this leaves from the terminal at Sant Miguel de Puy 3, next to the *Hostal La Montaña*, a two-km walk across the river and through town from the train station.

Pobla has a couple of *hostales* and *fondas*, some relatively expensive restaurants and ample groceries, should you want to stay the night and not chance the early morning connection from Lleida.

After threading through the impressive Desfiladero de Collegats, and passing the 9th-century bridge and Benedictine monastery at Gerri de la Sal, you should alight at Llavorsi on the banks of the Noguera Pallaresa; it will be nearly 1 pm.

Starting from the junction of the side road heading east along the Riu de Tor, it's 20 km to Tavascan and 18 km to Areu, the last villages in the Cardós and Ferrera valleys respectively. There is no bus, and little traffic, but what vehicles there are will pick up hitchers. A taxi to either community, if you can find one in Llavorsi, will probably set you back between 1500 and 2000ptas.

Rating

It's easy to moderate, though you'll need to put in some long walking days.

Duration

This is quite variable. Possibilities include: the first night at Planell de Boavi, the second and third nights at Estany de Sotllo with a day-hike up Pica d'Estats and the fourth night at Areu. Or: first night at Tavascan, second at Baborte refuge, third at Refugi de Vall Ferrera, fourth at Areu or even in Andorra somewhere – it's up to you.

Supplies

These are limited en route, so it's best to shop in Pobla de Segur, Barcelona or Madrid.

Map

Editorial Alpina No 211, *Pica d'Estats, Mont Roig* (1:40,000).

Stage 1: Tavascan to Planell de Boavi

Tavascan (1167 metres) is just beginning to realise its potential as a mountain tourism centre. There are two *hostal-restaurantes*, a back-street grocers' adequate for last-minute top-ups, and a camping site just before town. These are all handy should you be unlucky enough to have to walk the whole distance (and thus arrive around 6 pm).

Leave the village to the north-east, always sticking close to the Noguera de Lladorre, along the road which immediately loses its asphalt and dwindles to a track. After nine km of increasingly beautiful countryside, the track disappears at Planell de Boavi (1460 metres), a fine meadow studded with birch, fir and rhododendrons. In midsummer this is crowded, bug-ridden and trash-strewn, but at other times it provides a deserted and excellent camping site.

Day-hike to Certascan & Noarre

From Planell de Boavi, retrace your steps toward Tavascan for 10 minutes until you see a stone hut up on the right, and a bridge over a stream down and to the left. Follow faint traces up through the hut's meadow and find cairns in the forest margin. A trail soon appears but is badly deteriorated; you're very dependent on cairns as you wriggle up the east (true left) bank of the Riu de Certascan. Just under an hour along, you should see two waterfalls from a bend in the 'path'; veer away from the stream and climb sharply for 40 more minutes until levelling out on an upland slashed by small hogbacks.

A forest road is visible on the slope beyond; keep left (west of north), following

View west from Coll de Certascan

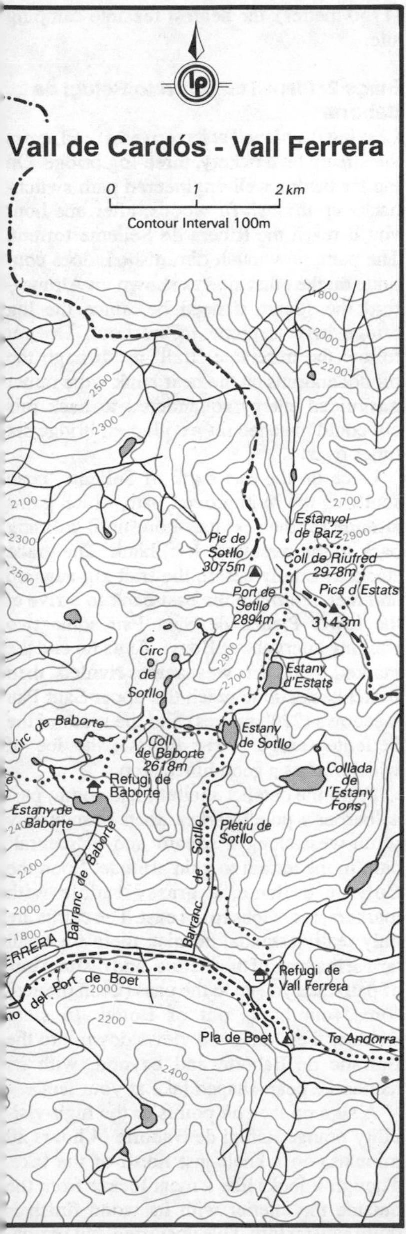

Vall de Cardós - Vall Ferrera

0   1   2 km

Contour Interval 100m

cairns on a roller-coaster course, past little tarns and under abandoned power lines. You meet the road a bit to the right (east) of where indicated on the Alpina map. Including the additional walk to a bridge, cement shed and signpost for the path up to the Llac de Certascan, allow 2½ hours for the climb from Boavi to here (at around 1900 metres).

If you plan to head up to Certascan with a full pack, it's best not to climb from Planell de Boavi, but to use the good, direct path commencing three km up the Certascan lake side road, crossed in the preceding description. The trail, wide and edged, ends just below the hut. The amount of road-walking (six km on the main riverside track, three km up from the turn-off) is the same as to Boavi.

Another hour-plus along the clear trail (except when snowbanks clog it) brings you to the FEEC shelter on the shores (2240 metres) of what is alleged to be the largest lake in the Pyrenees (perhaps in terms of volume – certainly not in surface area). The hut is open from approximately 24 June to 11 September; the current wardens – brothers, Joseba and Alejandro Gamarra – live in Vitoria (Gasteiz) in the off-season; reservations can be made there at tel (945) 25 42 26. The hut's capacity is 36, with bunk fees of 400ptas (250ptas for alpine club affiliates); set meals are a pricey 1000ptas, but cooking is allowed. As is usual, the wardens know much about the region and have put up a wall map with suggested excursions highlighted.

Leaving the refuge, skirt the lake clockwise, some 20 or 30 metres above the water, then veer off left (west) along the flank of the valley descending from the Coll de Certascan. The pass itself (at around 2600 metres) is reached 1 hour 20 minutes from the hut, skirting a tarn at the base of the incline and allowing for considerable snow before mid-July. A self-arrest device and crampons are helpful, but only mandatory with a full pack.

You can detour here for the obvious ascent of the Pic de Certascan (40 minutes up, at 2853 metres). Continuing from the summit, the safest and most interesting descent is via the rock slide just north of the spur plunging west from the trig point; backtracking to the saddle is inadvisable. You should end up on the shore of Estany Blanc, just south of the frontier ridge.

From the peak a full hour is required to pass the outfall of the lower Estanys Els Guerossos, and yet another, always on the left (east) bank of the drainage and entering the highest pines, to skirt an impassable cascade and the last tarn. You emerge on a broad meadow with ruined shelters and a few cairns at the far end; cross the stream dividing it where you can. Beyond the western lip of the meadow a bona fide trail resumes and crosses a brook at a waterfall; red blazes also should appear at the far end of the pasture.

At the end of a third hour of progress from the peak, much of it through attractive birch woods, you'll arrive at Noarre (1592 metres), roughly a dozen deserted houses. From the 'plaza' go down and left, cross a pedestrian bridge over the Riu de Noarre, and take the trail on the far bank which descends pleasantly for an hour to a modern bridge on the road serving this valley. The path is overgrown in spots but always followable, so be persistent. Along the way you've great views of cascades, farms across the valley, and (weather permitting) high peaks to the west.

The old trail continues below the road on the right a few hundred metres below the bridge, linking the last few farms perched above the river flowing toward Tavascan (reached after 45 more minutes). The path, initially difficult to find, glides along just above the water and enters the village over a medieval bridge. (It's only fair to say that the last stretch of road from the upper bridge is just as quick – there is a direct downturn into the middle of village from the 'suburb' just above the power plant). Either way, it will be suppertime, with return to Planell de Boavi in the dark at the end of a 12-hour day-hike!

If you use the Certascan-Noarre route to enter the Mont Roig area, go straight through Noarre hamlet on the obvious trail, rather than dipping left, to emerge above the loops on the road leading up toward a shallow pass into France. You would have to leave Planell de Boavi – or ideally the lake refuge – early enough for timely arrival at Pleta de l'Arenal (1750 metres), the nearest feasible camping site.

Stage 2: Planell de Boavi to Refugi de Baborte

Leaving the *planell* at its top (east) end, cross the stream on a rickety, three-log bridge. On the far bank a well-engineered path switchbacks up through fir woods; after one hour you'll reach the Ribera de Sellente torrent. The path, now much diminished, does continue on the other side as shown on Alpina – ford the stream if need be, since the log bridge here is prone to washout. Do *not* follow the miserable 'trail' up through the rhododendrons on the near bank – the rather misguided energy squandered to hack this out could have rebuilt a collapsed bridge six times over!

Once on the east bank of Sellente, head south up the re-improved path which gains altitude for the next half-hour until crossing back to the west (true left) bank. The grade slackens briefly before the trail zig-zags up and then returns to the east bank to arrive at the lower Planell de Sant Pau some two walking hours above Boavi. At its far end the marked route darts west across rivulets, then switchbacks up to reach the upper Sant Pau meadows (2240 metres) and the ruins of the Sellente refuge (three hours), the lee of which makes a good lunch stop.

From the derelict shelter head south, past a 'barber's pole' marker, then bear briefly south-west along a stream and a 'natural' path in the terrain to gain altitude. Soon the Coll de Sellente, a grassy saddle with markers, is obvious to the east. The cairns are only really essential in mist; there's a small tarn at the base of the incline, and distinct bits of path take you up to the pass (2485 metres) some four hours out of Boavi. In clear weather there are good views down into the Barranc de Baborte and beyond, with its namesake heart-shaped lake at your feet.

A sign on the *coll* points to the high-visibility orange Refugi de Baborte (4 hours 20 minutes) on a knoll just north of the lake. Though it looks like a meat locker from the outside the interior with its wood finish is quite satisfactory. This unstaffed, but perma-

Top: Pyrenees/Sant Maurici to Colomers – Els Encantats
Left: Pyrenees/Cardós-Ferrera – Estany de Sotllo, Pica d'Estats
Right: Pyrenees/Colomers to Ventosa i Calvell – Besiberri peak

Top: Pyrenees/Sant Maurici to Colomers – Estany Obaga from Coll de Ratera
de Colomers
Left: Pyrenees/Vall d'Aran – Unha church apse
Right: Pyrenees/Restanca to Benasque – Aneto from Aiguallut

nently open, hut has a rated capacity of 16 but comfortably holds eight people. There are blankets and a first-aid kit; you are kindly requested to send 100ptas to the UEC office in Barcelona – better to drop it off in person!

Stage 3: Refugi de Baborte to Vall Ferrera

From the shelter (2438 metres) head just east of north up the slope behind, but without gaining unnecessary altitude; you should be able to just see the string of tarns in the Circ de Baborte to the north-west. The Coll de Baborte (2618 metres) will be reached just

under an hour further along, with conditionally permitted good views of the Pica d'Estats and its neighbour the Pic de Sotllo (3075 metres). Descend 75 minutes to the shore of a large tarn in the Circ de Sotllo; follow its outflow east-south-east for the half-hour drop, mostly on turf, to the striking Estany de Sotllo (2532 metres) and pick up a clear trail on its west rim.

The lake lies astride the traditional route up to Estats, and if you're really serious about tackling the peak you should camp at the north end of the lake for a good morning start rather than stay at the Baborte shelter.

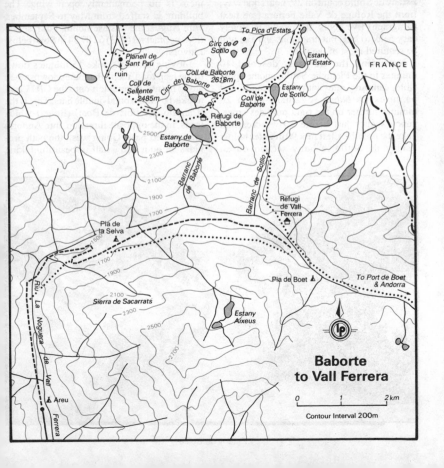

Baborte to Vall Ferrera

0   1   2km

Contour Interval 200m

Many climbers do the ascent as a long day-trip from the Refugi Vall de Ferrera hut.

The classic route continues north, past the Estany d'Estats – where all traces of trail disappear – and then up to the Port de Sotllo (2894 metres). From there you must descend a bit into French territory, but no further than the little Estanyol de Barz, and then double back right and east until you're between, though well below, Estats and Montcalm (3077 metres). For the final push up the gentler north slope, most people use the Coll de Riufred (2978 metres) en route to points 3126 and 3143. From a camp on the shore of Estany de Sotllo count on 2½ hours one way; from the Refuge de Valle Ferrera (see next paragraph) five hours. It's rated a relatively easy peak to bag, but crampons and axe will be required most of the year.

Resuming the traverse, descend 40 minutes to the Pletiu de Sotllo, another possible camping site with its cascades and pastures. A *balma* (overhang-cave) 20 minutes further on the right provides emergency shelter just before a river crossing. Take the uphill (!), left fork 90 minutes below Estany de Sotllo; a hairy section on an exposed rock face follows, but this can be circumvented if necessary by edging up a grassy detour. Having rounded the bend into the Vall Ferrera proper, proceed east without much altitude change until a metal 'Pica d'Estats' sign (2 hours 15 minutes) means the start of the sharp drop to the refuge (at 1940 metres and 2½ hours below the Estany de Sotllo).

This hut proves to have prices and policies similar to those at the Certascan refuge, though food is a bit more expensive. There are currently 21 spots in a nicely outfitted loft, though plans are afoot to expand it to 35; there is no permanently open wing. The building is staffed from May to September, with August the busiest month. For reservations contact tel (973) 62 07 54 in Sort (below Llavorsi).

Moving onwards, hike 15 minutes down to the jeep road, then 10 minutes downstream along it until turning left onto the GR11 trail marked by horizontal double bars. This is the 'Camino del Port de Boet' (Bouet) which leads, in the opposite direction, into Andorra via the said pass. Going west, the path provides an hour and a half of beautiful hiking

Estany de Sotllo

through fir and birch forest with amazing mushrooms most of the way, though the walking surface is frequently waterlogged.

You collide with the access road to the refuge just before the Pla de la Selva (around 1650 metres) where you could camp, but water's not obvious and it's best to make some more out of the day. Within 20 minutes, turn off the *pista*, just after a sharp curve, following GR bars onto a grassy track; soon this becomes a walled-in *camino* interrupted by two farm buildings. After 40 more minutes (for a total of 2½ hours from the refuge) you hit the road for the last time, staying on it for the final hour into Areu.

Areu (at 1220 metres) is a pleasant village with an excellent camping site (officially open during midsummer only but usable before then), a two-star *hostal*, and a small store. If this fails to appeal or is full up, Alins (5 km down-valley) has two *fondas* and is an altogether bigger place.

To leave Areu or Alins, it's often possible to arrange a ride with the *Copirineu* milk-truck which departs Areu at 9 am every day. This descends to Llavorsi and eventually Pobla de Segur; the driver, who has been doing the run for 15 years and is something of a local fixture, charges about the same as a bus (from 400 to 500ptas). The cab has space for a maximum of two with their luggage. Otherwise take a taxi to Llavorsi in time to catch the descending bus to Pobla which passes at 1.20 pm.

In theory it's also possible to continue along the GR11 as it diverges just above Areu to Tavascan, via the Coll de Tudela. This would be a long day, but would make a true loop possible, and the opportunity to store extra material in Tavascan.

PARC NACIONAL D'AIGÜES TORTES I DE SANT MAURICI

This national park is one of Spain's oldest and most spectacular reserves, with one of the highest concentrations of lakes and tarns in Europe. While the peaks are not spectacularly high, the countryside is sufficiently rugged to stymie, or at least dwarf, various attempts to tame it.

Most people enter the national park of Aigües Tortes i de Sant Maurici from Espot to the east; for keen walkers and those without their own transport, however, this route has several severe disadvantages. Firstly, Espot has no bus service; you must road-walk, hitch, or take a taxi 9 km up from the junction near the Torassa dam where the *Alsina Graells* service leaves you. Once in Espot you will pay premium prices for food and lodging as this is an up-and-coming ski resort, and to top if off, you will then have to shell out for a jeep-taxi 15 km into the park, either toward Estany de Sant Maurici or the Refugi J M Blanc at Estany Negre.

It is far preferable then, to approach the area from Capdella, the highest village in the little-known Vall Fosca. Facilities there are adequate, the walk in is mostly on trails, and you have a choice of onward itineraries from the group of tarns just south of the park boundary.

Supplies

Try Pobla de Segur or larger lower Catalan towns, as for the Cardós-Ferrera loop; there's nothing whatsoever available in Capdella!

Map

Alpina No 210, *Sant Maurici-Els Encantats* (1:25,000)

Getting to the Trailhead

You go to Pobla de Segur as for the Cardós-Ferrera circuit, but in this case take the 5.30 pm (except on Sunday) service run by *La Oscense* to Capdella. This departs from in front of the *Bertran* fabric store, exactly opposite the municipal tourist office, on the road to Sort in upper Pobla. If you miss the bus, or it's Sunday, you can easily cover the first 10 km on the C-144 road to Pont de Suert by hitching or a different bus, but the remaining 20 km up to Capdella is difficult to thumb or cover by taxi – there are few vehicles.

Capdella (Cabdella) is really two villages: the old upper quarter, without facilities and, 1.8 km below (where the bus turns around) the '*Central*' (one of the older power plants in these parts). Near the dynamo (luckily not audible), the *Hostal Energia* (tel (973) 65 00

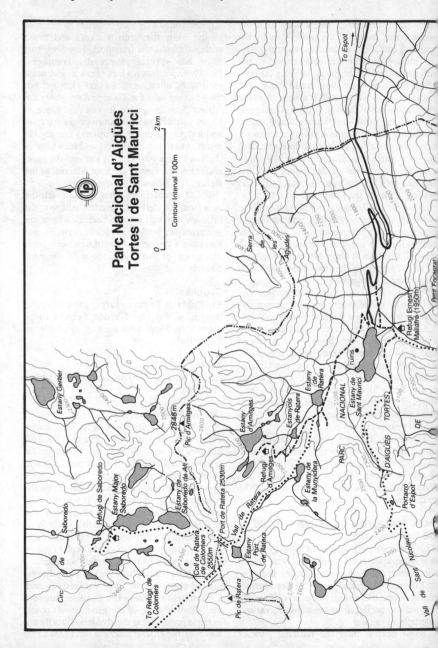

Parc Nacional d'Aigües
Tortes i de Sant Maurici

Contour Interval 100m

0   1   2km

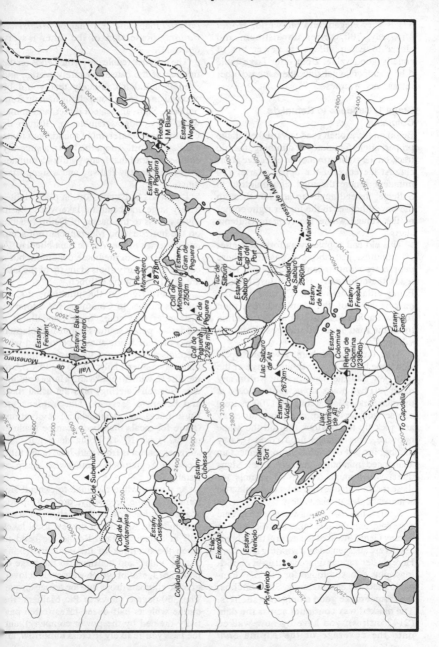

57) is very elegant and old-world; *Hostal Montseny*, 700 metres downstream and closer to Espui village, is newer but of equally good value. Both offer large table d'hôte suppers, vital since there are no other restaurants or stores.

Stage 1: Capdella to Refugi de Colomina

Begin on the asphalt road toward the village proper; after 15 minutes of climbing, the old track on the right provides an effective short cut. At the edge of the upper quarter (30 minutes), ignore the road sign pointing to Sallente; instead angle up and left through the lowest houses to the higher right corner of the village where the *camí* to Sallente starts.

This old and cobbled way forks left after 10 minutes, just above a pasture where people are wont to camp (down and right leads there instead). Have a last look at Espui village below the Central and the narrow head of the arable valley, then follow the Riu Flamisells past the treeline to hit the road again 90 minutes above the village.

After crossing the bare, ravaged dispersion zone below it, you should arrive at the ugly new Sallente dam (not shown on any maps yet) two hours along. A map board at the dam parking lot (at roughly 1700 metres) can set you on course; cross the causeway and pick up the obvious trail on the slope opposite. This zigzags up a *coma* (grassy incline) for just over an hour to intersect an abandoned miniature tramway line! Signs direct you through a series of tunnels for these tracks which served older hydroelectric schemes higher up the valley.

Just less than two hours above the Sallente reservoir, exit the last tunnel at the dam of Estany Gento (most of the natural tarns hereabouts are augmented by damming like this). Here cluster various dilapidated utility buildings, plus a locked lodge for FECSA (Fundació Electrica de Catalunya, SA) honchos; the former make good emergency shelters. The marked way continues across the dam (2142 metres); you have by now walked onto the coverage of the Alpina *Sant Maurici* map, and left that of *Montseny-Pallars* (possession of the latter is very optional).

The *telefèric* (cable car) which ends on the far side of the causeway rarely works, and even if it did it's unlikely that you'd be allowed on to spare yourself the haul up from Sallente. Signs indicate a direct, and somewhat risky, ridge-scramble to Refugi de Colomina; or a safer, more roundabout route via Estany Tort. Adopt the latter, a superbly engineered trail that leads within 45 minutes to yet another toy railway and a signposted junction.

Left leads to Estany Tort, in plain sight – a very large and beautiful lake whose basin gives access to the passes of Dellui (visible on the horizon) and Muntanyeta (not seen) and traverses to the Vall de Sant Nicolau. A *cabaña* here is in mediocre condition, but a couple of flat turfy spots at the tip of the lake are fine for camping or lunch.

Turning right at the junction, it's 20 minutes further to Colomina, for a total of just under five hours from Capdella at a moderate pace; sources reporting elapsed times of three hours should be viewed with scepticism. The refuge itself is a delightful unusual wooden chalet ceded by FECSA to the FEEC, with 50 bunks and a large cooking area (for self-catering) plus the usual meal and beverage services. The wardens are Enric Lucas and Anna Masip; reservations (more for meals than beds) can be made at tel (973) 68 10 42 Pobla de Segur. The summer season is from mid-June to the third week in September – otherwise camp at Estany Tort.

As a worthwhile day-hike to expend any remaining time or energy, proceed up the shallow ravine west of the shelter to Estany Colomina de Alt, one of the few local lakes still in a natural state. Round the bend to reach the overlook of the equally striking Estany Vidal, and continue up the ridge to point 2673, east of which a big wall beloved of rock-climbers drops into the refuge cirque. The 360-degree views to Pic Mainera, the cirque with its half-dozen lakes (often partially drained by the power company), and the pass you're likely to cross tomorrow, are superb. Allow two hours for the outing if you retrace your steps (which is advisable).

Stage 2: Refugi de Colomina to Estany de Sant Maurici

RatingThis moderate walk becomes slightly more difficult if conditions are adverse at the Coll de Peguera or if you avoid this by detouring via the Saburó and Monestero passes.

DurationTotal elapsed walking time from Colomina to the shores of Estany de Sant Maurici will range from six to seven hours, depending on snow and scree conditions; sources reporting a five-hour traverse should not be trusted.

Circle the *estanys* of Colomina and Mar on their west shores by an initially good and obvious path; at the far end of the latter lake, mount a grassy grade, though there are actual cement steps at the top. In less than an hour you should be level with the Saburó dam. The trail per se ends here, and the west shore of Estany Saburó is sheer and impassable.

Hang a left onto another green slope, assisted by a few cairns, and descend the far side of a small pass, assisted by more cairns

and faint traces. Cross the inlet of Estany Saburó and bear north, in stages, up to the obvious Coll de Peguera (2726 metres), reached 2 hours 15 minutes from the hut.

Metal signs point to the refuges one is coming from/going to; the north side of the pass itself is notoriously nasty, with a steep incline of several hundred metres. If it looks beyond your capabilities, the unnamed *coll* (2774 metres) just to the west, while higher and a longer way around, is reportedly gentler. In either case, crampons and a self-arrest device are all but mandatory before midsummer.

From the saddle to the first slackening of the grade count on taking 90 minutes if there's snowpack, an hour in the warmer months over the bad scree lurking below. Once past the relatively flat area, there's another drop to the right (east) of the watercourse, down a slope with boulders; surprisingly a faint trail helps you much of the way. Count on 75 minutes more to the turfy floor of the Vall de Monestero (Monastero).

Within 20 more minutes the path trickily crosses to the west (true left) bank of the stream draining the area, where it stays all the

Els Encantats, Estany de Sant Maurici

way to the largest and most attractive meadow of this beautiful canyon, just beyond the Estany Baix de Monestero. Rhododendrons on every side hint at the weather hereabouts; but with the sun out this is a fine lunch stop. Since the pass you have been officially within the national park; camping is theoretically forbidden but universally practised and tolerated for one-night stays.

Estany Feixant is hardly more than a swelling in the Riu Monestero; shortly after some ruined stone military barracks on the far side of Estany de Sant Maurici pop into view. The famous pinnacles of Els Encantats become recognisable on the right as you draw even with them. After a final descent through pines you arrive (75 minutes beyond Estany Baix de Monestero) at the Refugi Ernest Mallafré.

Small and cramped (rated for 36 persons but more realistically for 20), this has the virtue of being open year-round except during late January (tel (973) 63 50 09 for reservations). However the warden can be so brusque that you may, as I did, elect to camp at one of a number of spots just up the river. Despite a possibly anticlimactic finish, this is an appropriately wild and scenic introduction to the park proper.

Alternate Itinerary

If you have an extra day to spare, you can vary your entry to the Monestero valley as follows. From the Estany Saburó dam, head east to the Collada de Saburó (2560 metres) and then descend slightly to loop around the Cap del Port and Gran de Peguera lakes to slip over the Coll de Monestero (around 2750 metres). From there you would descend relatively gently into its namesake valley. This route would be somewhat longer, and it might be prudent to break this into two sectors, with an overnight at or near the Refugi J M Blanc.

Stage 3: Estany de Sant Maurici to Refugi de Colomers

This stage offers an exciting alternative to the usual jeep-track traverse – a variant of GR11 – over the Portarró d'Espot to Estany Llong and the Vall de Boí. Most of it follows a particularly spectacular section of the principal GR11 trail.

Rating This is a short, easy trek with modest elevation changes.

Supplies As for the previous two stages.

Map Alpina No 210, *Sant Maurici-Els Encants* and No 209, *Montardo-Vall de Boí*, both 1:25,000.

From the vicinity of the Mallafré shelter, get over to the north-east side of the dam (1900 metres), where there's a parking lot and a variety of wide gravel drives. You want the one marked '*Refugi d'Amitges 1 hr 30*'; a trail short-cuts the first switchback, after which you're forced onto the steadily rising track along the north shore of the lake. Views south to the Pic de Feixant, Els Encantats and the valleys of Subenuix and the lately traversed Monestero are unsurpassed, though FECSA has been known to fiddle with the water level in Estany de Sant Maurici, transforming it into a muddy bog.

Just beyond the Estany de Ratera, bear right onto the fork toward Refugio d'Amitges, and then make a quick left off the road where a GR11 signpost points back toward Mallafré and Espot. Here at its resumption, the trail (shown too far southwest on the Alpina sheet) is intermittent but cairned, and occasional red-striped poles make it impossible to get lost as long as you follow the north-east bank of the stream draining the Estany de Munyidera. This, just at treeline, is postcard-picturesque but a bit early for a lunch stop; the grade stiffens briefly at the top of the Vall de Ratera where sits the Estany del Port de Ratera, less attractive but better situated for a break, 2½ hours into the hiking day.

The Port de Ratera is the obvious saddle north-north-east of the upper lake, at 2530 metres, a mere 50 metres above the water level. The GR11 proper is marked to go due west above the lake, but especially with snowpack it's easier to use the *port* itself. Look down into the Circ de Saboredo (two lakes and the east end of the Vall d'Aran are visible), then traverse west along the flat, easy top of the ridge to the Coll de Ratera de Colomers (at around 2550 metres) and again find the characteristic red and white GR bars.

Here you should switch maps to the Alpina *Montardo-Vall de Boí* sheet as you begin the well-graded descent into the spectacular Circ de Colomers; suddenly several lakes, including the extensive Estany Obaga, appear. Snake down around the top end of Obaga (2242 metres), then continue north-west – the Alpina map is pessimistic in its depiction of the trail, which is in fact excellent.

Beyond Obaga, other shimmering lakes – Redó, Llarg, Cloto – appear in succession; the trail skirts the south-west shore of all but Cloto, closer to the water and narrower than Alpina's solid red line implies. Veer west after just a glimpse of Cloto and the low ranges behind the Vall d'Aran, and pop over a miniature pass to see the Refugi de Colomers at the far end of the dam with the same name. From the Estany Port del Ratera 2½ hours of walking should see you to the front door, for a total of five walking hours for the day, but what with stopping to munch, and gape at the fantastic scenery most people will take much, much longer!

The hut (at 2100 metres) has space for 30 and, with its wooden interior, is one of the more handsome ones. For the usual FEEC prices (400ptas non-club members/affiliates, 250ptas otherwise) you have the run of a cooking space and a stove-heated *comedor*; electric power cited in some guides is no longer available since FECSA disconnected it. More luggage space, and outdoor toilets/showers, are planned in the near future, but for now there's just a tap and an overhead shower pipe on the north wall and a privy-toilet perched over the dam (no swimming in *this* lake...). Josep Baques i Sole, one of the two wardens, is friendly and an experienced climber who also leads trekking tours in adjacent areas. There is no phone number for reservations; the summer season is from late June to late September.

Since the Port de Ratera you have been outside the national park boundaries, so there would be no objection to camping by the Estany de Colomers or any other nearby lake,

but be warned that level space is at a premium. More potentially useful is a permanently open refuge on the lake shore just south of the main building.

If you need to leave the mountains in a hurry, the village of Salardú in the Vall d'Aran is 15 km down a road beginning below Refugi de Colomers; see the Vall d'Aran section for more details.

BETWEEN THE PARK & THE VALL D'ARAN

The territory lying to the west and north of the national park is, if anything, even more impressive than the 'protected' area.

Stage 4: Refugi de Colomers to Refugi Ventosa i Calvell

There are actually two commonly frequented routes between these two shelters, of approximately equal length and difficulty, and which one you use will depend on your plans for trekking beyond Ventosa i Calvell. If you intend to strike out south-east toward Estany Llong in the Vall de Sant Nicolau (see end of this stage), you should adhere to GR11 for the more usual itinerary up to the Port de Caldes (Ribereta), then down a lake-studded valley to the second refuge, reached within five walking hours. If instead you opt to head north from Ventosa i Calvell to the Restanca hut and the Vall d'Aran, you will probably want to arrive at the former via the Port de Colomers leg detailed following. Choosing accordingly avoids excessive duplication of the route on the next trekking day.

Rating This trek is moderate for the basic route. Of the alternate onward options, taking Coll de Contraig is more difficult, Port de Rus less so.

Supplies There's no possibility of restocking until Boí so you must carry food from Capdella and/or patronise refuge kitchens!

Map Use the Alpina No 209, *Montardo-Vall de Boí* . The same publisher's No 214, *Pont de Suert-Escales* (1:40,000) is useful for the traverse from Taüll to Capdella.

Leave Refugi de Colomers on the GR11, then branch left almost instantly onto a red-dotted trail leading to the open refuge, leaving this just as quickly to follow a stream up toward a visible gap to the south-west. Slightly different red dashes now mark the way to the Port de Colomers, though this does seem to be a less popular route than over the Port de Caldes.

Cross the outlet of Estany Mort, pretty and alive with frogs despite its name ('dead'); head up-valley towards the visible and audible waterfall cascading from the lip of the Circ de Colomers. You will see, but should ignore, the Port des Caldes visible due west; where the red blazes cease and the trail appears to bear down and left (east) toward another lake, use common sense and keep a southerly course, following scarce stone cairns to ford the inlet of the lower lake between two sets of small falls. Thereafter the path improves and cairns multiply as you pass east and above Estany Bergils, just over an hour along.

The trail disappears again as you skirt two more nameless tarns, still on the east (true right) bank of the drainage, until arriving at the Estanyets del Port, scattered across the cirque. The inlet of the westernmost one is the Alpina-designated point for crossing to the west bank and beginning the climb to the pass, but in practice most people seem to switch sides long before, angling up to the obvious notch in the ridge rather than attacking it perpendicularly.

You reach the Port de Colomers (2591 metres) 2½ hours after leaving the Colomers hut; crampons are nice after a severe winter, but not essential. From the top of the pass you're rewarded with views west over the savage-looking Besiberri ridge and assorted lakes in the valley at your feet; prospects over the terrain just covered are not nearly so dramatic. Descend via a cairned trace to the marshy flats of Tallada Llarga, and reach the first of the Estanyets de Culieto 45 minutes below the pass.

The Refugi Ventosa i Calvell lies another 90 minutes beyond; the alternate dotted route shown on the Alpina map is trail-less and rather arduous, with the view over the name-less lake just above Estany Negre only partly compensating. It is better to follow the trail leaving from the outlet of the first Estanyet de Culieto; you will pass close to the lower anonymous lake anyway, a good lunch spot (and possible, though boggy, camping spot). Total trekking time for the day will be 5¼ hours, not three hours as reported in some accounts.

Situated at 2200 metres, the CEC Ventosa i Calvell refuge (also known as 'Estany Negre' after the huge lake just below) is a clean, friendly, 'state-of-the-art' shelter with supplies delivered by helicopter. Though rated at a capacity of 80 persons, the staff readily admits that a non-emergency quota of 50 is more realistic. Bunks are expensive – up to 700ptas for non-club members – but food is slightly cheaper and better than in many of the FEEC refuges. As in the other CEC establishments, you are not allowed to cook in the *comedor*, but may do so in the vestibule or on the outside terrace. It's worth noting that the supposedly 'open' ENHER refuge perched 200 metres west on a hillside is now locked except for the rather grubby basement; if you can't or won't stay at the refuge, your only alternative is to pitch a tent at Estany Xic just above (with space for one or two parties) or camp up by the tributary lakes previously noted. The main refuge is staffed from mid-June until the end of September; for reservations contact tel (937) 64 18 09.

Ventosa I Calvell to Boí

If necessary you can interrupt or end your Pyrenean traverse here quite easily. A good *camino* descends within 90 minutes to the Cavallers dam roadhead (1725 metres), and from there you've four km of road-walking to Caldes de Boí (a spa with luxury hotels), then four more to Boí (Bohi) village at 1282 metres.

The latter is much more distinctive, with its 12th-century Romanesque shrine of Sant Joan. It's flanked by two other settlements, Erill and Taüll (Tahull), whose respective churches of Santa Eulalia, Santa Maria, and Sant Climent (of the same era) are even more imposing. Taken together, these are the finest small Romanesque monuments in Catalunya and are well worth detouring to see. Boí has five *hostales* in the one and two-star category; a daily bus (*La Oscense*) runs from Boí to Pobla de Segur via Pont de Suert.

Ventosa I Calvell to Capdella via Contraig

From Ventosa i Calvell there is yet another possible, though far more strenuous, return to Capdella. Backtrack to the second, large lake in the valley (above Estany Negre) and cross the flat, turfy area to pick up the cairned way up to the Coll de Contraig (2770 metres). A warning: keep packs light and bring full regalia (axe, etc) since this north-west-facing pass is snowed up until early summer. Once over, descend past the Estany de Contraig to arrive at Refugio d'Estany Llong after six to seven hours (despite what you may read to the contrary – these are hut wardens' estimates).

From the Estany Llong hut (elevation 2000 metres, managed by the national park, maximum 53 customers, meals and self-cooking possible), a well-defined *camino* climbs to the Estany and Collada de Dellui (2550 metres) and thence past the lakes of

Neriolo and already-visited Tort en route to the Refugi de Colomina. This would be a moderate (five-hour) but satisfying day. The territory between the two passes, incidentally, falls within the national park; to be sure of space at Estany Llong contact Joaquim Merlos or his representative in Boí (tel (973) 69 02 84); the continual staffing season is from mid-June to mid-October.

Taüll to Capdella

Alternatively you can trek back to Capdella from Taüll (1495 metres), following the forest road above until it becomes the old *camino* over the Port de Rus to Capdella. This would be a six to seven-hour hiking day, but the surface is reported to be in good condition since this was a traditional approach to the spa at Caldes de Boí.

Boí to Espot via Estany de Sant Maurici

Barely worth mentioning, but included for completeness, is the supposedly 'classical' traverse from Boí to Espot via the Portarró de Espot (at around 2400 metres) and the lake at Sant Maurici. The first four-plus walking hours up to Estany Llong are on asphalt and forest road, as is the final stretch between the

Montardo d' Aran, Estany de Monges

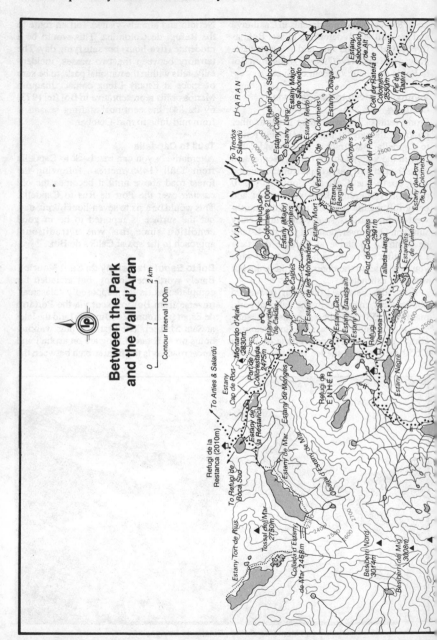

Between the Park and the Vall d'Aran

Contour Interval 100m

0   1   2 km

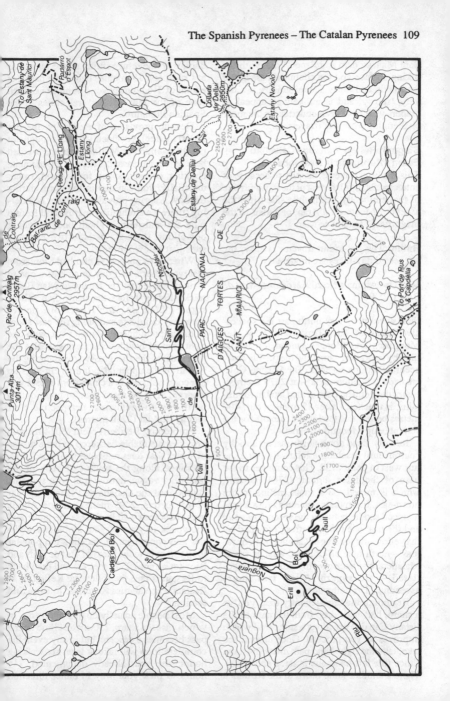

Sant Maurici dam and Espot. What with the hiking surface and the continual passage of jeep-taxis and noisy school groups, it's not very 'sporty' and is unlikely to appeal to readers who have been undertaking the more challenging *travesías* (traverses).

Stage 5: Refugi Ventosa i Calvell to Estany/Refugi de la Restanca

This is a brief traverse, happily so because of enticements to fill the rest of the day with one of two eminently worthwhile side trips: the ascent of Montardo d'Aran, or a visit to the magnificent Estany de Mar.

Rating The hut-to-hut traverse is easy; the suggested day-hikes are moderate.

Map Use Alpina's No 209, *Montardo-Vall de Bol* (1:25,000).

First wend your way north past the successive lakes of Xic, Travessani, Clot, les Mongades and Monges guided the whole time by legions of cairns and the (in this case) accurate Alpina tracings. The Port de Coll-crestada (Güellicrestada – at 2475 metres), easily the gentlest pass in the Catalan mountains, is reached 1 hour 45 minutes out; 400 metres before it is the logical turn off for the scramble up Montardo d'Aran.

Initially, head north-north-east up a rocky couloir until reaching a relatively flat zone just west of point 2728. This continues to the base of the false summit (2781 metres), which is turned via a small incline to the north-east. From there you must cross a pronounced saddle between the secondary peak and the true one (2830 metres), crowned by the yellow and red flag of Catalunya. Panoramas – north over all of Aran, west as far as Maladeta, and back over the cirque just negotiated – are superb. Allow two hours ascending, 1½ hours down.

Resuming the cross-country trek, you've a sharp, half-hour drop from the pass to the Estany Cap de Port, along a stony trail which improves as you proceed. Once around the lake, take the right-hand path *away* from the sluice (the left-hand one is steep and slick). There's another jump down to the Restanca

dam, with the refuge sitting on the far end as at Colomers, 75 minutes below the pass, for a total of 3½ hours beyond Ventosa i Calvell (one of the few 'correct' trek times in the Spanish literature).

Despite provision of electricity, the hut (2010 metres) is decidedly rustic, though not nearly so much as Mallafré, but the warden here is very pleasant. There is an adequate cooking counter, space for 40 and, rather unusually, you can nap in the dorm during the day. A spring provides water for laundering (there's a clothesline nearby) and feeds a pipe for showering – both body-numbing operations; there are perhaps two camping sites just below if needed.

Whether or not you've climbed Montardo, reserve either a half day or an entire one to visit, or circle past, the Estany de Mar. Backtrack slightly across the dam, then follow signs ('*Llac de Mar*') past old power company buildings and along the east shore of the impoundment. A good path, with one tight spot of boulder-clambering, scales the first bluff to the flat, grassy area flanking the outfall of the upper lake. It then zig-zags up a second palisade to a chute from where you emerge, after no more than an hour, onto a north-east-to-south-west perspective over Estany de Mar (2230 metres).

Forbidding Besiberri Nord (3014 metres) provides a suitable backdrop to the expanse of water that does not belie its name, 'sea'. Continue along the south-east bank of the lake on a vague, narrow trail with sporadic cairns until the Collada de l'Estany de Mar (2468 metres, 2495 metres on one Alpina map) becomes visible. Assess the grade and snowpack in view of your ambitions, abilities and equipment for tackling the popular loop trip over to the lakes of Tort de Rius and Rius (at around 2350 metres) and then back to Restanca (see the following Refugi de la Restanca or Valarties Roadhead to Boca Sud section.)

Most people actually do this in reverse, in which case the sharp, 250-metre climb up the pass becomes a descent, but in any event the complete loop will take at least six walking hours: the hour already documented, 1½ hours to pick your way in either direction along the rugged shore of Mar, one hour up to or down from the pass, another to skirt the two Rius lakes, and a final hour along the leg of GR11 paralleling the Barranc de Rius.

Stage 6: Down to Arties and Salardú

By now you may have been trekking for up to six days, and a break for rest and reprovisioning will be a priority. If you have not interrupted your journey at the Colomers or Ventosa i Calvell huts, the Refugi de la Restanca is the next obvious place, since west of it there will be no opportunity for three or four more hiking days!

Map Alpina No 228, *Vall d'Aran* (1:40,000) covers this area.

From Restanca it's less than an hour on the north-east-bound GR11 down to the roadhead at Pont de Rius (at around 1700 metres). The Camí del Port de Rius is conveniently marked with a GR no-entry sign which you will disregard when you return for the remainder of your westward trek.

The dirt track continues down along the Riu de Valarties on a fairly stiff grade for 45 minutes until it reaches a bridge, the divergence of the GR11 up and right (which you ignore), and the start of stabilised macadam (not really asphalt) to Arties village. Allow another hour at a brisk clip to arrive at the latter. Heading downhill is no chore, but when resuming course with a restocked backpack some days later, you'll want to take a taxi back up to the roadhead, or thumb it – the summer sun is already a trial at 10 am!

Arties (1144 metres) is unfortunately not so well equipped for independent travellers despite the presence of a *parador*, a couple of hotels, and three *cambres* (Aranés for 'rooms') outfits. Of the latter, *Montardo* is the cheapest but noisy given its setting above a bar on the main road; *Portola* and *Ma Jesus* have doubles only. Also, there seem to be no meals available for less than 2000ptas, and only one store.

After having a look at the triple-naved 13th-century cathedral (the famous nearby thermal baths are shut) and the unmissable church of San Joan across from the

Montardo, you're better off continuing 2.2 km east up the valley to Salardú (1268 metres), a bigger place large enough to have more choice of amenities, but small enough not to be a zoo (except in August or peak ski season).

Salardú

For accommodation, in ascending order of price, first of all there's the *albergue* (youth hostel) – always open except between 1 September and 15 October. It's very cheap and has inexpensive meals, but you need an IYHA (International Youth Hostel Association) card and reservations are advised. Then there's the popular *Fonda Barbara*, in an historic house on Carrer Major, often full but offering huge, excellent meals for all comers. There's also the *Bar Comidas* which also has beds, above supermarket *Solei* next to the *Fonda Barbara*; a *casa de huéspedes* next to *Supermercado Sol y Nieve* on the way up to the CEC lodge; rooms above the *Bar*

San Andreu de Salardú

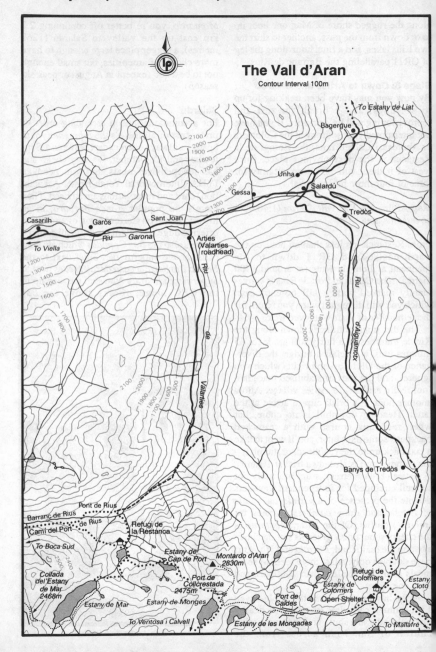

The Vall d'Aran
Contour Interval 100m

Top: Pyrenees/Vall d'Aran – Unha with Maladeta to west
Left: Pyrenees/Benasque to Viadós – Maladeta/Ixeia seen from Collado de la Piana
Right: Pyrenees/Ordesa – Circo de Cotatuero from Faja de Pelay

Top: Pyrenees/Panticosa to Sallent – Ibón Azul, Piedrafita peak
Left: Pyrenees/Bujaruelo to Panticosa – Ara bridge at San Nicolás
Right: Pyrenees/Panticosa to Sallent – Refugio de Piedrafita

Montaña, across the street from the *Fonda Barbara*; and a handful of expensive *hostales* that do a good job of publicising themselves.

Of particular interest to hikers, and very moderately priced, are two other establishments. The *Refugí Rosti* (tel (973) 64 53 08, summer season from 1 July to 15 September) in a 300-year-old building on the main square has character and evening set dinners. The management is often resident outside of the indicated dates. The CEC-managed *Xalet-Refugí Juli Soler Santaló* (tel (973) 64 50 16) is 100 metres from the youth hostel; it's more institutional but good value, with 80 made beds (not bunks) – half in quadruples, half in dorms, and priced per bed. The food is satisfactory (the only lunches in town incidentally) and unlike at the alpine CEC establishments there is a generous space for preparing your own meals. The manager, Lluis Ibañez, is helpful and very knowledgeable about most nearby regions of the Pyrenees.

In the event that Salardú is completely full (possible in August), you have one last nearby recourse: the *Bar/Fonda Saboredu* in Tredòs, a 15-minute walk away via the signposted *camí reiau*.

Three grocery stores – *Bazar* near the CEC lodge, *Sol y Nieve*, and *Solei* (cheapest) near the *Fonda Barbara* – between them should have all but the most exotic items, though the nearest butane gas is in Betrén, near Viella (Vielha). If you're running low on cash, there are two banks open for exchange at peculiar hours (from 12 noon to 2 pm and from 5.30 to 8 pm).

Getting to/from the Vall d'Aran

Should you need to leave the area or just get to Viella, *Alsina Graells* buses roll daily from Barcelona (8 am) and Pobla de Segur (11.30 am – same vehicle as to Llavorsi) to Salardú (2 pm) and Viella (20 minutes later) via the Port de Bonaigua. The return bus departs at 11 am, though there's no through service between November and April when Bonaigua is snowed up. *La Oscense* plies the route from Viella to Pont de Suert and Pobla once daily at 5 am, with the reverse itinerary

scheduled at a more civilised hour. (Boí-Pont de Suert services connect with these.)

THE VALL D'ARAN

As noted in the introduction to the Pyrenees, this upper valley of the Riu Garona (the Garonne once inside France) is a consequence of a brief overlap in the two Pyrenean chains. Like nearby Andórra, it was long an isolated realm with an idiosyncratic and independent history but, unlike its neighbour, has not been paved over as a duty-free parking lot.

'Aran is *not* Catalunya' graffiti, in the local language, is much in evidence, and if you refer to Aranés as a dialect locals may bristle. Reading the bizarre roadsigns may convince you otherwise. Other than having the superficial similarity of being a Romance language significantly influenced by Basque and old Gascon, Aranés differs markedly from French, Spanish and Catalan.

Most of the people themselves are unconcernedly trilingual speaking Aranés, Spanish and Catalan (often French as well). They're overtly friendly to outsiders, even positively voluble by Spanish standards – initiating conversations, volunteering information, etc. This is all the more amazing considering a swelling flow of warm-weather tourists and the giant Baqueira/Beret ski complex which looms four km east of Tredòs.

On the surface, the Cap d'Aran/Alto Aran/Nautaran (in Catalan/Castilian/Aranés respectively) seems unchanged and pastoral; laundry is still often done in the village trough-spring, and even in season you have to make appointments with innkeepers to get supper. But the scythe-wielding hay-reapers of summer are juxtaposed with vacation chalets for city folk which sprout at the edge of every village. However rigorously traditional in building style, these new structures represent an ominous trend and many locals have not been able to resist the temptation of selling 'extra' pasture at astronomical prices to developers. Visit soon.

Salardú, the 'capital' of Nautaran, is ideally placed for undemanding strolls to the surrounding villages of Bagergue (2.8 km), Unha (Unya – 1½ km), Gessa (1 km – there's also a trail from Unha), and Tredòs (take the short path previously noted). All these are centred on wonderful Romanesque churches, with the traditional domestic architecture hardly less appealing if not quite as venerable.

Arties' examples have been cited; Salardú's 13th-century church of San Andreu is a good basis of comparison for those in Unha (13th/18th-century), Gessa, Bagergue (12th/15th-century), and Tredòs (some of whose interior is in New York). If lintel plaques are anything to go by, most houses date from the 16th to the 18th centuries.

In terms of hard-core alpine walks, the sierra north of the valley is distinctly lower than that to the south just traversed and only the eight-hour (round-trip) *camino*-ramble up to the Estany de Liat (2130 metres) near the French border can be recommended. The pertinent trail starts in Bagergue (1419 metres), the most countrified of the settlements here.

From Tredòs (1348 metres) you can road-walk 7½ km up the beautiful Riu d'Aiguamotx valley to the *banys* (hot springs) of Tredòs (around 1700 metres), but the water, in one rustic pool by the ruined spa build-

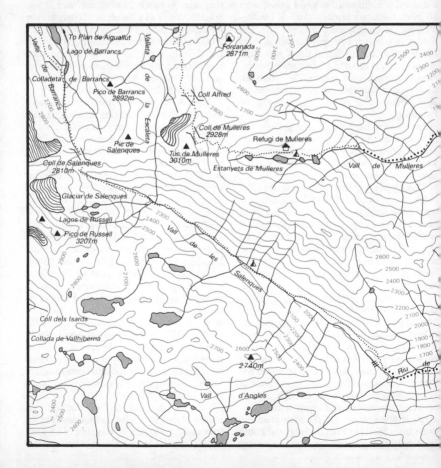

ing, is tepid and the deerflies amazingly vicious even by Pyrenean standards. You are more likely to appreciate your bath if you're coming *down* from the Refugi de Colomers, tired and dirty, or can hitch or take a taxi in at least one direction – not out of the question since the meadows surrounding the old *balneario* are popular picnic grounds. But frankly the real pleasure in an Aran interlude, especially after a week's trekking, is the pace of life and the gentle, green scenery presided over by Maladeta/Aneto rearing up to the west.

LA RIBAGORÇA & INTO ARAGÓN

Transition from Catalunya to Aragón is gradual, and for most trekkers it means crossing the headwaters of the Noguera Ribagorçana. Like so much of the high Pyrenees, this is wild, thinly populated country; be aware of, but not put off by, the busy highway forging up toward the Viella tunnel.

Rating

From Valarties or Restanca to Boca Sud it's easy, while from Boca Sud to Aiguallut it's

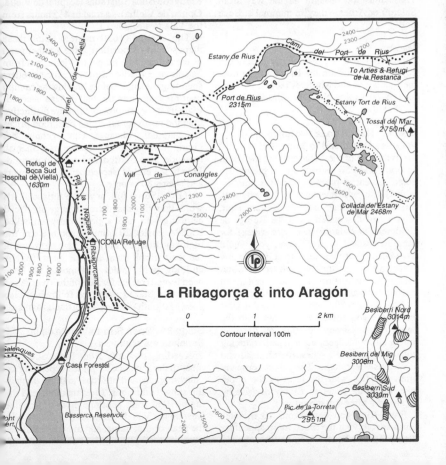

difficult via Mulleres and somewhat less so via Salenques.

Duration

If you proceed directly from Restanca, you should easily reach the Mulleres tarns or the Salenques meadows on the first day of progress. Either is a viable alternative to Boca Sud. If you begin from the Vall d'Aran, you should stop in the Ribagorça valley somewhere and take an extra night on the way to Aiguallut.

Supplies

These must be brought all the way from Salardú or Arties – they're minimal at Boca Sud!

Map

Alpina No 208, *La Ribagorça* (1:25,000) covers the area from the Rius lakes to both the Salenques and Mulleres passes; thereafter rely on Alpina No 207, *Maladeta-Aneto* (1:25,000).

Stage 7: Refugi de la Restanca or Valarties Roadhead to Boca Sud

From the end of the Valarties road it's about an hour, and 250 metres, up the previously noted 'no-entry'-blazed trail to the junction with GR11, which enters on the left, with little altitude change, from the Restanca hut. If you had descended from the Refugi de Colomers to Salardú (and vice versa) for supplies instead of from here, you would have been able to use this direct link. In any event, the lower trail is well-trodden and cairned so there is no great disadvantage in visiting the Vall d'Aran from Restanca.

After another 80 minutes, always due west on GR11, you should draw even with the outlet of the Estany de Rius; on the way ignore all cobbled, engineered paths enticing you to go up and left – these merely dead-end at various waterworks. The power company often meddles with the level of the upper lake, diverting water to Estany de Mar by means of a three-km tunnel.

From Rius you can detour 10 minutes south-east to visit the much more appealing Estany Tort de Rius, if you haven't already

done so as part of a Restanca-Mar-Rius-Restanca day-hike. These are the last substantial lakes you'll see for several days.

It takes 40 minutes to skirt Rius en route to the Port de Rius (2315 metres), from where the Pont de Suert-Viella road is plainly seen. The trail drops sharply in switchbacks with the Mulleres massif to the west progressively more evident. As you descend through the Vall de Conangles, pines yield to beeches and 70 minutes below the pass the path meets a bulldozer track. For once GR markings pointing off to the left are best ignored as you adopt this track for the final 20 minutes to the Refugi de Boca Sud (alias Hospital de Viella, Opitau de Vielha) – a total of 4½ hours from the Valarties roadhead.

The shelter (1630 metres) takes these names from its position at the southern end of the automobile tunnel to Viella, and from its role as a medieval hospice for travellers spending the night before braving the *camino* over the ridge into the Vall d'Aran. Accordingly its stone architecture is more distinctive than the norm for an alpine hut; food prices are marginally cheaper, with a genuine bar giving it more the atmosphere of a Spanish roadside inn. Staffed and open from mid-June to the end of September, it has showers and sleeps 80 people.

If Boca Sud is full, or you're antisocial, it's worth knowing that there is a large unofficial camping site and a perennially unlocked ICONA chalet 20 minutes south along the highway. Just past the Km 152 marker, you'll see tents in the trees, and the giant ICONA building (with tables, but most beds have been looted) on the far side of the river. A red and white blazed path (see following) also goes past both, so they're difficult to miss.

Stage 8A: Boca Sud to Valleta de la Escaleta via Mulleres

Proceeding onwards from Boca Sud, you must make a choice of routes depending on your interests and abilities, and the prevailing snow conditions. Most trekkers, and the main GR11 trail, continue more or less due west up the Vall de Mulleres (Molieres), past the peak of that name, and over the Mulleres pass into the Valleta de la Escaleta. However this is quite an expedition, with altitude changes totalling 2400 metres, and cannot be recommended unless you have a light pack and (until late summer) crampons and axe.

The route as far as the three Mulleres lakes (at around 2350 metres) – where there is an orange, eight-person, permanently open refuge and several camping sites – is uncomplicated and well-marked. It's a four-hour ascent from Boca Sud and, considering what awaits you the morrow, it's best to stay the night near the tarns.

The next day you work off breakfast with a two-hour climb up to the Coll de Mulleres (2928 metres), entirely over rock varying from huge slabs to slippery scree, and sooner or later on snow. This is the highest and one of the steepest passes on the whole Pyrenean traverse, and its difficulty should not be minimised. Those with sufficient time and energy may leave full packs on the ridge here and make the half-hour detour south to bag the Pic (Tuc) de Mulleres at 3010 metres.

Next you've a short crest traverse toward the so-called Coll Alfred, from near where you should use the best opportunity to descend to the highest tarn of the Valleta de la Escaleta. Count on 2½ hours more down to near the first ponds where camping would be feasible.

Stage 8B: Boca Sud to Plan de Aiguallut via Salenques

If the prospect of the foregoing is intimidating, an alternative spur of GR11 exists, via the Vall de les Salenques (Sallencas). Starting from the Refugi de Boca Sud, don't road-walk – turn off the asphalt after 200 metres, following red and white blazes pleasantly through a fir wood for 25 minutes to the ICONA building and the camping site. Complete an hour of hiking by clearing the latter, adopting the east (true left) bank of the Noguera Ribagorçana, crossing back to the west bank and (briefly) the road via a sluice, before reaching a dilapidated *casa forestal* overlooking the Basserca reservoir. Here a GR11 sign, cemented into the ground, tells you some things already known ('*Ospitau Vielha, 1 hr; Restanca 5 hr*' – more like six!)

and points down the road to your destination – '*Vall de Salenques*'.

GR markings lead you across a metal footbridge at the Riu de les Salenques' entry to the huge dam, and then cease. The trail steadily worsens until, 45 minutes along, it widens slightly as a flattish patch affording views of point 2740 and torrents from the Anglos valley. Here is the only practicable crossing to the north-east bank of the river and the continuation of the trek up to the Coll de Salenques.

Once on the far side you must first skirt waterfalls, then hunt for a faint, intermittent trail (sporadically cairned) through a nasty mix of boulders draped in rhododendron and studded with pine saplings. The going is rough and the scenery indifferent until Pico de Russell and the Coll dels Isards pop into view. Then all vegetation ceases but treacherous boulder-hopping remains the norm; finally, over three hours above the river ford, a brow of hill means the edge of several high, well-watered meadows with good camping. You should take the opportunity if there's less than seven hours of daylight remaining.

From the camping site, continue on a manageable grade and surface for two hours to the point where the valley narrows and the base of a grassy slope circumvents a cascade. It's possible to avoid rockfalls much of the way by keeping to turf or a blend of turf and compacted boulders. A sharp slope and then a long, relatively level approach to the base of the pass incline takes up another hour, and you should reach the Coll de Salenques (2810 metres) within 90 minutes to two hours more (depending on the snow-to-scree ratio). Crampons, gaiters and a self-arrest device are strongly advised, though not strictly mandatory; I met a party of five Germans, including a seven-year-old leashed like a lap-dog, slipping and sliding down the bank, with only three axes between them!

Up top, a small *vivac*-style shelter is convenient for lunch and for views north over the Valle de Barrancs to the peaks along the French border. To the north-east, the ridge swooping down from Mulleres separates the Aran watershed, and Lleida province, from the Río Ésera basin and Huesca province, yet to be entered. The view back is oddly disappointing, because the Salenques valley is so narrow and its lower reaches are out of sight.

Keep the crampons on for the descent over virtually permanent snowfields, then switch to normal footwear for the slight climb up to the Colladeta de Barrancs (2480 metres), necessary since the Lago de Barrancs just east is sheer-sided and impassable. Cairns resume at the *colladeta* (90 minutes below the big pass) as you descend in jumps to the edge of a glacial debris basin; Aneto, highest point in the Pyrenees at 3404 metres, and its massive glacier appear above and to the left.

The pertinent Alpina map shows much of the 45-minute drop to the Torrente de Barrancs incorrectly, some way left (west) of the actual course. Assisted by the timely cairns, cross the river and use the steadily improving path on the east (true right) bank for the final 45 minutes down to the Plan de Aiguallut(s) – pronounced 'Aye-gwa-lootch' locally.

This gorgeous meadowland (at around 2050 metres) is tailor-made for camping, but suffers from the demerits of the usual insects and the fact that it's crisscrossed by two rivers. When they're in full spate, as on a sunny afternoon in early summer, fording is difficult if not impossible, limiting movement and choice of tent sites, in a place already very popular with Spaniards. The best spots, at least some of which are accessible no matter what the water level, are near the base of the conical Pico de Aiguallut (2710 metres) which dominates the upper end of the meadows.

The tributary to the east of this hill is that descending from the Valleta de la Escaleta and the flank of Mulleres; the approach to Aiguallut from that direction is covered in the day-hike sections below. Assuming that you need it and can reach it, a green metal refuge – essentially a bare shed for eight or 10 persons – perches at the far (downstream) end of the *plan*, overlooking the Cascadas de Aiguallut. These plunge into the Forau d'Aiguallut, the mouth of a subterranean river which bores through a bed of karst, re-emerging four km north-north-east at Artiga de Lin.

The *cabaña* also marks the beginning of a faint trail over the shallow Coll de la Renclusa (2270 metres) to the refuge of that name. Frankly, the Aiguallut area is a far better base for non-technical day-rambles and you should plan on staying here for at least two nights.

THE UPPER ÉSERA VALLEY

This alpine basin is a good 500 metres higher than the Vall d'Aran and thus has no permanent habitation. Like many of the similar headwaters in these mountains, it abuts the Franco-Spanish frontier, but unlike those to the west, its flanks are relatively low in altitude and breached by several passes or viewpoints. These permit you to undertake various interesting day-hikes and have made the Ésera area popular – perhaps too popular – with campers and *excursionistas*. Still it's worth interrupting your advance toward Benasque for a day or two to sample the following.

Rating

All basic walks described are easy, especially as day-hikes, so you won't lack for company. Loops through Artiga de Lin, and detours to Cregüeña, rank as moderately difficult. Track-walking between the Plan d'Estanys and Benasque doesn't merit any classification other than tedious.

Map

Alpina No 207, *Maladeta-Aneto* (1:25,000); is the most relevant.

Day-Hike to the Frontier Ridge

It's less than an hour along the broad, easily followed *camino* down to the roadhead and the 'Zona de Acampada' above the Plan d'Estanys (Estan), but in summer the *zona* is merely a tent-tenement for hundreds of car-campers, and you wouldn't want to cover the full distance more than the single essential time.

Instead, 15 minutes past the impressive *forau*, in the middle of a sharp, stepped descent in the principal path, bear right to cross the stream and head north to join up with the zig zags labelled *'Excursión 9'* on

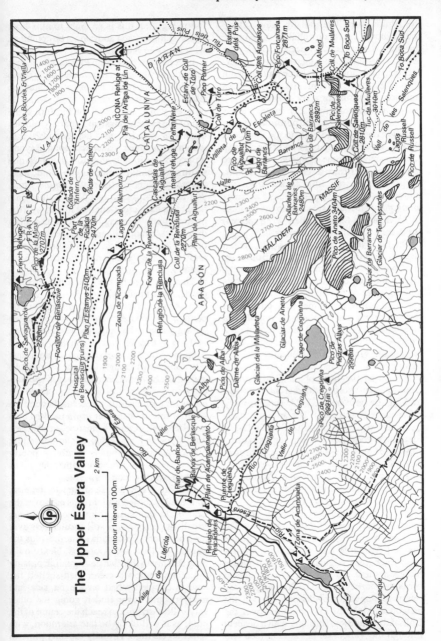

The Upper Ésera Valley

Contour Interval 100m

0   2 km

the Alpina map. The initially faint link-up trail is shown too far downhill on the Alpina; the cairned route actually passes close by the lower Villamorta pond, then climbs to intersect (after 40 minutes) the main path up from Plan d'Estanys at about 2100 metres (the junction at least is correctly shown).

Follow this, and after 25 minutes there's an obvious forking: left and north-west to the Portillón de Benasque, right to the Port de la Picada. Visit the former first, skirting a reedy tarn and arriving some 45 minutes later; there is potable water from a spring near the crest. Surprisingly there's little to see from the windy gap; you must press on for 45 minutes along the well-made side trail to the summit of Salvaguarda (Sauvegarde – 2738 metres) for decent views in all directions.

On the French side the smooth, green slopes above the three lakes called Boums du Port, with the little French alpine hut nearby, form a startling contrast to the jagged facets and contours of the entire Maladeta massif stretched before you to the south, once again demonstrating that frontiers are not always so arbitrary as they might seem. Count on a total of 2 hours 45 minutes one-way from Aiguallut, via lower Villamorta, without getting lost.

Return to the base of the Portillón de Benasque and some ruined stone huts and pick up the path marked '23' (presumably a French GR number). It's an easy half-hour east to the Port de la Picada (2470 metres), a good place to see eagles wheeling overhead on a summer afternoon. Another 20 minutes on the well-grooved-in trail will bring you to the Collada de l'Infern, virtually on the frontier, and just past the *clots* (ponds) of Infern.

Thereafter, though, you'd have about a 1000-metre drop over the three-km length of the Pomèro valley – ie a 33% grade – to the Pla de l'Artiga de Lin, where the subterranean river from Aiguallut exits, and where there's a small unlocked ICONA refuge to break the journey if need be. You might vary return to Aiguallut by looping up via the canyon and lake of Puis and then over the Colls dels Aranesos, finishing with a descent through the Valleta de la Escaleta (see text

following), but this is an eight to nine-hour undertaking in itself and cannot be combined with a visit to Salvaguarda.

Instead, turn back from Picada, and almost immediately bear left (down and south) onto the old *camino* which historically linked the Ésera valley with that of Aran. After 20 minutes you'll be back at the big fork at the top of the switchbacks, and after 15 minutes more you veer left onto the secondary trail which skirts lower Villamorta pond. Beyond it the path is virtually invisible, but keep due south and within 10 minutes you should meet the stone 'stairs' on the main *camino* which you left some hours ago. Save a little time here by cutting cross-country to join with the proper path coming up from the Plan d'Estanys roadhead and car park visible below; it's from 35 to 45 minutes accordingly up to the Refugio de la Renclusa (2140 metres).

This, managed by the CEC although technically well inside Aragón, is open roughly from April to October, with places for 107 people; an adjacent annexe is kept open during winter. The hut is crowded at Easter, on June weekends, and for much of July and August – you can reserve space in Benasque (see following) though fees are between 10 and 15% above the norm. Power is sporadically supplied by a generator, but there are hopes for permanent current. Just beyond the outdoor toilets is another *forau* marked by a small chapel. Again it must be emphasised that, if you're not a technical climber setting off for Aneto, the hut is relatively poorly placed to serve as a base for either day-hikes or as an overnight on a traverse.

Leaving the Renclusa shelter to the east, an initially cairned trail threads east over the Coll de la Renclusa, from where there are excellent perspectives still further east over the Pomer and Forcanada summits, plus the saddles of Tòro and Aranesos. Next you'll drop sharply to the Plan de Aiguallut, passing the aforementioned green shed-shelter; the path is decidedly bad on the far side and many people never find it going the other way. Allow an hour to reach the centre of the *plan*; as it will likely be late afternoon, with water levels high, virtually the only place to ford the two rivers is just upstream from their confluence near the *cabaña*.

Other than as the completion of a day-hike, this route would be of most use for full-pack traverses *from* Renclusa *to* Mulleres or Salenques and not vice-versa. Returning to the *plan* by this secondary path means the end of a moderately strenuous walking day of over seven hours.

Day-Hike to Valleta de la Escaleta

If pressed for time, this can be done as a morning's outing before the descent to Benasque (see following), but to do it justice – and to engage in any reconnaissance or scrambling on Mulleres if you haven't already come that way – the following really demands a full day.

From the south end of the Plan de Aiguallut, head upstream along the torrent feeding it from the east. A cairned, well-designed trail conquers some narrows on their south side (to the right as you're facing them) and leads up to the Valleta de la Escaleta – a mysterious, tarn- and cave-pocked landscape confined by the peaks of Aiguallut, Forcanada and Pomer. Mist permitting, you should (40 minutes along) see the gentle Coll de Tòro and cairns indicating the side trail to it.

Complete an hour of hiking arriving at this small pass (2235 metres) and the pretty figure-eight-shaped lake of Coll de Tòro, hemmed in by Pomer (east) and Peña Nere (north). Skirt the lake on its north-west shore, following cairns but no path, and within 20 minutes reach a lone camping site and still another point overlooking the Aran watershed. Despite a steep drop ahead, this is probably the shortest direct route between Aiguallut and Artiga de Lin and could be useful in devising loop routes.

Return to the main Escaleta path and quickly pass a meadow suitable for camping, then snake up and around a rocky bluff to reach a high vale containing three tarns. Bear left after the first of these and go up the obvious spur to the long, jumbled Coll dels Aranesos (at 2455 metres; 45 minutes from the Tòro detour and 90 minutes from Aiguallut). You have nose-up views of

Forcanada (2871 metres, usually only climbed from the other – south-face), hints of Mulleres behind and Pico Pomer directly to the north. But the most arresting vistas are those north-east over the Vall de l'Artiga de Lin all the way to the peaks separating the Vall d'Aran from France.

From the pass there's a sharp drop, with elusive cairns, to the Estany dels Puis (Pois); thereafter the grade along the Riu dels Puis is gentler, making this the recognised (though lengthier) southern leg for completing loops involving the Port de la Picada. Descend to Aiguallut within 90 minutes on a trail which is actually better than the Alpina map would have you believe.

Stage 9: Aiguallut to Benasque & a Possible Detour

You can cover the distance from Aiguallut down to the roadhead in 45 minutes; the crowds there may come as a bit of a jolt after days of relative solitude in the wilderness. A tiny stall sells a very random selection of items – olives, beer and wine, salty snacks, etc – to the multitudes, but can hardly be called a supply point.

Just past a shepherds' shelter, some 15 to 20 minutes below the car park and in the middle of the Plan d'Estany itself (1870 metres), the old Puerto de la Picada-Hospital de Benasque camino re-emerges on the right for the 45-minute walk to the ruined *hospital*. In all frankness, however, the recently paved road along the length of the Ésera valley renders strictly third-rate any nearby walking; you could hardly be blamed for arranging a ride the 16 km down to Benasque.

Whatever you do, resist the temptation to follow '*Excursión 4*' of the Alpina map to short cut the asphalt between the *hospital* and the Plan de Baños. The trail climbs perversely for the first 40 minutes, and is in such bad repair that you will certainly get lost before reaching the highly forgettable spa. When you finally do get there, you've a boring road or a knee-jarring cross-country descent to the Plan de Baños.

If you cannot or will not get a ride, do turn off the asphalted road at the Plan de Baños

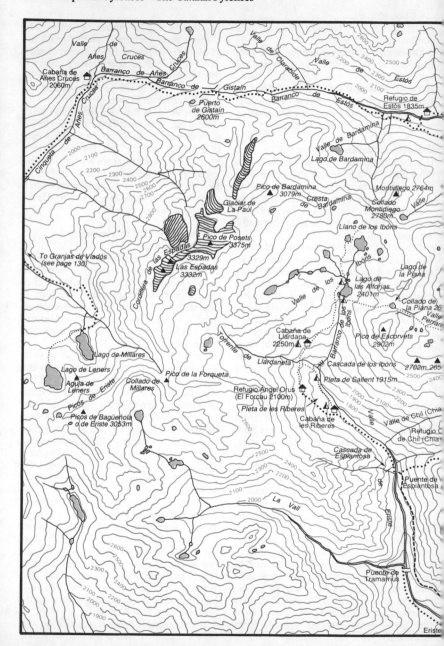

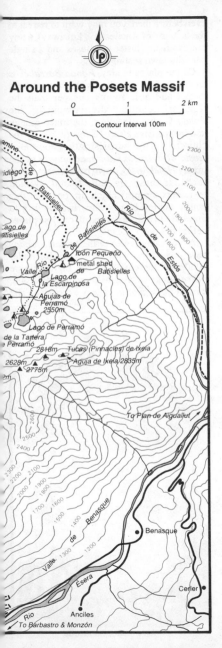

Around the Posets Massif

0   1   2 km

Contour Interval 100m

about halfway down, and take the forest track – part of the old *camino* – on the east (true left) bank of the Ésera river; this at least spares you being buzzed by exhaust-belching traffic and meeting some dangerously narrow tunnels up ahead.

From here down, the river is flanked by enormous, bizarre *acampadas libres* (free tenting-down areas) for car-campers, where densely packed Spaniards (and some French) reside *en famille* for weeks at a time. Doubtless, when a tunnel is finally bored through the ridge north of the ruined Hospital de Benasque, these sites will all be spruced up and commercialised. There's no incentive for you to stop until you reach the relatively low-key Plan de Acampamento, some three hours below Plan d'Estany and with a Refugio de Pescadores for the tentless, since this is the closest overnighting point to the trailhead for Lago de Cregüeña.

The path begins, wide and cairned, just before the bridge south of the camp; allow six hours for the round-trip, with an extra two or three hours to descend the final stretch to Benasque – ie an extra day. Although the lake, the third largest (volume-wise) in the Pyrenees, is only some 3½ lateral km from the Río Ésera, the time given is accurate owing to a 1200-metre altitude difference. The setting, a savage cul-de-sac occasionally broken out of by technical climbers aiming for the south face of Maladeta looming overhead, is ample compensation for the stiff climb in.

Upon returning to the bridge-trailhead, you can keep to the old track, past still another *acampada libre*, to within 3.8 km of Benasque and the point where you leave the coverage of the *Maladeta-Aneto* Alpina map. Whether or not you make the side trip to Cregüeña, tempers will have been calmed a bit by missing out on six km of asphalt.

The Aragonese Pyrenees

AROUND THE POSETS MASSIF

Although second in elevation to its eastern neighbour Aneto, the Posets group is arguably more scenic, and offers more to the non-technical climber. Certainly it is less popular, though undeservedly so – two of the three alpine refuges are all you could probably want in the way of such, opportunities for camping and day-hiking are almost limitless, and the region is as easy to get to as any of the better known Pyrenean magnets.

Benasque (Benasc)

While the Noguera Ribagorçana marks the official separation between Catalunya and Aragón, there exists an area – 'La Franja' (The Margin) – extending about 25 km west, along the entire river, where historically, linguistically and commercially Catalan influence is strong. Here in this transition zone you may still encounter spoken and toponymic Catalan; Benasque is one of the largest villages in the Pyrenean portion of La Franja.

With its cobbled streets, medieval two and three-storeyed mansions, and 13th-century church, Benasque (1138 metres) makes an excellent place for a couple of days' relaxation and reprovisioning before pressing on. Besides the predictable places to stay & eat, there's a bakery and pastry shop at which to stuff yourself silly; an outdoor unheated pool in which to work out the kinks in your legs; and, most importantly, a wide range of outdoor-oriented shops for replacing or repairing worn-out equipment. There's also the only bank and post office you are likely to see until Bielsas.

For the moment, Benasque is (relatively) unexploited, with local farmers still trundling hay-wagons through the square, but the writing is definitely on the wall: cranes and derricks hover over the last vacant lot near the bus stop, T-shirts and window-stickers everywhere agitate for a tunnel to French Luchon. If these boosters get their way, and even before then, you may want to retreat to the 'suburb' of Anciles (1.8 km away), a tiny but exquisite cluster of houses and a single bar with lawn seating.

Of the places to stay, *Fonda Barrabés* is an old budget standby, with bare-mattress dorms and attic rooms cheaper than the 'regular' doubles. Alternatively try the *Fonda Solana* next door; the much quieter and inexpensive *Hostal Salvaguarda* by the church; or the surprisingly good-value *Hostal-Residencia Valero*, an annexe of the luxury *Hotel Aneto*, down by the main crossroads. If these are full, *Hostal Avenida* represents the next notch up, but after this you're talking luxury digs. In August you may have to traipse around all of these places before finding a vacancy.

As for eating, most of the *hostales/fondas* have *comedores* with set menus for under 1000ptas; for closer to the higher figure *Barrabés* gives you a lot of typical food, though *Salvaguarda* is less expensive. The

Torre Juste, Benasque

only exception to the pattern is *Bar/ Restaurante Bardanca*, which serves very filling *platos combinados* and roast chicken for considerably less. It, and the nearby *Sayó*, are the only places in town where you can sit outside over a coffee without being run over by traffic.

Among the various mountaineering equipment shops, *Deportes Aigualluts* is one you're likely to have dealings with. Well-stocked even by Madrid standards, it's a good place to replace dead boots or lay hands on an altimeter or crampons. Alberto Lacau, the proprietor, is a mine of information and in addition controls the radio for reserving places at the Renclusa and Estos refuges (but not at Ángel Orus (El Forcau) which is on the wrong frequency); tel (974) 55 12 15 for doing this remotely.

The *libreria* (bookstore) nearby has the complete line of Alpinas, so you can buy maps for upcoming areas, as well as some minor photographic gadgets. At *Commercial Perez* you can find Alpinas and butane cartridges, but more importantly they rent crampons and axes and also sell them second-hand. *Regalos Cristhais* also has butane and, uniquely, high-quality boot sole inserts. *Galeria Barrabés* stocks most of the above items, but has premium prices and rather impersonal service. *Auto-Servicio Asunción* is not only one of the better of a half-dozen groceries, but also handles boot repairs – ask for Señor Palacín. However he always has a big backlog of work and requires two or three days' notice.

Rating
From Benasque/Eriste to Batisielles, the trek is moderate; from there to Granja de Viadós is easy, despite its long duration.

Supplies
Buy food in Benasque, at Viadós shelter (haphazard) and in villages of the Gistaín valley (see Viadós to Bielsa via Ordiceto or Pardinas).

Map
Use Alpina No 206, *Posets-Perdiguero* (1:25,000) even though it's particularly

error-ridden. No 205, *Bachimala*, is briefly helpful, particularly if you're dayhiking near Granjas de Viadós and/or continuing west.

Getting to/from the Trailhead
Should you wish to interrupt, or start, a trek at Benasque, buses operated by *Compañia Altoaragonés* leave from the main commercial street at 6.30 am (not Sundays) and 2.15 pm for Monzón (closest train service) or Barbastro (no train, but there's a bus connection to Huesca). Coming uphill, the bus leaves Monzón at 10.30 am, passing Barbastro 15 minutes later.

Stage 10: Benasque to Valle de los Ibóns via Valle de Eriste
Conventional 'wisdom' dictates backtracking four km from Benasque to the mouth of the Estós valley and following the jeep track most of the way up to the Estós refuge, but as is usually the case such advice is best dispensed with in favour of the more challenging itinerary described here.

Rather than follow the main road on the west bank of the Río Ésera to Eriste, take the side road to Anciles, and follow the initially cobbled *camino* on the far side of the hamlet. Quickly make a right turn onto a shady lane, which leads through hayfields to a bridge over the Ésera and a power plant across the asphalted C-139.

You should be in Eriste (1118 metres) within an hour; go through the central square, past the church, and up to the top of the village where the trail up the ravine behind starts. Eriste shows its most photogenic side as you climb above it – rooflines, hayfields and the head of the Linsoles reservoir with its occasional sailcraft hide the industrial scars.

Just under another hour's walking will bring you to the old Puente de Tramarrius (1245 metres); cross to the east (true left) bank of the stream, where the trail ends for a while. Alpina and other sources indicating a path between the river and the dirt road just overhead are strictly nostalgic; it has long since been buried by land-slides and overgrown into oblivion.

Count on a bit more than another hour, or

a total of two hours from Eriste, past an abandoned pyrite mine to the Cascada/Puente de Espiantosa (1505 metres), where various signs by the parking lot give an accurate duration ('*1 hr 30*') to the Orus refuge and point to the unvisited Clot de Chil (Chia) hut. The rocks on either side of the bridge, or the falls just beyond, make an excellent lunch stop.

Local wildflowers are every bit as spectacular as at points east, and there's even the odd rhododendron in the canyon. But already the terrain is harsher, the forests sparser and more coniferous, and low-altitude vegetation decidedly scrubby. A glance at the monthly rainfall charts in the Alpina *Posets-Perdiguero* guidelet tells why.

Within 20 minutes, at about the 1700-metre contour, the path levels out briefly and affords the first glimpse of the refuge and the head of the Valle de Eriste. Complete the fourth hour of walking by arriving at the Pleta de les Riberes (1815 metres), with a *cabaña* and the possibility of camping, and consider forking left (following a sign on a tree) to the Refugio Ángel Orus at 2100 metres.

This FEM facility (also known as 'El Forcau') is cramped – 25 is a more realistic capacity than its rated 40 – and expensive (750ptas for non-club members) for what it is, in spite of its relatively recent construction. It's open and staffed from July to September (for reservations tel (974) 55 11 59), but those cooking for themselves must do so outdoors. If on a traverse via the Piana pass you are probably better off overnighting at either of the spots described below instead of gaining, then losing altitude by detouring to the hut.

From the signposted tree at Pleta de les Riberes, a less used, cairned way heads straight across the grassy slope, paralleling the river, to the Pleta de Sallent (1915 metres), 1 hour 40 minutes from the bridge. There are only one or two level camping sites down by the water; if daylight permits it is far better to climb for another 90 minutes up to the Pleta de la Llardana. A cairned trace keeps initially to the left (west) of falls in the main watercourse, then slithers up an incline

to join an indistinct route coming over from the refuge. You're never quite walking on a path, but the surface of turf-embedded boulder is good.

Cross the Torrente de Llardaneta at about the 2150-metre contour (Alpina shows it too low and too far east, near the confluence of the streams) and find the recently refurbished Cabaña de Llardana (at around 2250 metres). This accommodates four plus their baggage in relative comfort, has abundant water from nearby seeps, and is one of the more appropriate stopping places on the way to Viadós.

Your final overnight alternative, and the goal of this section, is up at the Valle de los Ibóns (*ibón* means tarn in Aragonese dialect). Bear north-east, again over turfed-in boulders but this time somewhat to the west of the Alpina tracing, to overlook the double Lago de las Alforjas (2401 metres). Descend and reach fording points at the outlet some 90 minutes past the *cabaña*, or a total of 7½ walking hours from Benasque.

There are two or three good spots for a tent along the canal between the two parts of Alforjas, one of a dozen lakes tucked east and south of the just visible Posets and Bardamina crests. Allow an extra 90 minutes (round-trip) for the day-hike visit to the upper lakes of the Llano de los Ibóns, a mere 100 metres higher in altitude but involving scrambles over rough surfaces.

Stage 11: Valle de los Ibóns to Valle de Batisielles via Collado de la Plana

This leg is beautiful, with some of the best views of the two highest Pyrenees summits. Though downhill much of the way, it is surprisingly demanding.

From Alforjas allow 75 minutes to reach the obvious Collado de la Piana to the east (2660 metres), just north of Pico de Escorvets (2902 metres). The often-frozen tarn of Piana at its very foot should help you locate it if in doubt; there are few cairns on the way. From the saddle enjoy panoramas west to the Posets crest, second highest in the range at 3375 metres, and even better ones east to Maladeta and the Ixeia pinnacles.

The descent to the Lago de la Tartera de Perramó takes about the same time; it's

Maladeta, Ixeia from Collado de la Piana

another quarter-hour to the Lago de Perramó itself (2270 metres). The pertinent Alpina outlines the former incorrectly. Do, however, trust the Alpina regarding the route down from the pass – do *not* be seduced into following cairns leading from Piana towards tarns in front of the Agujas de Perramó! Otherwise you'll be faced with a steep, loose-rock incline from this upper plateau to the Perramó area. If necessary take advantage of the several camping sites by each of the larger lakes, where lush turf contrasts with the often lunar expanses on the other side of the pass.

A tough, though cairn-assisted, 90 minutes separates Tartera from the Lago de la Escarpinosa (2040 metres). Much of that time is spent wriggling between granite slabs and wrestling with rhododendron; the first few paces to postcard-pretty Lago de Perramó are deceptively easy. Alpina is once again mistaken; there is no route on the true right (east) bank of the Lago de Perramó's outlet.

Escarpinosa is a popular – too popular – overnight spot; a proper trail resumes here for the final 30 to 40 minutes down to a gorgeous meadow ringed by pines in the Valle de Batisielles (at around 2000 metres).

Although only five walking hours may have elapsed since quitting Alforjas (6½ hours from Llardana), you may well want to camp here, especially if you had a late start after a day-hike up to the Llano de los Ibóns or, wish to explore the Batisielles area.

A green metal shed-shelter for the tentless perches conspicuously on a knoll, but it's far preferable to choose from various camping sites (the best and driest are on the 'island' between the two forks of the Río de Batisielles.) The reedy Ibón Pequeño has an adjacent trash-clogged stone shed and a sign indicating the forest trail to the Refugio de Estós (see next stage). From any unobstructed vantage point in the valley, the Ixeia crags (at around 2835 metres), stars of many a postcard on sale in Benasque, loom to the south.

Just before the flats and 'island', a cairned trail diverges west up to the Lago de Batisielles (2250 metres), and onward to a high pass (at around 2800 metres) giving onto the upper Llano de los Ibóns. Some or all of this could be visited as a day-trip, or (done in reverse) used as a possible alternative to the Valle de Perramó approach to Batisielles. But it's scarcely used as a traverse route, and the 2½-hour round trip walk up to the lake will complicate the long day outlined following, or mean an extra night spent at the Estós hut.

Stage 12: Valle de Batisielles to Viadós via Valle/Refugio de Estós

This is a long, but generally enjoyable, day with fine views from the initial and final stretches of the *camino* which sandwiches a strangely claustrophobic pass.

At the Ibón Pequeño cabaña, turn up onto the cairned and red-blazed 'Camino de Batisielles'. After an intial climb, there is little net altitude change for the next 1½ hours, but the whole way you have fine vistas across the Valle de Estós (Astós) to the peaks of Gías and Aô which hover over the refuge. This itself becomes obvious toward the end of the day's first 90 minutes and near the turn off for the 20-minute crossing of the river.

The Refugio de Estós (1835 metres), recently rebuilt after a devastating fire, bills itself as the 'most modern and best equipped in the Pyrenees'. While all such claims are subjective, there's no doubt that more is on offer here than at most huts. It's quite luxurious (hot water), large (180 places), and even has an on-premises phone (tel (974) 55 14 83) for reservations which are unlikely to be necessary, and also available through *Deportes Aigualluts* in Benasque. Dissenters tend to camp (messily, as usual) in the grove and meadow just upstream at about 1800 metres.

If you are still on the south bank of the Río Estós, you should cross as soon as practicable to the opposite bank, since the only through path up to the Puerto de Gistaín is on the north side. Alpina mistakenly indicates a route on the south bank. Trails cairned beyond the camping meadows on the south bank in fact only lead up to the Valle de Bardamina and the Paúl glacier, the standard approaches to Posets peak.

The Clarabide stream meets the main Estós watercourse some 90 minutes above the refuge at about 2050 metres; cross to stay with the main river and collect some of it, since oddly enough this is the last dependable water for some time. Allow two hours more to reach the Puerto de Gistaín (at around 2600 metres), the southernmost of the three apparent passes visible. You approach for the final few hundred metres on the south flank of the Barranco de Estós. The saddle is surprisingly disappointing for views, with little visible of the drainages behind or ahead of you, but is a good place to spot chamois.

There's really a double pass here, with an intervening moor, and the initial descent west is easiest done to your far left-hand (south) side. After this, you angle down gentler grass slopes to meet the 'main' trail dropping uncomfortably sharply from the top of the Barranco de Gistaín. You should soon see sporadic horizontal bar-blazes and '*Senda Pirenaica*' inscriptions on the rocks as the trail improves along the one-hour drop to the confluence of streams at Añes Cruces (2060 metres). A *cabaña* here, adequate for emergency stays, is conspicuous on the far hillside.

The Alpina sheet is drastically wrong here; the onward trail is on the west or true right bank of the Cinqueta (Zinqueta) de Añes Cruces, below the *cabaña*. The east side is impassable after a few hundred metres, and even on the correct bank there are a pair of huge erosion zones which must be skirted. Otherwise, however, the path is straightforward and, as you slowly round the mountain, the point of the day's exercise becomes clear – unsurpassed perspectives of the entire west face of Posets. Allow 1 hour 45 minutes down from the river junction to the Granjas de Viadós (a hamlet of a dozen scattered farms at the end of a road) and its hut, for a total of over eight hours since Batisielles.

The Refugio de Viadós (1760 metres), though privately owned, is unusually reasonable and well outfitted. The 39 bunks on the two floors of the main building (plus six in a separate annexe) cost only 375ptas; there are indoor toilets and hot showers (for an extra fee), evening electricity and a cozy *bar-comedor*. Meals are the Pyrenean refuge standard, both in terms of price and quality; the warden can sell you basic foodstuffs, and usually *Cointra* gas, for a modest (33%) mark-up. Those cooking for themselves do so in the annexe but are welcome to eat in the

Campers at Granjas de Viadós

comedor. The continual staffing season is 1 July to 20 September, though the annexe kitchen is always kept open; at other times contact the warden, Joaquín Cazcarra, in Gistaín village (tel (974) 50 60 82).

The shelter is actually more rustic than it sounds, and has an impressive setting; new arrivals often spend hours gaping at Posets from the hayfield in front. People are allowed to camp there as well; an outdoor privy and trough-spring caters for them. Although the refuge is just west of the Alpina *Posets-Perdiguero* map coverage (a marketing gimmick for the next quad?) there's no problem finding it, since like the Estós hut it's squarely astride the main trekking route.

Day-Hikes Around Viadós

The best day excursions from Viadós are the full-day one up to the Lago de Millares (2400 metres) below the Pico de la Forqueta, with a path the entire way; and the half-day hike to the Señal de Viadós (2600 metres), north-north-east of the refuge, affording stunning 360-degree vistas. The long day-trip to the lake of Ordiceto, described in the following section as part of the high-level traverse to Bielsa, is worth doing as such if you opt instead for the low-altitude traverse.

POSETS MASSIF TO BIELSA

West of Posets you will be venturing into hard-core (literally and figuratively) Aragón; gone are the meadows and forests of the central and eastern Pyrenees – the rocks of the west usually refuse to support them. So if, particularly at Batisielles and Granjas de Viadós, you have an urge to linger the extra day, you should indulge it. The bleak marches of Ordiceto, Ordesa and Panticosa are spectacular in their own way, but hardly inviting or conducive to throwing your pack off onto the turf – of which there will be little or none.

Rating

It's easy from Viadós up to Ordiceto, but tedious if you have to road-walk down from there. Lower routes, whether directly from La Sargueta or along the entire *camino* from Gistaín, are also easy going but longer.

Duration

Allow an extra day for visiting the Gistaín valley villages. Setting off from there you may also be forced to spend the night in Bielsa rather than, more conveniently, up the Pineta valley.

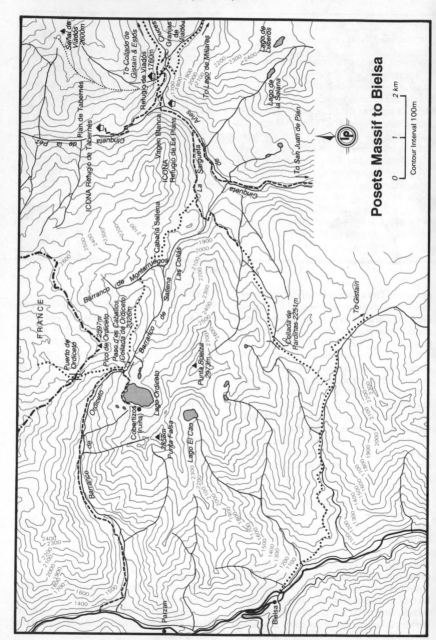

Posets Massif to Bielsa

Contour Interval 100m

0   1   2 km

Map

Use Alpina No 205, *Bachimala* (1:25,000).

Stage 13: Viadós to Bielsa via Ordiceto or Pardinas

Each of these routes ends in Bielsa, allowing a stop there for supplies; neither visits the three villages of the lower valley of Gistaín (alias Gistau, Chistén). These – Gistaín, San Juan (Chuan) de Plan, and Plan – are 600 metres, and a 12-km track-walk, below the Refugio de Viadós. There's a bank (in Plan), a post office, some supplies (including butane cartridges) and conventional accommodation, but no bus service to anywhere (though there is talk of instituting one). Whether these features, the distinctive uniform stone architecture, and the last vestiges of the old Aragonese dialect will motivate you to visit depends on your schedule and interests.

If you elect to proceed directly to Bielsa and Pineta by either the high or low-level alpine routes, the day's start is identical. Descend from Granjas de Viadós, using some stretches of path for short-cutting the road, to the schoolchildren's summer camp of Virgen Blanca, near the confluence of the Añes Cruces and Pez streams.

There is a large ICONA refuge (Es Plans) on the east bank of the river, but the commotion from the nearby camp is generally enough to discourage use. Another ICONA facility exists up the Cinqueta de la Pez at Plan de Tabernés. While it's more peaceful, it's out-of-the-way and only likely to be of interest to those subsequently hiking into France via the Madera or Pez passes.

It's just under an hour to the La Sargueta turn off (1540 metres), downstream from Virgen Blanca; take the side track which, after 40 minutes more, ends at a cluster of farms. Here's a three-way junction, and an important choice. Heading straight leads eventually to the Collada de Pardinas (2251 metres) and shortly after to the intersection with the old Gistaín-Bielsa *camino*; though no shorter than the high route to be detailed, it is gentler, with (on balance) a more enjoyable walking surface. If you're not confident about your ability to hitch out of the Ordiceto

area, and if extensive road-walking is unappealing, it's probably better to use the lower alternative. Allow seven hours to reach Bielsa this way.

For Ordiceto and the higher route, bear right at the triple fork (there's a cairn or two). Within 30 minutes you should reach the small pass and meadow of Las Collás, after which the trail (marked with red and white arrows) dips briefly as the Cabaña Sallena comes into view. The countryside is an appealing mix of piney ravines and turf with bare, 2973-metre Punta Suelza looming to the left as a sample of the landscapes to come.

The trail passes just beneath the *cabaña* some 20 minutes beyond Las Collás, then curves above and beyond it, adhering to red and white waymarks. Resist any temptation to dip left into the Barranco de Sallena (Solana) – the Alpina quad is correct and this is still the 'Senda Pirenaica', though the walking surface is in fact much better than the map's cross-country dots imply.

Cross the Barranco de Montarruegos (the last dependable water until the pass) 45 minutes later, and 3 hours 15 minutes from the Viadós hut. Next you angle up the ridge separating Montarruegos from Sallena, roller-coasting a bit in terms of altitude, and then slip through the Paso d'es Caballos (Collada de Ordiceto – 2326 metres) five hiking hours into the day. The dirt road encountered almost immediately leads left to the lake; the path bears obviously to the right (north), toward the Puerto de Ordiceto and France, just 500 metres away. Most foot traffic in either direction up here uses this latter pass.

Ordiceto (Urdiceto) dam (2369 metres) is a final 15 minutes distant; after the promise of the day's hike the lake is an anticlimax, prone (like its Catalan counterparts) to having its water level fiddled with. At the best of times the terrain is grimly rocky, and the pass west of Punta Suelza between Ordiceto and the Lago El Cao to the south (misleadingly labelled '*Itinerario*' on the Alpina) is strictly off-limits to most trekkers, making a direct traverse to Bielsa impossible. The main attraction is the panorama from the upper west shore of the mountains to the east. Here also are some turfy flat spots for a tent, around the unusable *cobertizos* (power company bungalows), but you may prefer to use up the day by hoofing it down the canyon, just north-east, to civilisation.

It's 11 km on the dirt road through the Barranco de Ordiceto to the main highway just above Parzan, and another four km south on the asphalt to Bielsa. Since the Lago de Ordiceto is strangely a popular destination for Spanish car-parties, there's a good chance of a ride down – it's no fun to walk it.

BIELSA TO THE PARQUE NACIONAL DE ORDESA

Bielsa itself (1023 metres) is an object lesson

in what happens to Pyrenean hill towns when tunnels are bored above them; the historic church, old bridge and town hall on the plaza are now drowned in a rash of tourist honky-tonk far worse than anything in Benasque to date. At least there are three or four good *supermercados* and a bank for stocking up, and a pair each of relatively expensive hotels and *hostales* if you're craving sheets.

The Valle de Pineta

If Bielsa doesn't appeal, it's fortunately not too difficult to wangle a ride up the road penetrating the Valle de Pineta past one of two camping sites: the reasonable and well-amenitied *Pineta* at Km 8, or the public

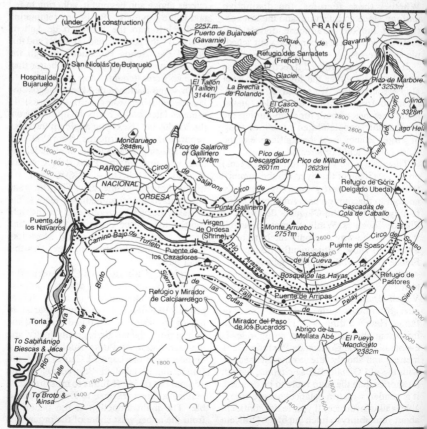

meadow at Km 14, opposite the *parador*, virtually free (70ptas) but with no facilities. Both sites are convenient to the trailhead for the Collado de Añisclo at Km 12.

The valley itself is the first of the giant glacial troughs which distinguish this part of the Aragonese Pyrenees. There are only two, *steep* ways out for trekkers intent on reaching the Ordesa national park (Parque Nacional de Ordesa). The first, up the *circo* at the valley's head to the Balcón de Pineta and then over the permanent snowfields of the Cuello del Cilindro (3100 metres), requires snow- and ice-equipment 10 months of the year and is not described in detail here. The other option via the Añisclo pass, while

scarcely less strenuous, is more generally accessible and is outlined following.

Rating It's moderately difficult trekking from the Pineta valley floor to Añisclo, moderate thereafter along the recommended route (though long hiking days). Possible itineraries via the Cuello del Cilindro and the Balcón de Pineta, especially reversed, are likely to be difficult.

Duration Allow three days from Pineta to Bujaruelo via the head of Añisclo, and an extra (fourth) day if you attempt to go through the Cuello del Cilindro.

Bielsa to the Parque Nacional de Ordesa & Various Routes through Ordesa

Supplies Shopping in Bielsa is better than in Torla. You can't buy anything in the Valle de Pineta or at Bujaruelo.

Map Use Alpina No 204, *Ordesa-Vignemale-Monte Perdido* (1:40,000), even though it's marred by the various errors noted.

Stage 14: Valle de Pineta to the Valle de Añisclo

The Pineta valley's elevation is roughly 1350 metres, and the Collado de Añisclo is at 2470 metres. This vertical increment over a lateral distance of less than a km yields a grade in excess of 100%! The Spanish army runs Mountain Artillery Brigade recruits up and down the trail linking the two, should you still doubt the calibre of this leg of the journey.

Despite the cruel climb it's actually part of our old friend GR11, and is thus marked (except where most needed, at the bottom) and heavily used over the whole distance. This means you can at least concentrate on putting one foot above the other, with the occasional wild strawberry providing additional consolation.

The trailhead for the Collado de Añisclo is signposted at Km 12 on the valley floor road. Cross the riverbed perpendicularly, as water levels permit, and make for the large, boggy meadow directly opposite. The red and white blazed trail, its start marked by cairns, begins at the upper left (standing with your back to the river) corner of the bog. Do not be lured astray by a path with brown and yellow waymarks parallel to the river – if you use this at all, it should be downstream into the previously noted meadow.

About three hours of climbing separates you from the valley bottom and the 2100-metre contour, where a wooden sign announces '*Bajada al Valle de Pineta*' to those coming from above. Allow another hour to the pass (2470 metres) and a fine view over the head of the Añisclo canyon. There is water and some level turf for camping at 50 to 100 metres below the ridge, an unspoiled spot with only sheep about.

The GR11 bears right, initially north-west, then south-west, from the pass but is repre-

hensibly routed and unreservedly not recommended. An extremely dangerous, 500 metre traverse of a sheer wall, through a hell of scree, snow and wet rock, is involved; one slip and it would be your last. It is incomprehensible how the GR committee has managed to get away with marking this 'trail' for general use. Four lightly laden individuals whom I met descending looked shaken and admitted that it was 'very difficult'; they had traversed it in 3½ to 4 hours from the Refugio de Góriz.

In the interest of staying in one piece resign yourself to losing a bit of altitude using remaining stamina and daylight to reach the prime camping sites in the Añisclo canyon. A trail well marked with cairns drops within two hours from near the pass to the dilapidated Choza (Cottage) de Cazadores at 1770 metres, and to the junction of the main drainage with the Barranco Arrablo, for a total of six hours for the day.

Stage 15: Valle de Añisclo to Refugio de Góriz

You've a choice of two routes up from the valley floor to the vicinity of the Góriz hut the shorter one is more difficult and doesn't permit you to see as much of Añisclo. All trail tracings on the pertinent Alpina map are quite misplaced, so directions are presented here in some detail.

Near the Choza de Cazadores (also shown too high on the Alpina), cross the river by bridge at about 1750 metres. A nasty, sharp scree-laden route, studded with sporadic cairns but never really a trail, ascends (in about three hours) to link up with the end of the itinerary outlined as follows.

It's preferable to continue down the west (true right) bank of the upper Añisclo canyon along a cairned trail not shown on Alpina; the way is occasionally demanding, requiring some handwork and scrambling, and you will look longingly at the clear main trail across the raging river. But at least no more altitude is lost as you climb slowly through the Añisclo narrows, high above the many day-trippers who enter from Ainsa village at the bottom.

Once around a rock overhang with drip

ing seeps (90 minutes beyond the bridge), matters improve substantially, and suddenly you find yourself in the clear, on a bluff overlooking the Barranco de Capradiza. The succession of cairns culminates in an easily passable wire fence and single red blaze.

The Alpina at this point is just plain misdrawn; the trail does not go anywhere near the tiny watercourse shown to the south of Capradiza. Neither is it even necessary to cross to the south bank of the Capradiza ravine, via the old stone bridge glimpsed in the stream bed. Moderately sloping uplands span the distance, and 700-metre altitude difference, between the narrows and the Punta Custódia defile (2300 metres). You'll need three hours to reach this with no trail; you won't miss one since it's fairly easy cross-country work.

From the saddle you have a good view northwards to the summits dominating the region: from right to left the Pico de Añisclo (3002 metres), the Sum de Ramond (3254 metres), the Morrón de Arrablo (2792 metres) and (weather permitting) Monte Perdido (3355 metres). A well grooved path with cairns suddenly reappears here also. The Collado Superior de Góriz (2343 metres) is reached after 20 minutes more, as you rejoin the GR11 so-called 'trail' coming down from the base of the peaks.

Allow another 45 minutes to get down to the refuge, having walked a total of 5½ hours from the bridge and *cabaña* (7½ hours from the head of the Valle de Añisclo).

Once you've reached the Refugio de Góriz (Julián Delgado Ubeda) at 2160 metres, you may well wonder why you've bothered. Though open all year, its 100-odd places are in great demand in July and August, when you've little chance of a ordering a meal, let alone a bunk, unless you arrive by 3 pm. Assuming you even get in the door, you can expect a suitably warm and hospitable welcome from the ever-friendly staff: 'There's no more to eat and no place to stay and get your daypack [containing my passport, notebook, sunglasses, etc] out of here' was openers for me.

No matter how many people have managed to squeeze into the undersized shelter, an equal or greater number are camped nearby – a spring is marked with a red flag but you're not supposed to use the hut's external WC. The result is a grim, garbage- and faeces-strewn scene, aggravated by the ban on camping within the nearby Ordesa national park. You might just want to forgo even asking for a space and camp at far better sites, 25 to 30 minutes east, just below the pass where a large stream flows through a meadow at about 2250 metres.

One of the reasons for the Góriz hut's popularity, besides proximity to the national park, is the large number of *simas* and *avencs* (sinkholes and shaft-caves) which riddle the predominantly limestone strata hereabouts. The geology also makes springs slightly less frequent than in the rest of the Pyrenees, but with the usually unstable weather here you can count on finding some sort of potable water year round.

Alternate Routes

Unfortunately the Refugio de Góriz and its immediate environs are also squarely astride several main routes besides those just discussed: up to France via the Brecha de Rolando, to Pineta via the Cuello del Cilindro, and down to the Ordesa canyon – and is thus unavoidable if travelling along GR11 or any of its alternatives. If you are lucky enough to get a bunk, or can stand to camp for two nights, the most popular daytrip is up Monte Perdido, third highest in the range. Allow seven hours for the round trip; ice axe and crampons are required all year. The main route is a cairned path as far as the tiny tarn of Lago Helado (at around 3050 metres), reached some three hours out. Then you turn sharply south-east for the final ascent up a couloir and then a rock-strewn snow ridge to the summit.

From this side of the range a traverse to the Valle de Pineta, completing a loop if desired, may be more appealing since the worst elevation differences in the area will be experienced going downhill. After getting over the Cuello del Cilindro (3100 metres) and down the reportedly temperamental glacier on the far side, you will arrive at the frozen lake of Marmoré and probably elect to break the journey and camp on the flat Balcón de Pineta. Allow seven hours to this point, and another 3½ hours the next day to descend the clear trail to the head of the Valle de Pineta.

VARIOUS ROUTES THROUGH ORDESA

The Valle de Ordesa is justifiably the pride of the Aragonese mountains, and the park protecting it is one of Spain's oldest national reserves. A lush mixture of coniferous and hardwood forests adorns the floor of this 13-km-long, 800-metre-deep trough. Today the swift streams draining the main valley, and waterfalls plunging from hanging valleys to the side, swell with year-round rains and constitute a legacy of the glacial processes which shaped the limestone palisades.

The park is one of the best spots in Spain for raptor-viewing; those who come prepared with field guide and binoculars may be rewarded with sightings of the golden eagles, lammergeiers and griffon or Egyptian vultures who nest in the Ordesa cliffs. Chamois, known in Aragonese dialect as *sarrio*, are also a common feature, and are indeed so successful that they outdo the rare Spanish ibex (*Capra hispanica*) here as well as in other regions of Spain where their ranges overlap.

From the Góriz area you have a choice of itineraries through this most famous canyon of the Pyrenees. If you are just visiting the national park which contains it, you can do two of these back-to-back for a thorough tour; in any case the Faja de Pelay route is the best one.

Stage 16A: Refugio de Góriz to Senda de los Cazadores via Faja de Pelay

Leaving the hut, heading due south on the blazed trail, it's from 45 to 50 minutes down to the 1900-metre contour just above the Circo de Soaso, and an apparent forking. Avoid bearing right toward the now-abandoned *clavijas* (metal stakes in the cliff for letting yourself down hand-over-hand) route, and continue straight following the GR11 waymarks toward the zig zag portion

of trail ahead. (The bypass of the *clavijas* is not shown correctly on the relevant Alpina map).

Some 20 to 25 minutes down the switchbacks, an obvious side trail on the left links up with the main Faja de Pelay path coming up from the meadows of the Circo de Soaso; this short cut saves you considerable altitude loss but again is not marked on the Alpina map.

From the link-up with the wide, immensely enjoyable Faja de Pelay *camino* allow between 2 hours 45 minutes and three hours to the Refugio y Mirador de Calcilarruego and the final descent to the Puente de los Cazadores. While not a true corniche (cliff-face) trail, the route is exciting enough. It turns from one ravine after another, though rarely exceeds 1900 metres in elevation (despite what the Alpina map says). The whole way you're treated to great views: initially back to the Cola de Caballo falls at the head of the Circo de Soaso and Monte Perdido, then the wedding-cake flanks of Monte Arruebo, and finally – and most impressively – the Circo de Cotatuero and its cascades, with the Brecha de Rolando and its flanking peaks behind.

Adding to the list of Alpina map idiosyncrasies, the Fuente Fria o del Abé is dry and the Abrigo (lean-to) de la Mallata Abé is a good 3 cm too far east; water is only available from an unmarked spring just before the Calcilarruego hut, a good lunch spot.

Most of the day's descent is covered in the next 75 minutes, as you drop 600 metres on the tight switchbacks of the Senda de los Cazadores. Emerge from the forest just opposite its namesake bridge; if you intend to leave the park from here, it is suggested you bear left along the south (true left) bank of the canyon and follow the instructions in Stage 17, Puente de los Cazadores to Torla or Bujaruelo.

Stage 16B: Puente de los Cazadores to Circo de Soaso

This is the easiest and most popular walking trail in the Ordesa national park. Frankly, it's best avoided in midsummer, though is listed here for the sake of completeness and for hose who have arrived from the plains of Aragón by car or bus.

The asphalt access road into the park ends 0 km beyond Torla village and just after the railhead for the Circo de Salarons, at a car park surrounded by the visitor centre, a restaurant and a forestry station. Upon leaving he car park on foot turn immediately right into the Puente de los Cazadores, and then eft again onto the path following the south bank of the Arazas river.

This route parallels the 'main', north-bank rail until re-uniting with it a few km up-alley at the Puente de Arripas, but is far less rowded than the thoroughfare opposite. Just under an hour along, the Mirador del Paso de os Bucardos offers the best views back oward the Salarons and Cotatuero cliffs, and s virtually the only point along the river that gives you much of a perspective on the valley.

Cross back to the north bank via the Puente de Arripas within a few minutes, and troll past the thundering Cascadas de la Cueva for 25 minutes more along the now-oint trail until reaching the distinct, but unmarked turn off to the Circo de Cotatuero see next stage).

Soon the forest thins out, and the canyon ssumes a decided U-shape as you leave the ark territory just before the crumbling Refugio de Pastores. This is the first place where you are allowed to pass the night (not hat you'd want to – wait until the Circo de Soaso) since camping within the park is forbidden, and the handful of *abrigos* within its boundaries are intended for emergency use only.

Some three hours along the progressively narrowing gorge you'll come to the meadows of the *circo*, excellent for camping, and cross the rickety Puente de Soaso, with the Cascadas de Cola de Caballo pouring off the abrupt head of the valley just north. From the bridge up to Góriz, along the route described in the Refugio de Góriz to Senda de los Cazadores via Faja de Pelay section, allow a little over an hour, for a total of just over four hours from the car park.

Stage 16C: Bosque de Las Hayas/Cotatuero Side Trail

To vary a return to the Puente de los Cazadores area, take the previously mentioned side trail toward Cotatuero . The path, initially through box, pine, fir and of course beech (the *hayas* of the *bosque*) roller-coasts halfway up the flank of Monte Arruebo, at about the 1700-metre contour. It crosses the lips of numerous hanging valleys, narrowing on occasion to clear rock overhangs. It's certainly wilder, and more authentic, than either of the valley-bottom *caminos*, and you've tremendous views of the waterfalls on the Faja de Pelay side.

Assuming no snow, it's two hours from the Bosque de Hayas to the bridge and *abrigo* below the Cotatuero cascades. These, and their namesake *circo*, come into view some 90 minutes along; allow another half-hour to get to the stream. From the tiny shelter it's less than an hour down to the main north-bank path; the junction is marked by the small shrine of the Virgen de Ordesa.

It would be easy enough, however, to follow the west-bound trail which continues along the base of the Punta Gallinero cliffs to meet the path leading down from the Circo

de Salarons to the park headquarters. Briefly join the latter, then bear right (west) again to reach the Río Ara at the point where the asphalt access road and the GR11 also meet (see next section).

Stage 17: Puente de los Cazadores to Torla or Bujaruelo

At the south end of the bridge, and the bottom of the descent from Calcilarruego, bear west and follow the south (true left) bank of the Arazas, guided initially by blazes. Ignore the faint turning up to the now-abandoned Camino Alto de Turieto, and instead keep right onto the Camino Bajo. You can detour to see several waterfalls from along this beautiful section of GR11, which rounds a bend in the Valle de Broto (containing the Río Ara, not to be confused with the Arazas) some 75 minutes from Cazadores area.

Shortly after, the park boundary is signposted, as are the forks for Torla – now visible to the south – and the Puente de los Navarros to the right (north). Just less than two hours out the *camino* blends into a sizeable dirt track; from here it's another half-hour, for a total of 2 hours 20 minutes, over the Puente de Glera and up muddy cobbles to the church of Torla.

Torla

It may not be worth the effort walking here – Torla has been utterly spoiled since my first visit in 1986. Vast new cement tower-blocks on the outskirts, including a handful of new hotels dwarfing the medieval core, tipped me off on approach. There are three hotels and two *hostales* (all expensive), and a couple of *casas particulares* (rooms in private houses) such as *Pascualeta's* over the *Bar Rebeco*; but you won't get a bed to save your life in summer.

If, by some miracle, they have space, *Fonda Ballarín* (tel (974) 48 61 72) is the friendliest and offers the best value in a community where many proprietors simply refuse to rent to solo travellers and/or for one night. Torla has two or three stores for reprovisioning but these are not up to the standard of those in Bielsa or Benasque. *Cointra* gas is sold at the *Hotel Ordesa*.

But all told, it's better to move on and o̶ (see the Getting to/from Ordesa Trailhead section following) before nightfall finds yo̶ homeless, or give Torla a miss entirely. If yo̶ insist, there's a camping ground three k̶ north of the village, but the inbound b̶ service gives you enough daylight to g̶ elsewhere to spend the night; Bujaruelo, f̶ example, is a far better jumping-off point f̶ the next day's hiking.

Getting to/from Ordesa Trailhead

There's a daily minibus at 10.50 am fro̶ Sabiñánigo (on the Jaca-Zaragoza rail lin̶ to Torla via Biescas; the downhill bus leav̶ Torla at 4.30 pm. The bus terminal i̶ Sabiñánigo lies 300 metres east (to the righ̶ of the train station as you leave it, though th̶ Torla vehicle tends to leave from two doo̶ west of the main garage.

Bujaruelo

Bujaruelo is most easily reached by takin̶ the north-bound option to the Puente de l̶ Navarros noted previously. GR waymark̶ lead you along this, down to the confluenc̶ of the Ara and Arazas rivers and then up th̶ Ara gorge. From the bridge the marked rou̶ follows the track for a while, then slips ove̶ to a bona fide trail on the east (true left) ban̶ of the Ara, until arriving at the ruined churc̶ and old bridge of San Nicolás de Bujaruel̶ some six km and two hours from the par̶ boundary junction.

On the west side of the bridge, a larg̶ camping site occupies a riverside paddoc̶ but best of all is the old *hospital* here, whic̶ has been refurbished as a *mesón/fonda* by th̶ Lardies family. This is essentially anoth̶ private refuge like that at Granjas de Viadó̶ though it's only open during July an̶ August. For 600 ptas you get bedding and̶ sink in four-bedded rooms, and hot showe̶ in the evening, supper is adequate but th̶ expensive refuge norm. There are no groce̶ ies for sale, so if you skip Torla deliberate̶ you need to have at least one more day's foo̶ on hand to see you through the next leg ̶ the traverse.

.RA VALLEY TO THE TENA BASIN

Today the hospital at San Nicolás de ujaruelo, as in the era of the lintel plaque dated 1848), sees a steady stream of travel-rs hiking to or from France, via either the 'uerto de Bujaruelo (Gavarnie) just above nd east, or the Col des Oulettes up at the ery top of the Ara valley next to Vignemale eak. Less commonly done, but no less seful, are long (eight hours and more) but easible traverses west to Panticosa, in the 'ena river basin. The easiest and briefest of nese is detailed following.

Rating

The fully described GR traverse via Ten-lenera is easy to moderate, tending toward ne latter only because of its length and occa-ional tedium of the route. Alternate tineraries via Espelunz or Brazato are liable o be moderate and moderately difficult espectively (more because of time required han surface).

Maps

There's a big gap in Alpina coverage here – ou must rely on the SGE sheets Nos 30-8 146), *Bujaruelo* and 29-8 (145), *Sallent de Gállego*, both 1:50,000. Except for the area vhere the Valle de Otal meets the Ara valley – where it's drawn way too far south – the asic GR trail is shown correctly on the SGE naps.

Stage 18A: Bujaruelo to Panticosa via Otal/Tendenera

Recross the old stone bridge to the east bank f the Ara and turn left, following a sign ointing to the Otal and Ara valleys. Because f the heavy foot traffic through the area, irtually all trails are blazed and care must be aken to follow the correct GR marks. After 0 minutes you reach a second (cement) ridge, which you cross to get onto the west ank again; red and white bars direct you up grassy slope to a wooden '*Refugio de Otal 30*' sign.

The trail west through *Vaccinium* bushes voids the worst of the dirt road up to Otal; fter 45 minutes more you emerge at the nouth of the valley, with the Collado de Tendenera obvious at the far end. Rolling grassy meadows are cleft by a stream, the whole framed by outriders of Pico de Ten-denera (to the south, 2853 metres) and Mallaruego (north, 2692 metres). It's a half-hour more, and so a bit less than 90 minutes from the sign, to the road's end at the shelter (an unusable cow shed at 1600 metres) and the resumption of the bona fide trail up to the pass.

Having completed roughly two hours of hiking from Bujaruelo, you bear initially right (north); next steadily up the valley; then counter-intuitively away from the pass, gaining altitude in long, roundabout arcs. Do not be tempted to leave the path and tackle the hillside directly; the GR markers know what they're about here. Allow two hours more to reach a meadow and a spring at about 2200 metres, just below the saddle. This makes a good lunch spot, safe above the cow pastures with their annoying flies.

The Collado de Tendenera (2325 metres) appears deceptively close, but you need another half-hour to hike from the spring and adjacent cascades to reach it. The view east is dominated by the border summit of Tallón (Taillon) at 3144 metres, guarding the Puerto de Bujaruelo, and Mondaruego (2848 metres) to its south, overlooking Ordesa. Looking west, nearby Pico de las Escuelas (2510 metres) occupies most of your field of vision, with some other summits separating Cadanchú from Canfranc, also discernible.

Descend from the pass, first on the north side of the watercourse at the foot of Escuelas, later switching to the south (true left) bank and rounding the bend for an excel-lent view (90 minutes below the saddle) over the Río Ripera valley draining the cirque and giant wall of the Sierra de Tendenera. You can glimpse the pronged peak of Balaitous (3151 metres) on the Franco-Spanish border to the north. Within 30 minutes more you cross the river and join up with the jeep track recently bulldozed up the west bank, and after another 25 minutes pass an ICONA *cabaña* (with one wing open).

By now the Picos das Argualas (at around 3000 metres) have replaced Balaitous on the skyline. The bulk of the day's trek (through

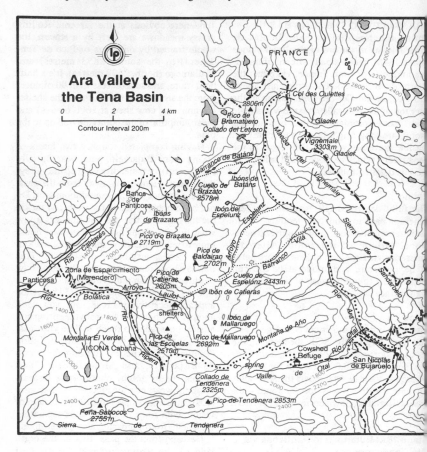

Ara Valley to the Tena Basin

0   2   4 km

Contour Interval 200m

FRANCE

2806m
Col des Oulettes
Pico de Bramatuero
Collado del Letrero
Glacier
Vignemale 3303m
Glacier

Barranco de Batáns

Ibóns de Batáns

Cuello de Brázato 2578m

Baños de Panticosa

Ibóns de Brazato

Ibón de Espelunz

Pico d'o Brazato 2719m

Río Caldarés

Pico de Baldairan 2702m

Sierra de

Barranco

Cuello de Espelunz 2443m

Panticosa

Zona de Esparcimiento (Merendero)

Pico de Catieras 2605m

Arroyo

Laulot

Ibón de Catieras

Río Bolática

shelters

Ibón de Mallaruego

Pico de las Escuelas 2510m

Pico de Mallaruego 2692m

Montaña de Año

Montaña El Verde

ICONA Cabaña

Cowshed Refuge

Ripera

spring

Valle de Otal

San Nicolás de Bujaruelo

Río Ara

Collado de Tendeñera 2325m

Pico de Tendeñera 2853m

Peña Sabocos 2755m

Sierra   de   Tendeñera

lonely, if not always startling, country with only the odd eagle or stock herder for company) is over; there remains only a considerable horizontal rather than vertical distance.

Cross back to the east (true right) bank of the Ripera on a cement bridge, and near some shepherds' huts you'll enter the area covered by the Alpina *Panticosa-Formigal* sheet. Within another half-hour, making a total of three walking hours from the pass, meet the Arroyo Laulot coming down from the Ibón de Catieras; cairns on the right mark the path discussed in the Alternate Approaches to Panticosa section following.

For the moment, bear left onto the *pist* which parallels the joint streams, now calle the Río Bolática. A few hundred metres pas the chain blocking the road, a car park an the junction of the two higher rivers, there the potential to bear left onto a path dow towards the Bolática. This follows the wate fairly closely right into Panticosa town, an saves at least a half-hour's walking com pared to the usual route. It should only b attempted if enough daylight remains – an after considering what Panticosa has to offe

Staying with the jeep track, it's 75 minute to the 'Zona de Esparcimiento' ('dispersio zone' – as per Alpina) and the ICON *merendero* (picnic ground – as per the SGE sheet) just below the junction of the *pista* and the asphalted, valley-bottom road. A neighbouring children's summer camp (Las Viñas) can be noisy, but generally the ICONA recreation area, with a spring and picnic tables, makes a good place to tent for the night. If you don't manage to coincide with buses along the main road (see following) staying up here will save you the chore of hauling a full pack the extra distance to and from Panticosa. Allow 20 minutes more to reach town proper, making for a total of from 8½ to nine hours on the day.

Stage 18B/C: Alternate Approaches to Panticosa

Instead of veering left to follow the wooden sign above the second Ara river bridge, continue up the Ara valley at least another seven km along a trail on the east or true left bank) to the mouth of either the Barranco Vilá (1700 metres) or the succeeding Arroyo Espelunz (1800 metres). These both lead up, with a sharp turn south-west, to the Cuello de Espelunz (2443 metres), though the latter canyon is longer while the former route must negotiate an extra, gentle saddle (of Vilá, 2300 metres). Allow a good five hours from the cement bridge up to the pass. The drop on the Panticosa side is actually steeper, once past the Ibón de Catieras (camping possible). As you descend the Arroyo Laulot, you'll find two shelters, hook up with the cairned trail noted previously.

If you're really ambitious, and are willing to possibly camp a night en route to the Tena watershed, continue up the *camino* along the Ara valley some four hours to the mouth of the Barranco de Batáns (de los Batanes) at 2050 metres. With this gradual (but lengthy) elevation gain along the river, you cut the climb up to the Cuello de Brazato (2578 metres, two hours more).

Immediately west of the pass, and 200 metres below, is the surprisingly level cirque containing the two Ibóns de Brazato; you may want to camp there if you don't have sufficient daylight or stamina to reach the Baños (Spa) de Panticosa 90 minutes further on. If you have adequate supplies, this would

be the most adventurous and rewarding route to go for. The Ara gorge becomes more attractive as you climb up, with the unscaleable south-west face of 3303-metre Vignemale looming overhead, and the tarns of the Batáns valley provide a taste of what's ahead above Panticosa.

PANTICOSA & BEYOND

This route offers a two to three-day traverse of the westernmost zone of the Spanish Pyrenees which could be described as resolutely alpine. It's a spectacular finale: the landscape is spangled with lakes in a concentration not seen since the Aigües Tortes national park in Catalunya; includes two low passes if access to France is desired; and Balaitous, the westernmost of the summits over 3000 metres, dominates.

Rating

It's easy, except for the sticky Piedrafita pass, which boosts a traverse into the moderate category.

Duration

This route takes two hiking days, best apportioned as a half-day, a full day and a final half-day.

Supplies

Stock up on food in Panticosa.

Map

Use Alpina No 203, *Panticosa-Formigal* (1:25,000).

Getting to/from the Panticosa resorts

If you need to get out of the mountains, downhill buses to Biescas and then Sabiñánigo leave Panticosa spa at 4 pm and 7 am, passing the village 15 minutes later, reaching Sabiñánigo at 5.15 pm and 8.15 am respectively. The uphill bus links Panticosa village with the *balneario* (health resort) at 11.40 am and 7.10 pm; vehicles start originally from Sabiñánigo at approximately 10.50 am and 6.30 pm respectively. If you miss the buses, hitching (between the village and the baths, at any rate) is fairly easy.

Panticosa & Beyond

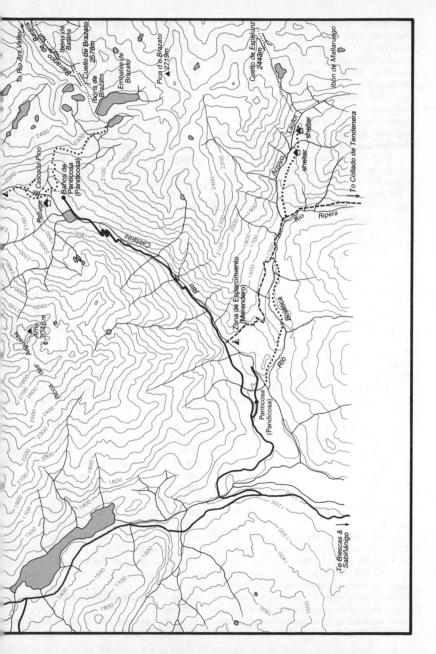

Panticosa (Pandicosa) Town & Spa

Panticosa, with its stuccoed exteriors, ornate windows on some older buildings and functional chalet architecture, smacks more of France or Switzerland than of any of the uniform *pizarra* (slate)-built villages of the Aran and Benasque valleys. Only the old Romanesque church, with its vaulting, square belfry and curious environment of vegetable patches, is worth a special detour. But Panticosa, as opposed to the 'new' Torla, has long been a major skiing and hydrotherapy resort, and so has had time to assume its touristic role more gracefully.

Be warned, though, that it's just as costly and no less crowded in summer. The two-star *Hostal-Residencia Navarra* is the least expensive place to stay. Singles cost from 1200 to 1500ptas, with only luxury facilities besides that – skiers are the usual clientele. The restaurant attached to the *Navarra* has the best value menu in town. There are also a couple of decent groceries; you can buy *Cointra* gas at *E Belio* and possibly at *Casa Brandes*. There's a post office, but no bank dealing in foreign exchange.

Surprisingly, you have (theoretically anyway) more chance of finding affordable lodging at Baños de Panticosa, eight km distant at the top of the Río Calderés valley. You'll find the one-star *Hostal Mediodía* and a mountaineers' refuge, *Casa de Piedra*, up behind most things. The spa is also a good base for short hikes; the information office hands out a decent sketch map for day-excursions. There are no groceries to speak of though – all shopping for the next phase of the Pyrenean traverse must be done in Panticosa.

Stage 19: Baños de Panticosa to Ibóns Azules

From the 'plaza' of the spa, in front of the tourist information post, bear right (east) up the stairs toward the Fuente de San Agustín and find GR blazes just across the bridge. Leave the various fountain-houses behind as the trail climbs north on an easy grade up to a large cement weir; just before is the hairpin right-turn leading up to the Ibóns de Brazato.

One half-hour above the resort you'll cross a bridge just above the Cascada Pino and climb for as much time again to a meadow (1900 metres), the first spot above the spa where camping is allowed. Within another 30 minutes, the base of the Cuesta d'o Fraile and the falls of the same name are reached; steep zig zags lead to the dam (2¼ hours) of the lower Bachimaña reservoir (2180 metres).

Here are a pair of shelters (one old, one new) and a camping site accessible by the catwalk across the dam, but it's best to continue along the GR trail. This gains some more altitude, allowing a view of the primitive five-person refuge across the higher main Bachimaña dam. (The direct 'trail' depicted on the pertinent Alpina is not advisable for those with full packs.) As it is, the GR route on the reservoir's west shore has some moments of scrambling before arriving (2¾ hours along) at the tarn at its north western tip, where there's good camping.

But again, if daylight allows, complete the third hour of hiking above the *baños* to an important, signposted three-way junction. Arrows point right (east) to '*Ib. de Bramatuero, Col. del Letrero*' (and the little refuge with a couple of camping sites adjacent, as well as the 2578-metre Puerto de Panticosa into France); south to '*Balneario de Panticosa*' (ie back the way you came); and west (left) to '*Ibones Azules, Picos de Infierno*'.

The lower Ibón Azul is merely 30 minutes away, but can offer only a doorless metal shed-shelter (and no camping space) beside the ugly dam; don't bother at a late hour unless you can make it for the 15 additional minutes to the upper lake. Unmarred by any construction, this is stunningly set below the peaks of Infierno and Piedrafita, which flank the obvious Cuello d'o Infierno just ahead, and offers the best camping this side of the pass. Accordingly, call it a short (less than four-hour) day, as the next stage is fairly challenging.

Stage 20: Ibóns Azules to Refugio de Piedrafita

From the campers' turf on the north shore of the higher lake, count on 75 minutes up to

Picos de Europa/Cares gorge – trekkers in a gallery

Top: Picos de Europa/western massif – Central massif from Vega de Ario
Left: Picos de Europa/Central – Los Urrielles pass
Right: Picos de Europa/Central – descending the Canal de Asotín

the Cuello d'o Infierno (2721 metres); the trail is distinct but crampons are useful if the approach incline is snowed up. The pass, nowhere near as hellish as the name implies, affords great views east over the lakes of Bachimaña and Bramatuero, plus the frontier ridge just above. To the west, vistas over the often semi-frozen Ibón de Tebarray, its namesake peak, and the border peaks behind Canfranc are even more impressive.

However the Collado de Piedrafita (2782 metres), 15 minutes away, is another matter. This, possibly the worst trekkers' pass in the Aragonese Pyrenees, has a nasty drop on the north side, either over scree or (more likely) snow which persists in quantity late into summer; crampons and some sort of self-arrest device are all but mandatory. Depending on conditions, it's 1½ to 2 hours down to the pretty Ibón de Llena Cantal (2450 metres) – should you be reversing this itinerary, there's good camping by the striped 'barber's pole' on the east shore, opposite the marked GR trail.

The grade relents and the hiking surface improves as turf reappears; descend another half-hour to a large meadow where the drainage of Llena Cantal (impassable) joins another stream entering from the south-west. Ford the main torrent, then leave the GR blazes when they return to the west (true left) bank; instead, angle down the grassy slopes to yet another barber's pole.

Just beyond it, cross the river flowing west from the Campo Plano reservoir, doing so upstream from the point where the water-course already negotiated becomes parallel to the new obstacle. There are trail traces, cairns, and (washouts permitting) an impromptu plank bridge. A more prominent path hops up the bluff overlooking the far bank, zigzagging to the Refugio de Piedrafita (formerly named Alfonso XIII; 2160 metres), finishing a walking day of well over five hours.

This stone igloo is in relatively good condition for an open, unattended shelter. It sleeps 25 on two cement platforms, but the nearest potable water is either in the river just forded, or the nameless lake some five minutes north-north-east where many people

choose to camp. The adjacent tarn is stagnant, and the shelter is shown on the wrong side of it on the Alpina map. Incidentally the GR trail eventually passes just west of the the hut, but the extra river crossings and circuitous approach seem to make it not worth considering.

From the shelter the shallowest pass into France, the Cuello d'a Piedra de San Martín (2284 metres), is only 90 minutes east, above the Campo Plano dam. The most popular all-day trip from Piedrafita, though, is the difficult ascent of Balaitous (Balaitús) via the Barranco de Respumoso and the south-east face.

Stage 21: Refugio de Piedrafita to Sallent de Gállego via Aguas Limpias

It takes 45 minutes, with no altitude loss and some occasional gain, for the GR trail to completely round the north shore of the Respumoso reservoir. Almost instantly you'll pass the grandiose, but half-finished and unusable, 'Nuevo Refugio' (misdrawn on Alpina) and then, assorted debris left by the dam-builders. The trail, shown way too far north on the Alpina, briefly becomes a stairway past a chapel (used as a refuge) beside the dam; upon entering the canyon of the Río Aguas Limpias it's transformed into a fine *camino*, presumably built for the project and its only attractive legacy.

At first it's a splendid corniche trail along the north (true right) bank, losing altitude steadily but not unreasonably, passing after an hour the lightly-cairned side trail up to the Arriel lakes and a slightly easier approach to Balaitous. At about the 1700-metre contour and the attractively forested narrows of Paso del Onso, the gorge bends sharply south so that the path is now west of the water.

'Civilisation' announces itself 2 hours 20 minutes along at the Llano Tornaliza, (misspelled on Alpina), which is packed with tents in summer; within another 20 minutes you arrive at the head of the Embalse de la Sarra with various signs pointing up the GR trail just used. You can postpone the inevitable for a while by taking the path threading a bit above the west shore and exiting as a dirt drive just beyond the dam, reached (in any case) three hours from Piedrafita hut.

Next there's an unavoidable stretch of asphalt to the junction just above Sallent de Gállego; a walled-in path here will deposit you by the village church after a walking day of less than four hours.

Sallent de Gállego

Sallent de Gállego (Galligo) provides some consolation for the rather anticlimactic end of the Pyrenees traverse – it's a pretty enough settlement, more uniform than Panticosa, if busier owing to the Formigal ski centre next door and the constant stream of cars from France. Count on two banks for exchange, three stores including a bakery, and the *Fonda Centro* (plus more sumptuous quarters). There are a selection of cafés and a park (by the old bridge) where you can wait for the afternoon bus down the hill.

Getting There & Away Bus services co-managed by *Hispana-Tensina* and *La Oscense* leave Sallent at 3.45 pm for Huesca, with a change at Sabiñanigo for trains or another bus to Jaca (usually within a half-hour). Since the bus and train stations in Sabiñanigo are so close together (300m), it's a simple matter to see which conveyance heading in the appropriate direction will leave first. If you miss the afternoon bus out of Sallent, there's a departure at 7am.

Coming up the hill, all buses bound for Sallent de Gállego (as well as Panticosa and Torla) leave Sabiñanigo at 10.50 am and 6.30 pm, with any necessary changes at Biescas.

Here finishes the Pyrenean high traverse, at least on the Spanish side. West of Sallent, any remaining high peaks are French, but more importantly high-tension power lines, asphalt roads and ski resorts proliferate. Also the rolling, lakeless green hills of Navarre are tame compared to the rocky grandeur of Aragón. The route has been vaguely palindromic, ending as it began, with dams and often superannuated power projects – some dating from the 1920s, but mostly from the Franco era.

The Respumoso and Sarra dams are harbingers of the giant Lanuza and Búbal dams farther down the Tena valley. In a scenario all too familiar in Spain, the inhabitants of Lanuza and Búbal villages were banished by the rising waters which inundated their rich valleys in 1954; today they stand three-fourths abandoned, perhaps awaiting the nouveau riche from the cities who will snap up the gutted houses at bargain prices to renovate them as 'lakeside villas'.

Northern Spain

The north of Spain seems expressly designed to confound any preconceived notions new-comers may have about the country. Green, misty, rugged, isolated, it seems displaced from some more northerly realm. A handful of passes funnels rail and road links through the successive mountain ranges separating the ocean from the *meseta*, but they seem to make scarcely an impact; 10 km from the through-routes the landscape will probably be wild, even primeval.

The north, one of the earliest regions of the peninsula to be settled by humans, served as a redoubt for indigenous inhabitants – such as the Basques and later the Visigoths – during every invasion of Iberia and today remains a last stronghold for various large mammals and smaller animals. One would not be overly surprised to meet the Spanish equivalent of the *yeti* or the *sasquatch* in some remote forest glade, such is the atmo-sphere.

Because of centuries of habitation, the countryside can no longer be classified as virgin – very little primary-growth forest is actually left – but compared to the rest of the peninsula it's a botanical Garden of Eden. Agriculture, at the higher elevations anyway, is sufficiently low-tech that massive doses of chemicals have not yet wiped out all of the smaller native flora. Further west, however, this underdevelopment – or backwardness, according to your point of view – has resulted in a grim human ecology. The Sierra de Ancares, particularly the Bierzo region near the frontier with the bleak Gallegan heath, is possibly the poorest and harshest corner of Spain.

Closer to Oviedo, the higher and fre-quently snow-capped Peña Ubiña (2417 metres) provides the focus of some hiking interest. There are any number of sub-2000-metre *sierras* which attract day-trippers from the northern towns, but the Picos de Europa, summit of the Cordillera Cantábrica, are lodestone and beacon for trekkers here. They are conveniently – perhaps symbolically – wedged in exactly halfway between the open Atlantic and the Pyrenees.

The Picos de Europa

Straddling the joint boundaries of Oviedo (Asturias), Santander (Cantábria), and León provinces – just 25 km inland from the Mar Cantábrico – the Picos de Europa are one of the most compelling mountain ranges in Spain. Though occupying a roughly square area only 40 km on a side (less than half of which is alpine zone) they must rank as a miniature masterpiece. Much of the attrac-tion derives from their geological status as a limestone anomaly near the eastern end of the mostly slate or granite Cordillera Cantábrica.

The Picos are generally considered to include the territory bounded by the Cabrales valley on the north and the headwaters of the Río Deva to the south. The latter curls around from a west-to-east course to a south-to-north one, bounding the mountains to the east. Another river system, the Sella and its tributary the Dobra, marks the western extent of the Picos, which are further subdivided into three massifs by yet more gorges.

Wedged between the Deva and the Duje river valleys is the Ándara group – the lowest (2441 metres), driest, least visited and the least interesting area. The Duje, as it flows north, then north-west, eventually meets the middle reaches of the Cares river, contained in the deepest and most impressive canyon around here. Between these two, rises the most spectacular and most frequented massif, the 'Central' or Urriello. Torre de Cerredo (2648m) marks the highest point in all of the Picos, but the perfect sugarloaf of Naranjo de Bulnes (2519 metres) is the most famous peak and virtually the logo of these mountains.

West of the Cares, whose sources are not far from those of the Dobra and the Sella, looms the Cornión – or 'Occidental' – massif, perhaps the wildest of the three. It's quietly impressive, if not always spectacular in the Disneyland fashion of the central group. The western summits culminate in Peña Santa (2596 metres) and its neighbour Torre de Santa María de Enol (2478 metres). Most of the Cornión lies within the Parque Nacional de Covadonga, established in 1918 both to preserve the fauna of the area and to commemorate the shrine at Covadonga in the northern foothills, from where the Christian Reconquest of Spain began in the 8th century.

The thick limestone beds of the Picos were heavily glaciated during the last Ice Age, and thereafter rapidly transformed into the karst which gives the mountains here their special character. Anyone who has visited the Italian Dolomites, the Aladağlar in Turkey, or many of the Greek mountains will be familiar with this sort of topography.

The strata are riddled with *jous*, the Asturian equivalent of *doline* or collapsed caverns; once the largest of these were lakes but today only those at Enol and Ercina in the western massif remain as reminders of the receding glaciers. Narrower cavities, some of them from 600 to 1000 metres deep in several stages, lurk in the karst dells – the delight of Spanish and overseas cavers who plumb their depths much of the year.

Since the Picos rise so abruptly from the nearby Atlantic coast, they act as a barrier for moisture laden north-east winds from the ocean. Snow lies thickly at the higher elevations from October to May, particularly after March. Mist or rain – sometimes both simultaneously in horrendous storms – is common for much of the rest of the year. The humidity fosters a deceptive green cover wherever soil permits; running water is actually scarce and, when the sun is out, the heat is formidable.

The Cornión massif manages to catch the most severe weather, and accordingly its foothill forests of alder, birch, ash, linen, beech and oak extend up to about 1300 metres. In the Urriello and eastern groups the climate is drier and the treeline (at 700 to 800 metres), lower. Vast low-altitude meadows of wildflowers provide havens for the numerous species of butterflies, a hallmark of the Picos.

The most obvious fauna, however, are the *rebeco* or chamois, particularly numerous in the central massif at Jou sin Tierre and Vega de Liordes; they seem to mock you with their bouncing gait as you toil along on two feet. Wild boar root about in the forest margins, and the *asturcón*, a breed of wild horse, frequents the area around the Ercina and Enol lakes. Various kinds of birds of prey, including golden eagles, falcons, kestrels and vultures, nest in the high pinnacles and also on the walls of the river gorges.

Mention should also be made of the

domesticated sheep of the range, source of the fermented *cabrales* cheese and whose unearthly cries sound almost human; I have never heard anything like it in Greece or Turkey, and in the mist it's easy to imagine that the souls of the damned are lost in a limestone hell.

It must be stressed that the Picos, while impressive enough, are not automatically a walker's paradise. In addition to the previously mentioned weather conditions, which often force you to spend an extra day holed up in your tent or a mountain hut, you will have to contend with the térrain. The sinkholes are a special hazard, since it would be easy enough to suddenly disappear down even a small one in the frequent mists here. Stay on the trails, or at least on the marked routes – at the best of times karst badlands form natural mazes, ideal terrain for wandering in circles for hours. Camping is usually difficult, surfaces and grades are punishing (especially above 1500 metres) and hikers are heavily dependent on cairns and refuges. You may soon miss the middle-altitude forests and abundant springs of the Pyrenees, only partly compensated for by the dramatic profiles of the bare alpine zones.

Approaches and planning are similarly complicated. A ring of villages (up to about 1100 metres) allows access to various points of all three mountain groups but, because they fall within three different provinces, public transport is bewildering. With some forethought, and an eye to bus schedules, it is certainly possible to work out satisfying traverses with villages as end or mid-points.

The central group has the greatest concentration of refuges and foothill villages to both north and south, though those in the Deva valley are considerably more touristified. The villages of the greener western massif tend to huddle to its south-western flank, technically a submassif known as the 'Precomión' where some excellent, middle-altitude *caminos* of great antiquity run parallel to the Dobra to link several communities.

The central and western ranges can be visited simultaneously without necessarily descending to inhabited areas, as they are each linked with the Garganta de Cares (Cares gorge) by a few *canales* – steep ravines. Because of the unavailability of supplies in the highest settlements, such a strategy requires that you carry four or five days' supply of food at a time. It is perhaps best to resign yourself to the task of repositioning to start shorter, two to three day traverses. Village sojourns are apt to be pleasurable as their economies, unlike those of the ski-resort communities of the Pyrenees, have in most cases not yet been warped by tourism. Most foreign visitors are currently British cavers, Belgians (Asturian immigrants to Belgium have told them about the area), Dutch and French.

But the future of the Picos de Europa seems uncertain. Already developers have partly destroyed a 1000-year-old trail in the Bulnes area, and assorted money-losing, 'prestige' nonsense such as more *teleféricos* to complement the one at Fuente Dé are under consideration. When you meet, however briefly, inebriated and noisy daytrippers who stumble away from the top of the existing cable-lift to buy more drink at the nearest refuges or, have similar experiences at either end of the Cares gorge, you are seeing the Ghost of Christmas Future. (Surprisingly, trash – that bane of the Pyrenees – is minimal and is handled well by the refuges.)

If you enjoy your time in the Picos, and object to the more drastic sorts of proposed despoliation/exploitation, you can write, on behalf of the Colectivo Montañero por la Defensa de los Picos de Europa, to: D Bernardo Fernández, Consejería de la Presidencia, Gobierno Regional del Principado de Asturias, Suárez de la Riva 11, 33004 Oviedo. Time is short, the mountains delicate, and tourist-dollar spending preferences are reportedly taken into account in planning decisions.

Duration

Almost infinitely variable. The most representative schedule might be: Day 1, La Hermida/Urdón to Sotres; Day 2, Sotres to Vega Urriello; Day 3, Vega Urriello to Vega Liordes; Day 4, Vega Liordes to Bulnes via

Cordiñanes and the Cares Gorge (mostly downhill so not so bad); Day 5, a day-hike out of Bulnes; Day 6, descent to Arenas and perhaps Cangas; Day 7, transfer to Enol/ Ercina lakes and hike in to Ario; Day 8, reposition to Vega Redonda, walk to Mirador de Ordiales if time permits; Day 9, traverse to Llago Huerta; Day 10, descend to Sajambre via Vegabaño; Day 11, Senda de Arcediano to Amieva.

Certainly the Picos deserve at least 11 days to do them justice, and many different itineraries are possible by mixing and matching the sections discussed in the text.

Season

Trekking above 1000 metres is viable only from May to October; May and June are often stormy and September, while clearest, is the hottest month.

Maps

There are several to choose from, but because of idiosyncrasies of coverage and conflicting data it's advisable to have more, not fewer maps. In any case you will need a 1:25,000 sheet apiece for the western and central groups, and a 1:50,000 quad showing the entire area for route planning – relationships between villages are shown poorly on most of the large-scale (detailed) maps.

As usual Editorial Alpina makes its bid with No 303, *Picos de Europa I, Macizo Occidental o de Cornión* and No 304, *Picos de Europa II, Naranjo de Bulnes, Macizos Central y Oriental* (both 1:25,000), but there is the usual quota of errors, and frustratingly the Cares gorge is sliced up at the meeting of the sheets, neither of which includes the Cordiñanes area.

Better choices if you can get them are *Mapa Excursionista del Macizo Central de los Picos de Europa* by Miguel A Andrados (1:25,000), and *Mapa del Macizo del Cornión* by José Ramón Lueje (1:25,000), the latter containing the least number of errors of any map gazetting the Picos.

A few comprehensive 1:50,000 sheets by various publishers seem to be in circulation; mine, published by GH Editores in Madrid, available in Cangas de Onís, and (like the

Lueje map) originally part of a book, is fair enough.

Equipment

Bring the lot, as mentioned in the equipment list in the Facts for the Trekker chapter – the training shoes and PVC mineral-water bottles so beloved of Spanish trippers are not going to cut it at the high altitudes! There seems to be one store in Oviedo (*Deportes Tuñon,* Campoamor 5/7) which will have a range of suitable articles, including the suggested maps.

Getting to/from the Trailheads

Considering the three Picos massifs roughly from east to west, the villages or towns of Potes, Espinama, Urdón/La Hermida, Arenas de Cabrales, Sotres, Valdeón, Caín, Sajambre, and Cangas de Onís are the principal jumping-off points for rambles in the mountains.

Eastern Access From Santander, capital of Cantábria, a weekday bus leaves at 5 pm (4 pm Saturday and Sunday) throughout the year, bound for Potes via Unquera (a 2½-hour trip). From 1 July to mid-September there is an extra service out of Santander at 9.30 am. Unquera is an important station on the north-coast FEVE narrow-gauge railway, and it's possible to pick up onward bus services from here; the stop is just in front of the *Restaurante/Bar Granja,* opposite the train station.

From Potes, there are services at 8 am, 1 pm and 8 pm (from 1 July until 18 September) up to Fuente Dé via Espinama village; the latter two departures use the same coach that came from Santander. The return service leaves Fuente Dé for Potes 45 minutes after the cited times.

Buses begin the reverse Potes-Santander itinerary from the *Bar Gomez,* with departures daily throughout the year at 5.45 pm and at 7 am (from Monday to Friday), in summer also at 8.30 am (Saturday and Sunday), and 9.45 am (Monday to Friday).

All of the Santander-Potes coaches pass through La Hermida/Urdón, the start (or end) of the steep walk linking it with Tresviso and

Sotres. They also pass Panes, a village marking where the C-6312 road west to Arenas de Cabrales splits off from the southbound road up to Potes. Two buses a day serve this route, starting from Colombres (2 km east of Unquera) at 8 am and 5.30 pm. This 45-minute trip is the only way to reach Arenas de Cabrales by public transport directly from Santander province.

Northern Access All services within Asturias, including the runs across the provincial border into Cantábria, are handled by EASA, which has headquarters at Calle Jerónimo Ibrán 1 (tel (985) 29 00 39) and issues handy schedule leaflets and booklets on request.

Arenas de Cabrales is most usually reached from Oviedo/Cangas de Onís, far to the west, or the beach town of Llanes, just north. Buses leave Oviedo, the Asturian capital (passing through Cangas exactly an hour later) at 8 am, 12 noon, 4 pm and 6 pm from Monday to Friday; on Saturday, only 8 am and 6 pm departures exist, with Sunday services from Oviedo to Arenas only at 8 am and 4 pm.

Coaches leave Arenas for Cangas and Oviedo at 7.45 am, 8.45 am, 4 pm and 6.15 pm from Monday to Friday; only at 8.45 am and 6.15 pm on Saturday; with no 7.45 am service on Sunday. The journey from Cangas to Arenas takes 90 minutes in either direction.

Llanes-based buses leave for Arenas at 8 am and 5 pm Monday to Saturday, with no Sunday departures; departure times for the return journey are at 9 am and 6 pm.

From Arenas de Cabrales there is a fairly expensive Land Rover 'taxi' service along the six km south to Poncebos; from there it is 12 more km, hitching only, up to Sotres.

Southern Access From León, capital of its province, there is daily service via Riaño to Posada de Valdeón, taking 4½ hours; from there, another Land Rover shuttle plies the few km north to Cordiñanes and Caín. From Riaño there are just two weekly (currently Thursday and Saturday) services to Cangas de Onís via Sajambre, and back.

Western Access Between Cangas de Onís and Soto/Oseja de Sajambre, there is one daily service (two hours) in each direction, leaving Cangas in the late afternoon and Oseja at 9 am.

From Cangas up to Covadonga, there are four services, actually starting in Oviedo, between 15 June and 15 September, but only one of these (passing Cangas at 11.15 am) continues the full 26 km (and 1½ hours) to the lakes of Enol and Ercina. If you take, for instance, the coach passing Cangas at 10.30 am, there's a 45-minute stopover at the shrine of Covadonga while you wait for the through bus. Seats on this route can be hard to come by in season, and from Cangas are usually allotted on a first-come first-serve basis, so get any departure you can if there seems to be a space problem.

THE EASTERN & CENTRAL (URRIELLO) MASSIFS
Approaches from the Deva Valley

Potes At around 500 metres, this main tourist centre on the south-east side of the Picos is big, busy and commercialised. Still, it can make a useful stopover as it's the last point where you'll find anything resembling a range of groceries, and where you can change money. You can also get some of the recommended hiking maps at *Fotos Busta-mente* or various kiosks in the plaza if you haven't already done so.

If you need or want to stay the night, choose from among the *Casa Cuba*, *Casa Cayo* (both in the centre), or the *Casa de Huéspedes Gomez* (next to the bus stop on the edge of town); there's also a half-dozen relatively luxurious establishments.

Espinama At 877 metres, and 20 km up the Deva valley, this more untouched, 'real' village makes a good alternative for an overnight stay. The Nevandi stream, a tributary of the larger Deva just below, gurgles past rickety old farmhouses and under wooden bridges frequented by stray livestock.

For accommodation you have the *Fonda Maximo* and the *Fonda Vicente Campo* at opposite ends of the village; if they're full, choose between the *Hostal Remoña* and the

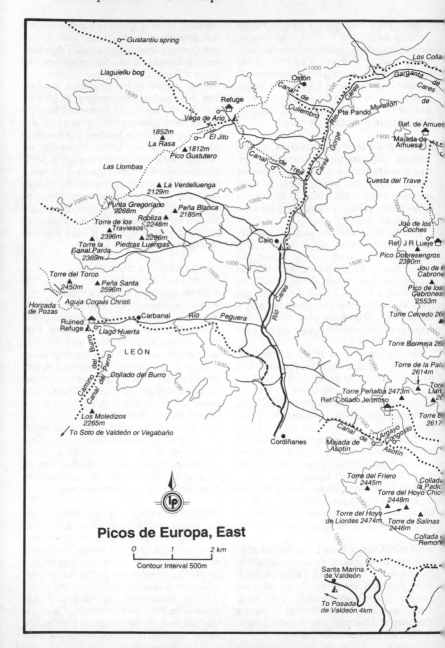

Gustantiu spring

Llaguiellu bog

Los Colla

Garganta de Cares

Ostón

Canal de Culiembro

Cares Gorge

Pte Pando

Murallón

Refuge

Vega de Ario

Ref. de Amues

Majada de Amuesa

1852m
La Rasa

El Jito

Canal de Trea

1812m
Pico Gustutero

Cuesta del Trave

Las Llombas

La Verdelluenga
2129m

Punta Gregoriano
2268m

Peña Blanca
2185m

Robliza
2248m

Torre de los
Traviesos
2396m

2296m
Piedras Luengas

Caín

Jou de los
Coches

Ref J R Lueje

Pico Dobresengros
2380m

Torre la
Canal Parda
2369m

Jou de
Cabrone

Pico de los
Cabrones
2553m

Torre del Torco
2450m

Peña Santa
2596m

Torre Cerredo 26

Aguja Corpus Christi

Carbanal

Río

Peguera

Río Cares

Torre Bermeja 26

Horcada
de Pozas

Ruined
Refuge

Llago Huerta

LEÓN

Collado del Burro

Torre de la Pala
2614m

Torre Peñalba 2473m

Ref. Collado Jermoso

Torre
Llan
26

Los Moledizos
2265m

To Soto de Valdeón or Vegabaño

Cordiñanes

Majada de
Asotín

Canal de
Asotín

Argayo
Congosto

Torre E
2617

Torre del Friero
2445m

Collad
la Padic

Torre del Hoyo Chic
2448m

Torre del Hoyo
de Liordes 2474m

Torre de Salinas
2446m

Collada
Remor

Picos de Europa, East

0   1   2 km

Contour Interval 500m

Santa Marina
de Valdeón

To Posada
de Valdeón 4km

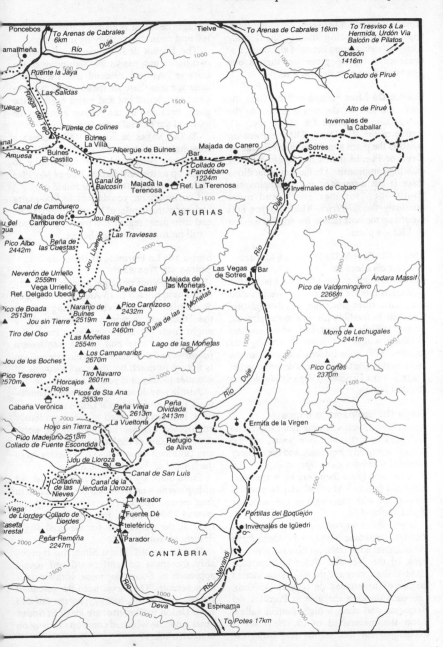

Hostal Nevandi in between. All of the lodgings offer evening meals, the *Vicente Campo*'s menu being the most elaborate. For emergency top-up groceries, there's one *Spar* franchise near the *Nevandi*.

Fuente Dé Most visitors will continue the final four km on the morning bus, to the cul-de-sac at Fuente Dé (1100 metres), source of the Río Deva. (Disagreement on whether the place should be called Fuente de Deva or Fuente d'Eva has resulted in the existing compromise.) In the way of facilities there is but a *parador* and a camping site (both open summer only), and most famously the *teleférico* which lurches 800 metres up the cliff face to the edge of the Jou de Lloroza plain.

Stage 1A: Fuente Dé to Jou de Lloroza or Vega de Liordes

Masochists and/or gung-ho hikers tackle the altitude difference on one of two well-graded trails: the three-hour one up through the Canal de la Jenduda Lloroza to the plateau, or the slightly gentler and wider *camino* climbing within 3½ hours to the Vega de Liordes. For more information on Lloroza and Liordes, see the pertinent descriptions in Stage 3: Vega Urriello to Vega de Liordes via Jou de Lloroza.

Stage 1B: Espinama to Sotres

Alternatively, you can walk from Espinama to Sotres in just under five hours, but the surface is entirely jeep track and the scenery subdued when not downright dull; the Land Rovers (mostly on their way to or from the luxury Refugio de Aliva) which pass you and shower you with dust might best be put to use if you thumb a lift.

If you insist on walking, leave Espinama through the arcade next to the *Bodega Peña Vieja* and take the track on the east (true left) bank of the Nevandi. After an hour-plus climb to the spring and the all-but abandoned hamlet of Invernales de Iguëdri (1300m), you pass through the gate at Portillas del Boquejón and enter a high, flattish valley. Soon the watershed of the Nevandi is exchanged for that of the Río Duje; the

Refugio de Aliva is visible 500 metres to the left and could be a satisfying lunch stop.

The Ermita de la Virgen (1450 metres), two hours out, marks the high point of the traverse. As you descend into the Duje's drainage area there are meadows by the river good for picnicking and views north of the gorge enclosed by the Ándara group to the east and the central massif opposite.

At Las Vegas de Sotres (1080 metres), a seasonal roadside bar sells *sidra* (cider), and sometimes people take the opportunity to climb up to the tiny, hidden lake of Moñetas to the south-west (a six-hour round trip).

Continuing on, you drop to the 900-metre contour at the hamlet of Invernales de Cabao, and then must regain 150 metres in altitude – still on roads – to reach Sotres.

Stage 1C: La Hermida or Urdón to Sotres via Tresviso

If Sotres is your principal goal, it is frankly better to approach from Arenas de Cabrales as detailed in the previous Getting to/from the Trailheads section, or more daringly to alight from the Santander-Potes bus at La Hermida, at one end of the *desfiladero* (narrows) of that name. La Hermida village is not up to much but there are a couple of *hostales* to stay at if you've arrived late.

A little way down the gorge, two km northwest, is the power plant at Urdón and the start of a spectacular climb up an ingeniously engineered *camino* hacked into the north (true left) bank of the Urdón river. This takes you (in about three hours) 650 metres up to the hamlet of Tresviso (900 metres).

From there a jeep track similar to that out of Espinama wends much more gradually, in four hours, to Sotres via Pirué ridge (at around 1300 metres); just past Pirué take a right at the major fork for the final slight descent to Sotres.

Despite the stiff initial climb, this is probably the most straightforward and scenic approach to Sotres for those without their own vehicle. The views from the so-called Balcón de Pilatos, halfway up the *camino* from Urdón to Tresviso, are ideal. In Sotres I met a couple who had come up this way on mountain bikes!

Sotres

Although this is one of the better bases for exploring the eastern and central Picos, the village itself (1050 metres) is rather unattractive, seemingly in a constant state of excavation and cement-mixing. The *Pension Cipriano* is the best value and has an extremely popular *comedor*; if you're really broke, an unmarked *fonda* next door has dorm bunks – but these are often block-booked by school groups. The third and last *pension* across the plaza is over-priced and to be avoided.

Casa Gallega is the one store, but is well-stocked and its bar section will fix good meals with an hour or two's notice. The local specialty – expensive, an acquired taste, but potentially addictive – is *cabrales* cheese, similar to roquefort and cured for six months. It is made only in five villages (Sotres, Tresviso, Bulnes, Tielves and Camarmeña) at this far eastern edge of Asturias.

Should Sotres be your last stop in the Picos, or if you just want to go on day-hikes for a while, the traverse to Urdón – only 5½ hours downhill – would be the obvious choice. From the fork mentioned just above Sotres, *caminos* also short-cut the right-hand jeep track leading rather circuitously to Beges village (600 metres), in the Corbera river valley south of Urdón; from Beges another *camino* leads sharply but directly down to La Hermida.

Stage 2: Sotres to Vega Urriello

This is perhaps the easiest approach to the most popular alpine area in the central Picos; a more difficult route is described in Stage 7A: Bulnes to Vega Urriello following.

Rating This stage is moderate.

Supplies Buy these in Sotres.

From Sotres, proceed down to Invernales de Cabao (900 metres) and cross the river via an old stone bridge, if it hasn't been buried by the rubble from road-building activities. Currently available maps will not show the ugly new track which will eventually reach Bulnes, switchbacking up the west bank of the Duje. However, from the first bend the fine old cobbled trail, perhaps dating from the Visigothic era, re-emerges.

This gains altitude sharply through rank vegetation, crossing a potable stream after 45 minutes; in the next quarter of an hour, it collides twice with the new road – cross perpendicularly to the resumption of the trail each time. You should see a pair of green '*UR*' (for 'Uriello') waymarks to guide you, but unfortunately you may also encounter some vandalism in the form of dead branches blocking the onward path at the road-crossings.

Just over an hour along, the trail finally succumbs to the bulldozers; you must use the new track for the next 45 minutes past the *majada* (pastoral hamlet) of Canero to the Collado de Pandébano (1224 metres). Here, in AD 718, a skirmish between Visigothic Christians and Moorish stragglers from the recent battle of Covadonga reputedly occurred.

Today you can get tub-cooled beer just below the saddle at the *Bar Los Picos*, its character somewhat diminished now that it's accessible by road. From the pass proper the Majada la Terenosa is visible above and to the south-west, as is the north face of the Naranjo de Bulnes, which will be your intermittent guardian for the next few hours.

Even if the road is extended to Bulnes – in anticipation of that, the trail onwards to Bulnes is undescribed – the path from Pandébano up to Urriello will probably persist; it is obvious and was recently improved beyond Terenosa. Count on 2 hours 20 minutes to the refuge at Terenosa (1300 metres); if you can't tell which building it is, the lintel is clearly labelled.

The refuge makes a good target if accommodation in Sotres is full (not inconceivable in summer) – just leave sufficient daylight to reach it. The hut (with 20 bunks upstairs) is inexpensive, like most in the Picos – from 100 to 300ptas a head depending on whether you have club affiliation. Drinks and snacks are available but no full meal service; you can cook as well as eat in the downstairs *comedor*.

From Majada la Terenosa to Vega Urriello

allow 2 hours 45 minutes, for a total of five walking hours from Sotres. The renovated trail is well marked with red and yellow blazes; it affords great panoramas over Bulnes village down in the Tejo gorge, the Canal de Balcosín, and some horrendous chasms immediately to the right.

You'll see (and probably be glad you're not on) the tortuous trail inching up the far side of the Jou Lluengo canyon; it would be (literally) sheer madness to go up (and probably down) this with a full pack, and most walkers on it are indeed doing day-hikes up from Bulnes.

The present route gains altitude gradually up to about 1500 metres, then roller-coasts for a while through the so-called *traviesas* before the final climb, assisted by a few zig zags, to Urriello meadow (1950 metres), where there's a permanent spring and (weather permitting) magnificent views north over Asturias.

But it's the Naranjo de Bulnes (2519 metres) that dominates the scene, rearing straight up behind the antiquated refuge of Delgado Ubeda. There are 20 crowded bunks downstairs and 20 more upstairs, but the capacity is still grossly inadequate for the summer clientele – the overflow camps on the *vega* out the front or in a couple of *vivac* caves nearby. A bunk, if you can get one, is inexpensive but meals aren't; conveniently there is *Cointra* gas for sale and a small cooking platform in the equally tiny *comedor*.

A new refuge, double the size of the old one and with indoor plumbing, is scheduled to be built in 1990. It will probably stay open for the same season (from late May to early November) and have the same wardens (Gaspar and Tito Claudio Sánchez Moreno) who feel very attached to the sugarloaf overhead. They consider it unique in Europe, and imagine that what now seems like a surplus of shelters (theirs, Terenosa and Bulnes) will, in a few years' time, prove barely sufficient to handle the floods of walkers.

Stage 3: Vega Urriello to Vega de Llordes via Jou de Lloroza

This popular traverse cuts right through the heart of the central massif. While not involving much altitude change, you'll have to cross some difficult terrain, including a cable-assisted incline at the highest point. Fill water containers at the Vega Urriello

Through Garganta de los Boches

spring – there is no other reliable source for half a day.

Rating This trek is moderate to difficult – tending to the latter because of the cable-pull at Horcajos Rojos.

Within 45 minutes of leaving the Delgado Ubeda hut you should be halfway around the lunar Jou sin Tierre; dip slightly, then re-ascend to the Garganta de los Boches leading to the equally forbidding Jou de los Boches, to complete just under two hours walking.

Make a choice here: the trail heading left to the Horcajos Rojos (2345 metres) is shorter, but over a stiffer grade; the last couple of hundred metres is an exposed rock face with an anchored cable for pulling your-self up hand-over-hand.

The right-hand option, shown correctly on the relevant Alpina map, passes under the north-east face of Pico Tesorero to arrive at the Los Urrielles pass (2370 metres) three hours from Vega Urriello. You should expect some snow and plenty of scree, as well as occasional boulder-hopping, but the route is well-cairned and should present no problem with a light load.

Coming in the opposite direction, ie from the top of the Fuente Dé *teleférico*, you'd have to glance down at the cables from Horcajos Rojos to see which route you'd prefer; most north-bound hikers seem to choose the 'assisted' passage.

However you reach it, from the top you have unobstructed views south over another moonscape, relieved only by the green ridges of Cantábria on the far side of the Deva (itself not visible). You will also see the metallic surface of the Cabaña Verónica glinting on a knoll some 500 lateral metres away.

This, reached with a 20-minute descent, proves to be an old aircraft radar dome, which justifies much of its existence by selling cold drinks at a 300% mark-up amid the parched landscape (an enterprising assis-tant with an ice bucket at the trail junction below saves you the trip up to the 'hut' if you wish).

The shelter itself is open all year and sleeps eight in bunks with any degree of comfort; Mariano the warden will, with a straight face, cite a capacity of 18: seven more on the floor, plus three people in a drawer – like morgue specimens! In line with the fizzy-drink prices, everything at Cabaña Verónica is expensive; since there's no spring, even water has to be hauled in.

Another 45 minutes will bring you to La Vueltona and the path's end at a curve in a *pista* heading west to some mines. There's a deep spring in a cave above and to the right, shown correctly on the suggested GH map but way too high on the Alpina. To finish a traverse at Fuente Dé, head straight onto the track and skirt the Jou de Lloroza on its east to pick up either the trail or cable car down.

To continue toward Vega de Liordes, bear right to follow the *pista* 30 minutes to its end at the Collada de Fuente Escondida (the 'hidden spring' – aptly named since we didn't find it). Bear sharply left here, follow-ing *jitos* (cairns) over ramps of karst prone to be dangerously slick in wet conditions. The solid red line on the Alpina does not represent any existent path; in any case you should link up with the proper path coming west to enter the Canal de San Luís within half an hour.

Proceed up the *canal*, then veer abruptly left (south), always following the *jitos*, to the Colladina de las Nieves (2241/2226 metres on different maps). You'll take 75 minutes to reach this grassy saddle from your probable junction with the main trail. The Alpina does not show the route correctly; it actually goes much further up the Canal de San Luís than indicated.

From the pass, allow 45 minutes, again assisted by cairns, to the trail junction marked on the Alpina just above point 1946. For the whole way the broad Vega de Liordes teases you below and to the right, but there really is no viable route for getting down to it until the junction.

Straight on, via the clearest path, leads (within two hours, if you have the daylight and stamina) to the Collado Jermoso refuge. This shelter, open from May to October, sleeps 17 and has spring water plus an incom-parable location overlooking the western Picos. Unfortunately it is somewhat badly placed for trekkers; to continue onward (as

Trekkers huddle at Cabaña Veronica

outlined in the next section) you would have to descend the difficult Argayo Congosto and Argayo Berón ravines, or retrace your steps to the junction.

Most people will, by this point, content themselves with a good look at the route for the next day (down the Canal de Asotín toward the Cornión massif) and then double back initially almost 180 degrees onto the path leading down to the *vega*. Again the Alpina is misleading; there is no need to circle round to the Collado de Liordes to reach the turf. It takes half an hour cross-country or on livestock traces to approach the Caseta Forestal de Liordes (1880 metres).

This sleeps four at a maximum, but most prefer to camp in front near a stream which disappears into a cave-mouth. Despite the odd cow, the water has sufficient volume to be appetising and potable. Indeed, it would be a shame to hide in the *caseta*, since the Vega de Liordes offers some of the best camping in the central massif and the grass is a welcome contrast to most of the terrain for this seven-hour walking day.

In emergencies it is possible to bail out of a traverse here; negotiate the shallow Collado de Remoña (2030 metres) and drop down, mostly on *caminos*, to Santa Marina de Valdeón (1158 metres) within three hours. Santa Marina has two *fondas* plus a camping site, and is on the bus line from León to Posada de Valdeón via Riaño.

Stage 4: Vega de Liordes to the Río Cares via the Canal de Asotín

From the flat expanse of the *vega*, climb north-north-west until finding the yellow-blazed rocks which preside over the Collado de la Padiorna some 20 minutes along. The turf fades away, but traces and cairns persist over the next 45 minutes which are needed to draw level with the two deeply recessed (and invisible) lakes marked on the Alpina.

After less than two hours' progress, the still well-marked trail leaves the limestone dells and descends gently to the head of the Canal de Asotín. A torrent at about 1700 metres on your right might provide seasonal water, but cannot be relied upon; the first permanent water is found at the high end of the Majada de Asotín (roughly 1450 metres), where a weak spring seeps down the cliff face to your left as you reach the turf.

There's another seasonal stream in the corner of the meadow opposite the cliff-spring, and possible emergency camping on the sloping 'flats' near the mouth of the Argayo Congosto. Here wooden signs point back the way you came to 'V. de Liordes', and up the uninviting couloir to 'C. Jermoso'.

You enter the woods about 20 minutes below the centre of the *majada*; do not go directly down the Riega de Asotín, but bear left (south), following *jitos*, and slightly up onto the flank of the canyon. You leave the coverage area of either Alpina map as the route becomes a spectacular corniche trail (the 'Senda de Rienda') overlooking the headwaters of the Río Cares. The village of Cordiñanes pops into view, but is deceptively close; because of assorted bends plus ups and downs, it's fully 90 minutes from the Argayo Congosto juction.

Cordiñanes has no store but, oddly, three *fondas* at which to stay and eat; unfortunately the three-hour trek down from Vega de Liordes is likely to get you to the village well before the 2 pm lunch hour.

The nearest proper stores, a bank and three more *fondas* are three km south in Posada de Valdeón. If you intend to enter the western massif via the Canal de Trea, you virtually must devote the rest of the day to errands in Posada, as there are no supplies in any of the hamlets to the north. Spend the night in Caín to get a good start the next morning – it's not worth getting baked on the 1400-metre climb up to the Vega de Ario (see Stage 1A: Lago Enol & Lago la Ercina to Vega Ario...& Beyond in the Western (Cornión) Massif and the Precornión section following).

Stage 5: Traverse of the Garganta de Cares

Most people pass through Posada and Cordiñanes intending to hike the length of the Garganta de Cares, probably the most sensible choice for first-time visitors to the Picos. The chasm dividing the Urriello and Cornión massifs approaches 1000 metres deep and is nearly 12 km long. Best of all, an exquisitely constructed path, built to service a water and power project back in the 1920s, threads the entire distance between Caín and Poncebos, leaving you freer to gape at the

scenery instead of concentrating on every stride.

Rating It's moderate, mostly because of the distance involved.

Supplies Buy these in Posada de Valdeón.

The first 90 minutes of walking, from Cordiñanes to Caín, is humdrum enough – on a recent asphalt road – but at least it's downhill and the forest provides intermittent shade. On the way there is a shady fountain, an information panel and a reconstruction of a wolf trap used by the locals in former days!

Caín is a peculiar hamlet, packed out in summer with visitors who patronise two or three *fonda/bars* and pitch tents at 200ptas a go on a paddock where the nearby river is the only amenity.

Below Caín the entrance to the gorge proper, squeezed between abrupt mountain walls, is obvious; pass the camping site and almost instantly cross via a bridge to the east (true right) bank of the river, the first of four such crossings. The initial stretches of the canyon are the most fantastic – the interplay between the engineers and the environment is most marked here.

The *camino*, at times a tunnel through rock, at others a corniche trail, is apt to be disconcertingly noisy and crowded for the first few km; after that you can marvel and take pictures at leisure, but the gorge gradually opens out after the five-km mark and becomes less imposing.

After 40 minutes, cross the last bridge back onto the west (true left) bank and note the marked junction with the Canal de Trea route. An alternative route up to the Cornión area, the Canal de Culiembro, is passed some 35 minutes later. On the right, a steep minor path heads down towards the Pando bridge and the river, suitable for dips.

At intervals along this traverse you catch glimpses of the old trail, in poor repair and parallel to the water. It used to be the only way through the gorge before the higher *camino* was built. There's no shortage of drinking water – besides sporadic springs, there is the aqueduct, reason for the newer

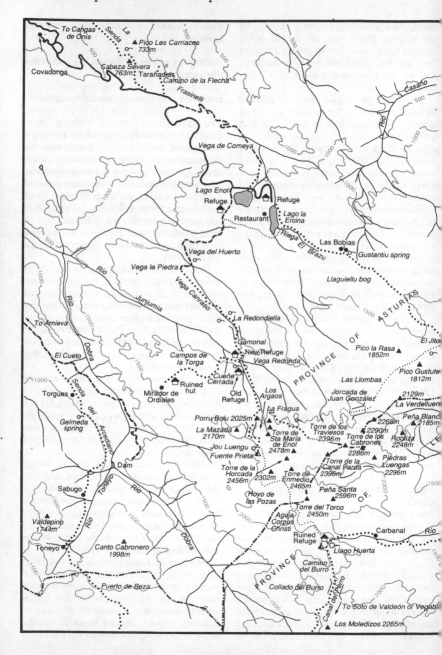

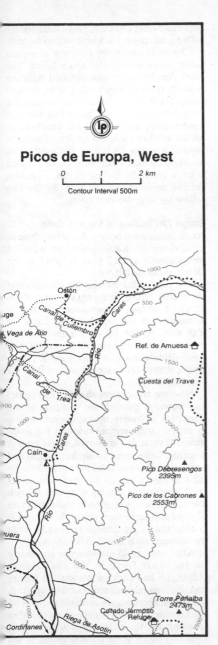

Picos de Europa, West

0   1   2 km

Contour Interval 500m

path's existence, which despite signs to the contrary has perfectly adequate drinking water when it's accessible.

The gorge gradually bends from a south-north orientation to a west-east axis, over the next 1½ hours. The spectacle has diminished and so have the crowds, but the Murallón de Amuesa on the opposite side of the river is still impressive.

Exactly two hours along there's a strategically placed drink stall, somewhat before the only substantial ascent – 'Los Collados' – on the downstream traverse. Near the top of this sits another makeshift bar (the cleverly named *El Espejismo*, 'The Mirage') and shortly after (2½ hours along) another junction marked only on the Lueje map.

Bearing left takes you, within 40 minutes, up to the village of Camarmeña, perched like an eyrie over the river and famed for its unique perspectives on the Naranjo de Bulnes. In addition to the *mirador* there's a bar and a *hostal*.

Most walkers bear right to stay with the main route, which finishes three-plus hours out of Caín at a roadhead clogged with parked cars and various signs pointing in different directions. *Fonda Garganta de Cares*, 400 metres down the road at Poncebos (a place name – not even a hamlet), has adequate meals and could be a good place to stay except for the constant car noise.

Alternatively there's the one-star *Hostal Poncebos* (book jeep-taxis to Arenas de Cabrales here), about as far again downstream and past the bridge and confluence of the Duje. But if you haven't already been up to Bulnes, it's far preferable to make the following detour as the finale to your day.

Stage 6: Poncebos to Bulnes via the Riega de Tejo

Rating It's easy walking up to Bulnes, moderate thereafter (as daypack hikes!).

Supplies These are limited in Bulnes.

Immediately to the right (south) and barely 100 metres past the end of the Cares gorge trail is the sharp downturn to the river and the ancient, photogenic Puente la Jaya (280 metres). Cross this and begin the intially severe ascent up the canyon of the Río Tejo (Texu), known in its lower reaches as Las Salidas. The trail, paralleling the river but often high above it, is good and there is no possibility of confusion until one hour along when you should ignore (for now) a bridge leading over to Bulnes El Castillo.

Just before and after the bridge are the sole possibilities for camping in the area; the only spring water in the entire Riega de Tejo comes from the slow seep of Colines, marked by ferns on the rock. Continue for 20 minutes more to Bulnes La Villa (750 metres), a red-roofed, stone-walled hamlet with various facilities for tourists.

Bulnes

Most obvious of these is an excellent *albergue* (inn) geared specifically to trekkers. There are only 20 comfortable bunks, though it is open year round. It's best to book in advance (tel (985) 36 69 32 or (985) 35 65 26). Alberto the manager claims that they'll never turn anyone away; people can sleep on dining room tables if necessary – comforting news since camping around this hamlet, studded with rocks and fernbrakes, is difficult.

Mains electricity arrived in 1989, and indoor plumbing is planned soon; meanwhile it's the bushes and a spring 200 metres away for your basic needs. You are allowed to cook in the *comedor*, but this is cramped and doubly difficult until the water arrives. Meals and drinks are offered at the usual refuge prices, as well as maps and guidebooks. The staff of this privately-run outfit makes no bones about being affiliated with CAREX, an Asturian trekking organisation, and promotes their services heavily.

Eating is actually better at the *bar/restaurante* next door; this building was formerly an old FEM refuge but is now also privately run and immensely popular with campers and passers-by. The *Bar Guillermina*, away from the central 'square', also does meals and has the widest range of foodstuffs (tinned goods, biscuits, sweets)

between Sotres and Caín, plus a mild, lightly salted goat cheese that keeps well on the trail.

Cheese is one of the fulcrums of a giant battle brewing over the area's future. The local cheesemakers, not satisfied with the road up from Invernales de Cabao, are agitating for a more 'direct' road through the irreplaceable Riega del Tejo! The Asturian government, for its part, has proposed to install another cable car up from Puente la Jaya to Amuesa via Bulnes El Castillo – an absolute disaster whether alone or coupled with a road. In the meantime, however, Bulnes remains an ideal base for the two following long day-excursions.

Stage 7A: Bulnes to Vega Urriello

As recommended before, this is best done as a round-trip day-hike out of Bulnes or, rather less prudently as a full-pack descent from the Delgado Ubeda hut.

The path up leaves from the *albergue* and its nearby spring, zig-zagging up a slope around a seemingly impassable waterfall to a meadow at the mouth of the Canal de Balcosín. At the far end, some boulders require scrambling over, but in general relatively little altitude is gained in the *canal*, which terminates in the cirque Jou Bajo (or 'Baju') one hour out.

Now the route veers sharply right (west) and upwards through the rockfalls of the Canal de Camburero, the path switchbacking to arrive (after another hour) at the abandoned Majada de Camburero, where there is a spring. Once more swing left (south) and keep climbing around the base of the Peña de las Cuestas; although the grade has slackened, this is still nothing to sneeze at, with the trail surface worsened by a constant rain of litter and scree from above. In summer it is essential to get through here early while the mountainside is still in the shade.

After another 45 minutes you are clearly on the west flank of the Jou Lluengo (Lluengu), and both the Naranjo de Bulnes and the remodelled trail coming up from Majada la Terenosa are constantly visible on the far side. The two paths join shortly after reaching the lip of the Vega Urriello, just over 3½ hours from Bulnes; owing to the occasionally slippery surface, the descent will not take much less time especially if you have a full pack.

Stage 7B: Bulnes to Refugio J R Lueje via Amuesa

The other prime day-trip from Bulnes, assuming the route has not yet been defiled by a *teleférico*, is up to the *jou* and refuge usually used as a base camp for ascents of Torre de Cerredo, the highest point in the Picos.

To be surest of finding the way, you might return to the bridge over the Tejo giving access to Bulnes El Castillo, but there is a very obvious walled-in trail, departing from near the *Bar Guillermina*, which connects the two *barrios* (districts) of Bulnes.

Once in the higher quarter, head directly west on a clear trail, taking on water from a spring at the mouth of the Canal de Amuesa. Most of the altitude gain occurs toward the top of the *canal*, reached 2½ hours after leaving Bulnes La Villa. Here's another spring, the last before arriving at the refuge; the Majada de Amuesa lies a bit to the north across the relatively flat pasture (at around 1400 metres). There is a rather makeshift shelter here for emergency use; it may be shut. (The keys are in Bulnes or with one of the shepherds.)

From the *majada* the route veers abruptly south and up over the Cuesta del Trave, the last turf to be seen; soon you're into the typical Picos moonscape, with cave mouths visible in the bluff skirting to the right and the enormous Jou del Agua below to the left. The path also fades badly around here, but there is always the timely *jito* to point the way.

Finally, slightly over two hours from Amuesa and nearly five hours from Bulnes, you slip through a miniature pass separating the Jou de los Coches from the Jou de los Cabrones to see the new stone hut of J R Lueje (at around 2050 metres) and a strong spring nearby. The refuge is staffed from May to October and provides for 18 people.

The return to Bulnes can be accomplished in four hours; obviously if you intend to tackle Torre de Cerredo, you will need to overnight at the higher shelter. The descent from Bulnes back to Poncebos takes 1¼ hours, or virtually the same as the uphill trip, owing to the often tricky trail surface and a certain amount of roller-coasting.

Arenas de Cabrales

The chief village of the Cabrales valley, situated where the Río Casaño joins the now tame Río Cares, is a far better base than either Potes or Espinama if you want to get to grips with the central massif quickly. Despite the legions of trekkers passing through in summer, the locals remain welcoming and it makes an excellent place to overnight either before or after a traverse.

If you're coming from points east, this may be your first extended sojourn in Asturias, and initial acquaintance with an architectural style shared with small portions of León and Cantábria but mostly with Galicia. The rainy, maritime climate dictates ornate wooden balconies, often glassed in to serve as solariums, and *horreos* (pagoda-like corncribs to keep grain above vermin and the damp); whimsical stone carvings often decorate the facades of older buildings.

In Arenas the bus stop is directly in front of the helpful tourist information kiosk and a drinking fountain. Across the way is one of the better and more helpful grocery shops; they may store baggage for you briefly if you do a major shopping expedition. An extra incentive to do so is that most of the central shops in Cangas de Onís (see following) are not nearly as good, and that most of the stores in Arenas tend to stay open throughout the day in summer – handy if you plan to move up the mountain on a weekend.

Behind the tourist office are three *fondas* within shouting distance of each other. Two (there's information in the butcher shop on the plaza for the rearmost one) are marked with '*F*' signs and are apt to be completely booked out in summer, though the *comedores* are open to all. Between these a third, unmarked one, *Meson Castaneu* (tel (985) 84 52 63), has particularly good a la carte lunches at *menú* prices, and just a few rooms which are more likely to be vacant since they're not advertised. There's also the

Hostal Naranjo de Bulnes on the main road – if that is also full, try the camping site one km east.

Two banks handle foreign exchange transactions, and you can also find *Cointra* gas and hiking maps.

THE WESTERN (CORNIÓN) MASSIF & THE PRECORNIÓN

Cangas de Onís

Cangas is a sizeable town and may come as a shock after a week in the mountains and the villages. In addition to a scarcity of groceries, it's even harder here than in Arenas de Cabrales to find a place to stay during the summer. Still, if you find yourself here the night before heading up to the lakes of Enol and Ercina, you can while away the evening quite pleasantly once you've found accommodation. No place of interest is more than about 400 metres from the bus terminal, a tiny alcove next to the *Café Colón*.

Of the less expensive places to stay, *Fonda/Bar El Chofer* (south of the main thoroughfare) and *Hostal El Sella* (by its namesake river) are likely to be full in high season, as is anything more luxurious. A reliable institutional lifesaver, almost certain to have space, is the *Residencia/Albergue 'Rey Pelayo'* just across the street from the bus office. Eight-bedded rooms with bath are much better value than the rather grim sleeping-bag dorms, though IYHA affiliation in 1989 may mean a new members-only policy. You can eat cheaply and rather plainly at *'Rey Pelayo'*, but it's really best to enjoy Cangas with a night on the town. First prize for atmosphere goes to the *Sidrería/Mesón Puente Romano*, next to the river and the handsome Roman bridge; here are cheap *menús* but more likely you can be initiated into the secrets of *sidra* (cider) drinking, the Asturian national pastime. Best value in food is currently had at *Río Grande*, again near the *Colón*. There is also a handful of other reasonable *sidrerías* and *comedores* in the vicinity of *El Chofer*, such as *Fidel* and *Latino 2*.

'La Senda Frassinelli'

Details on vehicle access to the lakes of the western massif, the trailheads for all traverses there, have been given in Getting to/from the Trailheads. However, if you're stuck for transportation, have your own, or are descending from the lakes, the itinerary that follows in Route Directions can be recommended.

'La Senda Frassinelli' was so named in 1987, on the centenary of the death of an unusual but wonderful individual. Roberto Frassinelli Burnitz, of Italian and German extraction, came to Asturias in 1854, perhaps fleeing from an unhappy love affair or an indiscretion involving the European revolutions of 1848. He fell under the spell of the Picos de Europa, particularly the western massif, and chose as his home the tiny village of Corao, five km east of Cangas de Onís. For the remaining 33 years of his life he made it his business to acquaint himself with every inch of the surrounding mountains, setting forth on regular, lengthy treks no matter what the weather.

Fortunately for prosterity, he was a person of great and varied learning – natural historian, draughtsman, archaeologist, horticulturalist, designer of part of the Covadonga shrine, poet, mystic – in the Renaissance mould, as well as a quintessential Romantic. He was certainly the first foreigner to celebrate the Picos and the locals still revere his memory. In 1977 his remains were transferred from the village churchyard of Corao to the monastery church of Santa Eulalia de Abamia, appropriately enough by José Ramón Lueje, an Asturian who similarly devoted his life to the Cornión range.

Rating Easy.

Route Directions

To begin a descent along this route, follow the drainage of Lago Enol north to pick up a path leading down to the enormous Vega de Comeya (at around 960 metres), dotted with springs and ponds which the local stockraisers take advantage of.

To continue on the dedicated route, leave the *vega* via the jeep track cutting through the middle; unfortunately this involves following the main Enol-Covadonga road (when encountered) for 500 metres. Ignore the first *camino*, that of Flecha (Frecha) – passed on the right – but take the second, that of Molledo (initial elevation 680 metres) marked on both recommended maps.

There's a brief uphill stretch as you reach the top of the tiny Sierra Mala (765 metres), with its fine views north-west over the valley containing the Covadonga shrine. Level off and pass the tiny sheepfold of Tarañadiós, before slipping through the saddle linking Cabeza Severa and Pico Les Carriaces (Las Carriazas), all roughly the same height as Mala. The trail is now locally designated the Camín del Rey' as it skirts the source of the Río Umandi on its way northwest to the *majada* of (U)porquera.

Now you leave the coverage area of all available maps, and the slowly broadening trail descends in earnest through El Poquirrín and El Pandal. By the time you reach the hamlets of Cueto and Aleos, you're on a full-fledged jeep track once more; the monastery of Abamia and the village of Corao (100 metres) are not far. The entire downhill trip should take no more than 5½ hours.

Stage 1A: Lago Enol & Lago la Ercina to Vega Ario ...

However you arrive at the lakes, the following is one of the two most popular onward trekking routes, and for good reason. Even if you don't plan to tackle the severe descent into the Cares gorge from the Vega de Ario, the fine camping opportunities and refuge – plus the spectacle of the central peaks across three km of thin air – merit the detour.

Rating Easy to moderate up to Vega Ario; difficult in any direction beyond.

Supplies Stock up in Cangas de Onís or Arenas de Cabrales.

Begin from Lago Enol at 1070 metres. If you need it, there's a rather grim (cement) 30-bunk refuge on the south-west bank. Meals and self-catering are available; the warden (Juan Luís Somoano) is a co-author of the recommended Asturian hiking guide (see the introductory Books section), but most people seem to prefer camping in the immediate vicinity.

The heat of midday is no time to begin the trip up to Vega Ario; you may as well have a swim in the popular Lago Enol, though Lago la Ercina (1108 metres) 20 minutes further on at the end of the road, is more attractive for hanging around.

Here there's a luxury refuge like that of Aliva in the central range, but more compellingly a *sidrería/restaurante* where you can fill up for the walk ahead; food's expensive but if you bring a picnic and order a litre from the barrel (always better than the bottled stuff) you can use the tables unmolested. If the tables are packed out, 10 minutes up the trail detailed below you'll find more private, shady spots next to some stone cottages, with a weak spring nearby.

Once on your way, skirt the lake (often alive with waterfowl) on the obvious eastshore trail which quickly bends east up the Riega El Brazu (Braxu). Incidentally, of all the suggested maps only the Lueje shows the route more or less correctly and, even on it, there are defects.

After an hour with no possibility of confusion the trail passes the spring of Gustantiu (at around 1200 metres), gushing from the lee of a turret-like rock just beyond the *majada* of Las Bobias (Les Bovies). Fill water containers here, from where the climb really begins; though a creek flows out of the Llaguiellu bog 20 minutes beyond, its potability is dubious owing to the presence of livestock.

The beech woods also end near Gustantiu, and you've two hours of steady climbing through karst dells, via El Jito pass (1660 metres) to the Vega de Ario (1634 metres). Beyond the spring the route is well blazed with yellow paint splotches, making a traverse possible even in mist.

The *vega* forms a natural balcony overlooking the Cares valley and the highest peaks of the Urriello massif, including the conspicuous Torre de Cerredo. In the late afternoon (a likely arrival time if the bus left you by the lakes at 1.15 pm), this is something to behold. There's good camping on the brow of the hill at the south end of the

Lago Enol

meadow near some stone sheds – parties of avid cavers exploring an adjacent shaft usually mark the spot – but it's well worth considering the excellent refuge at the opposite end of the pasture.

The 'Marqués de Villaviciosa de Asturias' hut (open year round and also known as just plain 'Vega Ario') has been recently renovated and holds 43 people comfortably. Bunk prices (from 100 to 300ptas) are the Picos standard, and you can be served meals or cater for yourself in the large kitchen and *comedor*. The only potential drawback is the status of the spring outside; this taps a subterranean river with a variable level, and is at its worst in July and August – coincidentally the months of greatest use. Arrive with a full water bottle and be prepared to brave long queues.

The helpful warden, Luís Blas, is the person responsible for the waymarks on the trail in, but he has fallen foul of the national park authorities for 'defacement' of the rocks. Consequently his program to do the same for the difficult Canal de Trea 'trail' to the Río Cares has been suspended partway through. In the meantime, sketch-map photocopies of the route are on sale at the shelter.

...& Beyond

In the best of conditions the passage of th Trea ravine takes three hours going downhill and five hours coming up; there's only on reliable spring en route, closer to the bottom than the top, and at several points scramblin is necessary. An alternative traverse, via th Canal de Culiembro and the *majada* o Ostón, has a marginally gentler grade bu requires more time to accomplish.

The more or less direct traverse to the Veg Redonda refuge shown on most availabl maps does not exist, or at any rate if followe as drawn could get you into a lot of trouble For those with good scrambling skills an light loads, the following points are thos actually linked by most mountaineers. Thi itinerary is again shown with (approximate! accuracy only on the Lueje map.

From the El Jito saddle, bear south-west t cross limestone badlands and slip over th Jorcau la Rasa (1792 metres), between th knobs of Gustuteru and Rasa. If the singl spring before the pass is running, fill up, a there will be no more reliable water for som hours.

From the *jorcau* (dialect for *horcado* 'saddle') bear more sharply south-wes cross Las Llombas, to the saddle of Juan González (at around 2080 metres). Veer somewhat more westerly again, and closely skirt the base of such peaks as Torre de los Traviesos, Torre de la Canal Parda, and Torre de Santa María de Enol. You then must find the Cuenllona (Cuenyona) spring, somewhere east of the wall of pinnacles named Los Argaos, and also a safe passage over the latter. From near the spring the route is likely to be marked, as this is (in reverse) the way taken by climbers headed from Vega Redonda to Torre de Santa María de Enol.

Once over La Fragua saddle it's a matter of minutes to the main path linking Vega Redonda and Llago Huerta, but the entire crossing from Ario is likely to take five hours and, frankly, will appeal most to those with a fetish for karst. In all honesty, no time will be saved compared with retracing your steps to Ercina and ascending to Vega Redonda by the usual way as described below.

Stage 1B: Lago Enol or Lago la Ercina to Vega Redonda

This is the most frequented route in the Cornión massif and in addition to being enjoyable in itself, gives walkers access to further hikes of all levels of difficulty.

Rating An easy stage.

If you elect to return to the lakes from Vega Ario, allow two hours for this. It is possible to short-cut directly past the south end of Lago la Ercina and emerge on the *pista* within sight of the Enol shelter, but owing to the problematic terrain this takes 45 minutes or barely a quarter hour less than looping around both lakes via the access road.

From the Enol shelter it's an hour along the jeep track up to the Vega la Piedra; no short cuts of the *pista* are possible. A spring 45 minutes along at the Vega del Huerto is more usable than the tiny vault-dip, on the left by the jeep track's end, at Vega la Piedra (so named for the enormous boulders interspersed among the cottages of the *majada*).

The trail now curves south-east, bordered by monolithic *jitos*, and aims towards the high peaks on the horizon. There's water most of the way, especially near the top of the Vega Canraso where surge the various springs of La Redondiella (Rondiella). Once over the Gamonal pass (1460 metres) you'll see the new Vega Redonda shelter (1485 metres), reached after a symmetrical dip-and-rise, and 90 minutes beyond Vega la Piedra.

The new hut, open all year, has places for 68. There are adequate bathrooms (including cold showers!) in both the annexe and main building, plus an unusually ample self-catering kitchen and fair priced meals and bar service. Tomás Fernández López is the affable warden in charge; his associate Erík Pérez is a certified mountain guide and the other co-author of the suggested Asturian walking guide. If you wish to contact either of them beforehand they have an office in Cangas de Onís at Calle Emilio Laria 2, 2° (tel (985) 84 89 16).

The new facilities rarely fill up but the old refuge at 1540 metres (the one actually

marked on all current maps) will be soon remodelled to provide 15 more spots and preclude any such problems. It is next to the main spring for the area; the flow is piped down to the new complex. Accordingly people camp near the old hut, on sloping ground.

Day-Hike: Vega Redonda to Mirador de Ordiales

Between the two shelters a plaque with the legend 'Mirador de Ordiales' embedded in the rock marks the start of the most worthwhile easy excursion to round out your day, should you elect to overnight at Vega Redonda. The side trail beginning here climbs gently, first west, then south up the Cueñe (Cuenye) Cerrada to a pass known as El Forcau (1600 metres). It then widens and swings upward in a wide arc through the Campos de la Torga, reaching (after just over an hour) the meadows of Ordiales, where there's a dilapidated ICONA shelter and the mirador itself at 1691 metres.

This affords a splendid look over the valley of the Río Dobra, 1000 metres below, the western ranges of the Cordillera Cantábrica, and (if you're lucky) even an expanse of ocean. The Marqués de Villaviciosa, founder of the national park, chose to be buried up here and his taste cannot be faulted. Owing to the terrain, the mirador is something of a dead end; retrace your steps to the refuge to continue anywhere else.

Stage 2: Vega Redonda to Llago Huerta

Rating /Duration Fair warning is given that the next leg of the trek should not be attempted with less than five hours of daylight remaining, and that extensive scrambling will be required. While not supremely dangerous, this leg of a trans-Cornión crossing is strenuous and challenging – perhaps you'll have a bit of skin missing from your hands at the end of the day.

Upon leaving the newer Vega Redonda hut, the main trail climbs steeply south; collect enough water for the rest of the day from the upper spring and say good-bye to the last bit of grass on the north side of the divide. Just over an hour along, take a right at a fork; the left option leads up toward La Fragua pass where you would probably have emerged near the end of a traverse from Vega Ario.

Next the path surmounts a rock livestock-barrier and artfully rounds the 'nose' of Porru Bolu (2025 metres) on the way up to La Mazada pass (a bit more than the gazetted 2030 metres), reached two hours out of Vega Redonda. Up to this point the trail has been of camino calibre, always well engineered and revetted when necessary.

The Fuente Prieta is shown incorrectly on all existing maps, being a few hundred metres further south-east than it's drawn; it should be about 100 metres below on your right, some 15 minutes along the now diminished path. To repeat, you will require nearly three hours of daylight to reach Llago Huerta from here; otherwise, you should set up camp now – some cavers are usually there already on the limited patches of grass.

What remains of the camino ends just past the spring; ignore a side trail heading up and left and follow jitos over a rigorous mix of limestone chimneys, ledges, sinkholes, ramps, pinnacles and scree piles. There's little net altitude change between La Mazada and Llago Huerta, but this landscape exact its toll.

Once over the Horcada de Pozas (2070 metres) and around the fist-shaped Aguja Corpus Christi, the worst is over and you should see the broad pass of Llago Huerta to the east. Make for it without dipping into the gulches on your right.

There are both lower and upper meadows accommodating perhaps a dozen tent between them – the area is popular with cavers. The ruined shell of an old ICONA igloo sits at the very highest point of the upper meadow; a slow but dependable spring oozes out among the rocks 100 metres east on the Cares side of the divide. With Peña Santa towering overhead to the north, the area makes a fine camp. Views over the central massif are not quite as impressive as those at Ario, but commendable nonetheless.

From a couple of hundred metres north of the ruined shelter, beyond the line of giant jitos on the knoll just behind, a good tra descends past a shack at Carbanal, onto the south (true right) flank of the Peguera ravine, and finally finishes at Cordiñanes after four to five hours. This constitutes a recognised and useful link, particularly if you've left a vehicle at the head of the Río Cares, but for most people the best continuation of a traverse will be as described following.

Stage 3: Llago Huerta to the Sajambre Villages via Vegabaño

Rating This stage is easy, since it's downhill as described and on good trails.

A cairned and yellow-blazed trail which climbs initially toward the west before veering south is the way down to Vegabaño. After 45 minutes of up-and-down along the 'Camino del Burro', you dip slightly at the Collado del Burro to enter the Canal del Perro, which ends abruptly after one hour in a veritable brink at the 2000-metre contour. The green foothills of León fill your field of view; the ICONA hut at El Frade, plus the Vegabaño meadow to the south-west are easily spotted below.

Another half-hour down switchbacks minimally complicated by scree, skimming the base of Los Moledizos, brings you to the grassy saddle (1760 metres) enfolding the El Frade refuge (locked, but with a permanent spring nearby). The vast valley of the Río Dobra opens out to the north-west; you are now off the Alpina coverage and onto the Lueje or 1:50,000 map of your choice.

You must also choose your exit route from the high peaks here. Going left on the obvious fork leads to Soto de Valdeón (and eventually to Posada de Valdeón) within 90 minutes. The main trail, curving slowly west-south-west, takes you to Vegabaño and the two Sajambre villages. A half-hour below the saddle (first through heather and fern, then amid mixed deciduous forest) you come upon a spring and over the next 40 minutes to Vegabaño, water is never far away.

The path temporarily ends at the hut (1350 metres), also locked like the one at El Frade – a shepherd in Soto de Sajambre has the keys, and there is never any meal/drink service. No great loss, as Vegabaño is perfect for camping.

From the refuge follow the jeep track to the north-west end of the giant meadow, marked by a cluster of pastoral buildings; here the *pista* hairpins south. No more than 20 minutes beyond the shelter, a wide, obvious *camino* begins the most direct descent to Soto de Sajambre. This is as pretty a one as you could hope to find, winding first through forest, then farms and fields, on an ideal surface for 40 minutes to the bridge and fountain at the edge of the village. Total walking time for the day should be just under four hours.

The Sajambre Villages

Soto de Sajambre (925 metres) is a pleasant hamlet which could be a fine base for light walking in the Precornión and the Dobra valley, except that there is only one *hostal*

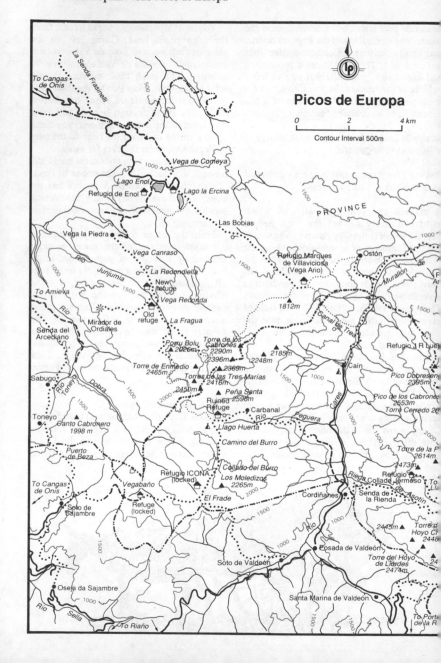

Picos de Europa

0   2   4 km

Contour Interval 500m

La Senda Frasinelli

To Cangas de Onis

Vega de Comeya

Lago Enol

Refugio de Enol   Lago la Ercina

Las Bobias

PROVINCE

Vega la Piedra

Vega Canraso

Refugio Marques de Villaviciosa (Vega Ario)   Ostón

Río Junjumia   La Redondiella

New refuge

1812m   Canal de Trea

Murallón

To Amieva   Vega Redonda

Old refuge   La Fragua

Mirador de Ordiales

Senda del Arcediano   Poru Bolu ▲2026m   Torre de los Cabrones 2290m   ▲2185m

2396m▲ ▲2369m

Torre de Enmedio 2465m   ▲2248m

Refugio J R Lue

Torres de las Tres Marias 2416m

Caín

Sabugo   ▲2450m   Peña Santa   Pico Dobresen 2395m

Río Toneyo   Dobra   Ruined 2596m Refuge   Pico de los Cabrones 2553m Torre Cerredo 26

Toneyo   Canto Cabronero 1998 m   Carbanal   Río Peguera

Puerto de Beza   Llago Huerta

Camino del Burro   Torre de la P 2614m

Refugio ICONA (locked)   Collado del Burro   ▲2473m

Los Moledizos 2265m   Riega   Collado Jermoso   Refugio   To Lle

To Cangas de Onis   Vegabaño   El Frade   Cordiñanes   Senda de la Rienda

Refuge (locked)

Soto de Sajambre   ▲2445m   Torre d Hoyo C 2448

Posada de Valdeón   Torre del Hoyo de Llordes 2474m   24

Osefa da Sajambre   Soto de Valdeón

Río Sella   Santa Marina de Valdeón   To Porte de la R

To Riaño

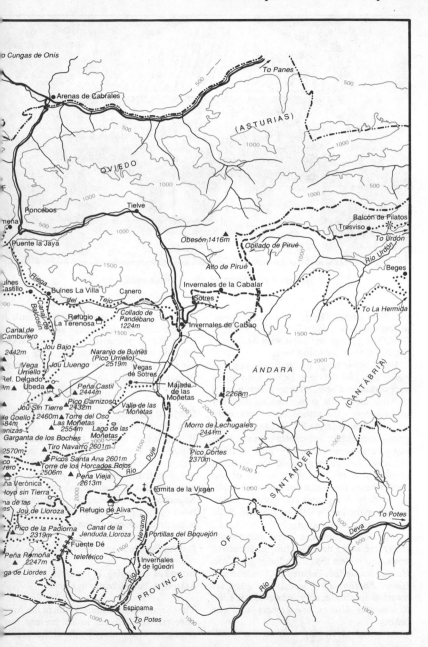

To Cungas de Onís

Arenas de Cabrales

(ASTURIAS)

500

500

OVIEDO

1000

1000

Poncebos

Tielve

Balcón de Pilatos

500

1000

Tresviso

Puente la Jaya

Obesón 1416m

Collado de Pirué

To Urdón

Riega

1500

Alto de Pirué

Beges

Invernales de la Cabalar

Bulnes Castillo

Bulnes La Villa

Canero

Sotres

del

Tejo

Collado de Pandébano 1224m

Invernales de Cabao

To La Hermida

Canal de Balcosín

Refugio La Terenosa

1500

Canal de Camburero

Jou Bajo

2442m

Naranjo de Bulnes (Pico Urriello) 2519m

Vegas de Sotres

ÁNDARA

2000

Vega Urriello

Jou Lluengo

Ref. Delgado

Ubeda

Peña Castil 2444m

Majada de las Moñetas

2268m

Pico Carnizoso 2432m

Jou Sin Tierre

2460m Torre del Oso 2554m

Valle de las Moñetas

Las Moñetas

1500

le Coello

84m

enizas

Lago de las Moñetas

Morro de Lechugales 2441m

Garganta de los Boches

Duje

2570m

Tiro Navarro 2601m

Pico Cortes 2370m

co rero

Picos Santa Ana 2601m

Torre de los Horcados Rojos 2506m

Río

1500

SANTANDER

ña Verónica

Peña Vieja 2613m

loyo sin Tierra

Ermita de la Virgen

1000

1a de las es

Jou de Lloroza

2000

Refugio de Aliva

Pico de la Padiorna 2319m

Canal de la Jenduda Lloroza

Portillas del Boquejón

To Potes

Peña Remoña 2247m

Fuente Dé

teleférico

Deva

500

Nevandi

Invernales de Igüedri

OF

Río

500

ga de Liordes

Río

PROVINCE

Espinama

1000

To Potes

1000

1000

(CANTABRIA)

Typical Leones/Asturiano house, Oseja de Sajambre

(the *Peña Santa*). There are reports of rooms in private houses, and a limited selection of food. The Cangas de Onís-Oseja de Sajambre bus detours for a stop here.

For a better range of facilities, you can easily press on to Oseja. Leave Soto on its access road and bear left onto a *camino* just past the 'city limits' sign, crossing the river immediately – the path is shown correctly on the recommended GH map. Climb gently to about the 960-metre contour, then negotiate some brambly and muddy stretches before beginning the equally gradual drop to Oseja. Despite any obstacles it beats the much longer road-walk, taking only 75 minutes and giving you an eyeful of the headwaters of the Río Sella beyond your destination.

Oseja de Sajambre, a linear community straggling along the road, has its attractive spots, and no less than three lodgings (*Casa Huéspedes La Rua*, *Viajeros La Fonseya* and *Hostal Pontón*). *La Fonseya* has good set meals at lunchtime only; otherwise it's the *Restaurante Alvarez*, one grocers' and one bakery.

As noted in Getting to/from the Trail-

heads, it's much easier to travel north to Cangas de Onís than south toward Riaño and León but, if you insist on moving south hitching is generally rewarding since people are aware of the scarcity of buses and taxi in that direction.

Stage 4: Soto de Sajambre to Amieva: The 'Senda del Arcediano'

If you intend to leave the mountains via Cangas de Onís (by far the most sensible choice, since from there you can easily reach the wonderful beaches of Asturias), and assuming that you can get lodging in Soto de Sajambre, the following route through the heart of the Precornión is certainly the most appropriate farewell to the Picos.

Rating Easy to moderate walking.

Supplies Shopping is possible in Soto de Sajambre, but it's better in Oseja.

The 'Senda del Arcediano' (Path of the Arch deacon) was laid out in its present form during the 17th century by the archdeacon of

Villaviciosa, but it seems probable that the route was already used in the Roman era. In any event, it was one of the main ways of getting between León and Asturias during the centuries before the construction of the C-637 road through the spectacular Desfiladero de los Beyos.

From Oseja the *senda* zig-zags up, with a northerly tendency, to the Puerto de Beza (1480 metres); this is the high point of the traverse as well as the border between León and Asturias. Next descend to the *majada* of Toneyo (1240 metres), source of its namesake river, sprawling between the peaks of Valdepino (1744 metres) and Cabronero (1998 metres), summit of the Precornión.

The *senda* now follows the river north-north-east, dropping in short stages between flat intervals, to the hut and chapel at Sabugo (1050 metres). Now that you're out of the shadow of Cabronero you can gaze at the peaks of the Cornión across the way before continuing across the Cuesta de Galgueral (Jarqueral) and skirting the dam at the confluence of the Toneyo and the Dobra.

The route then bends north-north-west, passing the spring of Gelmeda and the huts of Torgues, before colliding with the recent *pista* up the Dobra valley at the saddle of El Cueto (812 metres). From there it's just over two km, making a total of 6½ walking hours, to the village of Amieva (572 metres), where most walkers will call it a day.

If Amieva hasn't sufficient facilities for an overnight stay, and/or the bus to Cangas de Onís does not call here, the *senda* reportedly continues another hour to Ceneya on the main C-637 road, where you are less than 18 km from Cangas.

Balearic Islands

This archipelago of four inhabited islands and several smaller deserted ones spangles the western Mediterranean between Iberia and Algeria. Not merely a continuation of the Andalucian mountains, they are also a consequence of the African plate burrowing under the more static European one.

For such a small island grouping, there are appreciable differences between the individual islands. Menorca, the north-easternmost, is distinguished mainly by its ceaseless winds and prehistoric megaliths. Ibiza and Formentera at the south-western end of the chain are warmer, sandier and (more so with every passing year) trendier, sharing only their near-flatness with Menorca. Mallorca alone of the four major Balearics has the terrain and moderation of climate to offer anything exceptional to the trekker.

Mallorca

Largest and longest developed of the Balearics, Mallorca might not at first strike one as a walker's Mecca – too many 'winter sun one-week getaway' customers, you would have thought. But the island, like so many others in the Mediterranean, has a split personality fostered by its topography, and away from the fleshpots is still magically unspoiled, even beautiful.

Most of the south-east and north-east is low-lying, mantled with olive, almond and citrus groves, and with a sandy coast where the package development clusters. But the north-west of the island is dominated by an abrupt and imposing mountain ridge, the Serra de Tramuntana, heavily vegetated with oak, pine and other typical species of the Mediterranean maquis.

Limestone, uplifted from the sea floor by tectonic forces, constitutes the core of the range, and while there's not as much karst as in the Picos de Europa, it's fancifully – often forbiddingly – weathered. The mountains rise to over 1000 metres at numerous points, and fall abruptly to the rocky coast beyond, which along virtually its entire length is inaccessible. So while this is wonderful country for a hiking vacation, it is not really for those whose first priority is swimming.

Until recent decades, the Tramuntana (also the name of the north-west wind that howls overhead in the depths of winter) was primarily the preserve of olive-farmers distributed in a handful of tiny stone-built villages tucked just below the *serra*'s crest, and of charcoal-burners and snow-miners (see the Valldemosa Loop section following). In the highlands, at least, these industries have been abandoned, but many km of excellent trails linking settlements, farmsteads and high pastures still exist, now extensively waymarked by both local and foreign enthusiasts. The amount of walking information and documentation in English is impressive (see Books), and maps are also easy to get hold of. Butterflies, birds of all sizes and wildflowers can be expected, especially in winter and spring.

It would be tempting to pronounce Mallorca a walker's paradise, but some cautions are in order. Because of the limestone core of the island, water sources are frequently undependable and poorly placed at either the very beginning or very end of the hike. Owing to the neglect and isolation of the landscape visited, paths (even when marked) are apt to be clogged with vicious thornbush – bring long pants, even on a warm day, to protect your legs, and make it a pair you'll be happy to have shredded.

Season

Walking and swimming are rendered even more mutually exclusive by the weather – hiking is a chore between late June and early August, when the severe heat drives most people to the better Mallorcan beaches. The best months are spring (here meaning from late February to May) – when the country-side is in blossom or at least green, and the temperatures torerable – or autumn (here September and October), after the crowds have gone but before the rains arrive.

Winter walking is by no means out of the question, however, and many aficionados prefer it. Routes are occasionally enlivened with a dusting of snow, and the sparseness of some bus services is compensated for by your having the pick of other amenities. It rains mostly between mid-January and the end of February, when conditions can approach freezing at the higher altitudes.

Map

All of the recommended SGE sheets are available from the military mapping service in Palma at Ramblas Calso (Via Roma) 20, 3°, mornings only. The staff on duty, often soldiers native to the island, are friendly and helpful, and you should be able to transact your business in five minutes. At other times go to *Libreria Fondevila*, at Carrer Arabi 12/14, which has more normal opening hours

but their stock of particular sheets is often depleted and, of course, you may end up paying a slight retailer's mark-up.

Equipment

Most of the items listed in the equipment list in the Facts for the Trekker chapter will be put to good use; inland Mallorca is a wilder-ness, as will become apparent once you're there.

Getting There & Away

As one of the premier Spanish resorts, the island has extensive ferry-boat and plane services. Remember that the domestic ship-ping lines are grossly overpriced, and that it can actually be cheaper to book a round-trip domestic charter from Barcelona or Valencia on Spantex or Aviaco – ask at any on-the-ball travel agent.

If you are coming from Britain or else-where in northern Europe and intend to spend all of your vacation on Mallorca, the most rational solution is to buy a return charter to Palma; these can be had for as little

Palma, Mallorca

as £70 in the off-season. Coming from the USA, ask Iberia if they are still including Palma as one of the internal destinations thrown in free when you purchase an APEX ticket with them.

Ferries currently leave six days a week from Valencia, usually at 11.30 pm, arriving in Palma the next day bright and early. Barcelona-based services leave 10 times a week, most often at 11.45 pm but also at 12.30 pm.

SÓLLER

This attractive town, halfway along the length of the Serra de Tramuntana in a basin choked with low-acid 'candy'-orange trees, makes the best base for the hikes described in this chapter, which in turn are the most impressive on Mallorca. Public transport connections are good to excellent, accommodation of a high standard is available and the town itself, uniformly built of honey-toned masonry and boasting an idiosyncratic cathedral on the Plaça de Sa Constitució, is a (relatively) tourist-free delight.

Most of the tourist facilities are down in the Puerto de Sóller, one of the very few sheltered, sandy harbours on this coast and thus developed with a vengeance. There are too many establishments to list but it's enough to say that you'll have a slim chance of finding a vacancy in high season unless you've pre-booked on a package basis. Also there's precious little privacy on the tiny beach most of the year.

Sóller town proper, though with only three places to stay, is far more likely to have space, especially if you're an independent traveller. First choice would be the *Hotel El Guía* (tel (971) 63 02 27), very good value at one-star prices, and quiet enough, though just a hop and step from the train station. Alternatives are *Hostal Nadal* on Carrer Romaguera (tel (971) 63 11 80), and *Casa de Huéspedes Margarita Trías Vives*, Carrer Real 3 (with no phone – around the corner from *El Guía*). If you don't eat at *El Guía* – way ahead of anything else in the area – you can get fed at *Bar Oasis*, by the tram tracks just below the plaza. There is a handful of grocery stores around the square, plus a

bookshop selling most of the recommended local guides.

Deià, 10 km east, is a good fallback as a walker's base in the unlikely event that both Sóller and its port are full; see the end of the next section for accommodation details.

Getting There & Away

In this case getting there really is half the fun. There are buses from Palma run by *Autocares Llompart*, but these are hardly worth considering compared to the quirky rail service available. The trains depart from the left-hand terminal on the Plaça de Espanya, at the top of old Palma. The current timetable is: 8 am, 10.40 am (an expensive tourist excursion with a stop at a *mirador* overlooking Sóller), 1 pm, 3.15 pm and 7.45 pm. Return departures from Sóller take place at 6.45 am, 9.15 am, 11.50 am, 2.10 pm, 6.20 pm and 9 pm (the last journey only on Sundays/holidays). The rolling stock on this line is decidedly quaint, with wood and brass trim and green nauga-hide seats; the rattly but efficient journey which goes through a spectacular pass in the Tramuntana, lasts 80 minutes.

The train connects in Sóller with an equally anachronistic and rumbly tram which covers the five km down to the port and back 23 times daily between (roughly) 6 am and 9 pm. Most, though not all, departures from Sóller tend to be on the hour, those from Puerto on the half-hour, but there are pronounced variations at the beginning and end of the day, so always check current schedules.

SÓLLER TO DEIÀ

This walk links two of the most interesting communities on the island's north-western coast, and offers spectacular views of the sea en route. It is also short enough to make a good warm-up hike after a midday arrival in Sóller.

Rating

This is an easy trek.

Map

Use SGE No 38-26 (670), *Sóller* (1:50,000

Top: Picos de Europa/Western massif – camping at Vega de Ario
Left: Picos de Europa/Cares gorge – Puente la Jaya
Right: Picos de Europa/Central – roofs of Bulnes La Villa

Top: Mallorca/Balitx-Cala Tuent – Balitx d´es Mig, Coll de Biniamar
Left: Mallorca/Balitx-Cala Tuent – Sa Costera coast
Right: Mallorca/Cornadors Circuit – pilgrim steps above Biniaraix

Route Directions

Begin by finding the CAMPSA gas pump on the Palma-Puerto de Sóller bypass road; from the main plaza head west on Carrer Bauza and keep going as straight as possible, and you won't miss it. Once at the *gasolinera*, follow a dirt driveway exactly opposite. Within 10 minutes this dwindles to a fine stair-path, a bit overgrown but persistent.

After 35 minutes the cobbling has ceased and you go through a gate. Descend briefly among olive trees until, 45 minutes along, take the left of a fork, shunning a descending right option. Shortly after, keep straight to ignore a track heading off perpendicularly to the right; the correct bearing is still west-north-west, as it has been from the start.

Just under an hour out, pass another gate, and continue straight following a blue arrow; there are many of these, as well as yellow dots – red dots seem to be aimed at those coming *from* Deià. Eighty metres further, bear down and right along a partly bramble-blocked but revetted path – it's never nasty and this *is* the way, speckled with blazes and multiple gates heralding the estate of C'an Carabasseta. Cross a perpendicular track 70

minutes along and look for *'Deià'* signs on the grounds of C'an Carabasseta and just beyond.

You are now within earshot of the coastal road C-710 skimming just below, but this is rarely annoying and soon you're rewarded with fine prospects over the coast to the north. The path alternately pops through wooded glades and clings to the palisades hovering above the road and the sea, which looks close enough to jump into (but unhappily isn't). Shortly the cliffs of the Cala de Deià come into view to the west as you skirt some estates; there's no problem with the right of way which actually improves.

Just under two hours out of Sóller, immediately before a major climb, a smaller path pokes through a gap in the fence on your right to descend 100 metres into an obvious gully to a potable spring. Some minutes over the two-hour mark, the Son Coll C'an Amo Juan signals the end of all uphills going in this direction.

Lluc (Lluch) Alcari, a pretty cluster of a dozen coastal houses around a fancy hotel, is seen soon after. Skirt a dynamited boulder partially obstructing the path prior to emerging on an asphalt driveway 2 hours 20

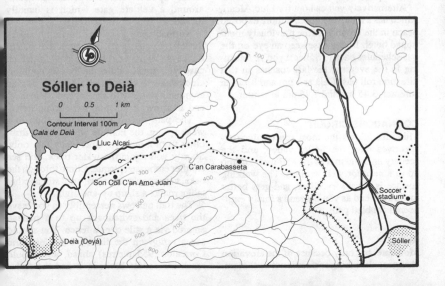

Sóller to Deià

0   0.5   1 km

Contour Interval 100m

Cala de Deià

Lluc Alcari

C'an Carabasseta

Son Coll C'an Amo Juan

Soccer stadium

Deià (Deyá)

Sóller

minutes along. You can short-cut this on a lane leading down to the main road. From this debouchment you've a 20-minute walk left to Deià, or an equal time to get right to Lluc Alcari.

Deià (Deyá), still basking a bit in the artist-colony reputation garnered by the prolonged residence of (among others) the late Robert Graves, has plenty of bars, eateries and grocery stores, though only two short-term places to stay: the *Fonda Villa Verde* (tel (971) 63 90 37) on the hill near the church, and the *Pensión Miramar* (tel (971) 63 90 84) on the far side of the main road.

If you want a swim you can continue walking to Cala de Deià; take the stair-street leading down from the laundry trough on the main road, staying with it as it changes into a driveway parallel to the stream bed and then ends at a gate. Just behind the gate a trail resumes, indicated by a painted *'Cala'* legend. Along here the water is less than 30 minutes away, as against more than an hour on the new access road.

Cala de Deià is crowded, with the human overflow perched on the boathouse ramps to either side of the cove, but at least the water's fairly clean and suitable for swimming, the most important thing at this point.

Alternatively you can opt for Lluc Alcari, which has a relatively good, if more exposed beach in the grounds of the previously mentioned hotel. In any case keep an eye on the bus schedules back to Sóller if you're returning in the evening; the last coaches in that direction roll past Deià at 5 pm and 8 pm in summer, 3.45 pm and 7.45 pm in winter.

CORNADORS CIRCUIT

This hike allows the most spectacular perspectives over the Sóller valley, and the scenery en route makes the 850-metre climb up to a *mirador* well worth it. The walking surface is always excellent, and gets better toward the end as you descend a finely engineered cobbled path.

Rating

Moderate, but only because of the elevation changes – the hiking surface is not a problem.

Map

Refer to SGE No 38-26 (670), *Sóller* (1:50,000).

Route Directions

Proceed past the *Hotel Guía* in Sóller, turn immediately right, take the second left, and then the first right to follow Carrer Pablo Noguera. Stay on it out past the cemetery, then take an initial left fork away from a bridge. Within 200 metres, hang a right to cross the stream by a second bridge, making another left turn as soon as you get to the opposite bank.

Once finally out of town there are faint, infrequent, red-paint blazes, but this is not a problem since there are no ambiguities along the well-maintained tractor track curling up first through olive terraces and later, stands of kermes oak. Some 75 minutes along, go through a gate to intersect another track in a T-junction; as you turn right you should see the settlements of Biniaraix and Fornalutx far below to the left.

After another five minutes, pass another gate and take the right of a Y-fork; the S'Arrom farm should be clearly visible overhead. The route bears left, then zig-zags steeply up to it – there is a pedestrian detour around a vehicle gate which is usually locked.

Normally you go around the farmhouse to the left (as you face it), but aggressive watch-donkeys (!!) may not let you pass, in which case you must circle the house counter-clockwise. Once around it, watch for an engraved stone with the legend *'Mirador'* and an arrow pointing up some stone steps.

The path thus reached comes soon to a weak spring, the Font de Ses Piquetes dribbling from a tunnel – emergency fare only. Shortly you rejoin the wider track, and see another embossed plaque. Climb through the oaks, very spooky in a mist, until still another tablet marks a sharp up-and-right.

The trail narrows perceptibly as you leave the trees and switchback up to a plateau entered via a stile over a fence. You should see a *refugi* on the flank of the left-hand Cornador (955 metres) ahead, and should reach the saddle between it and the right-

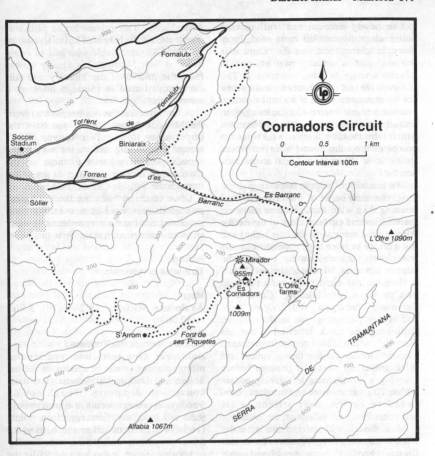

Cornadors Circuit

0   0.5   1 km

Contour Interval 100m

Fornalutx

Torrent de Fornalutx

Soccer Stadium

Torrent de

Biniaraix

Torrent d'es

Sóller

Barranc

Es Barranc

L'Ofre 1090m

☀ Mirador
▲ 955m
☐ Es Cornadors
1009m

L'Ofre farms

S'Arrom ●········ Font de ses Piquetes

SERRA DE TRAMUNTANA

▲ Alfabia 1067m

hand Cornador (1009 metres) 2½ hours out of Sóller.

There's a signposted junction; for now disregard the onward route heading straight and down, and bear left and up. From the shelter (with benches inside, nothing else) circle right to the *mirador* just on the far side of the summit of the lower Cornador.

This odd, round balcony overlooks the entire Sóller basin and pyramidal 1090-metre Ofre peak to the east. Since the Sierra de Tramuntana is prone to mist, don't be discouraged if you're 'socked in' on the way up or even on arrival – be patient and it will probably disperse.

Return to the saddle junction and descend 20 minutes to the green pasture of Ofre. Once through a gate, follow a jeep track to a cinder-block barn emblazoned with these signs: '*L'Ofre Mirador, Sóller 8 km*' (ie back the way you came) and '*27 km Lluc, por favor, no acampar, TOROS*' (no camping, please, bulls).

This onward route is no longer viable because the trail is disrupted from the Cúber dam onwards. Instead, turn perpendicularly left at the barn onto a path with the legend '*Sóller*', though first you might need to get water from a pillar fountain just past a gate by the easternmost house at Ofre.

The newly encountered trail toward Sóller, elegantly cobbled most of the way down, is known locally as the 'Cami d'es Barranc' and is actually part of the old pilgrim's route to Lluc monastery. The stream in the bed of Es Barranc usually runs dry by midsummer but, if it's still flowing, you can detour left some 40 minutes along to a small cascade and a pool. About 50 minutes below Ofre meadow there is a take-out tap on a pipeline coming down from a permanent spring in a side canyon, just at the first houses.

The marvellous 'pilgrim steps' keep dropping, changing banks of the ravine several times as they wind through some narrows; there's a second tap once clear of the defile. After a final crossing to the true right bank (on a bridge or stone lugs, depending on the water level), the route, now dirt, comes to the edge of Biniaraix, 90 minutes below Ofre.

Here various signs point back the way you've come, proclaiming 'Cami d'es Barranc', 'Lluc a peu', and 'L'Ofre'. Time and interest permitting, you might consider following the track labelled 'Cami es Marroig', which climbs gently from next to a nearby laundry pavilion through citrus and olive groves for about 20 minutes before reaching a downturning left giving access within 20 more minutes to Fornalutx, conceded to be the most attractive (if self-consciously so) village on the island.

Most, though, will prefer to turn left at the wash-house and amble 300 metres down into Biniaraix hamlet to the square, where there's a Spanish/Mallorcan rarity, a *taberna* (as opposed to a bar). The management serves fresh-squeezed orange juice, ice cream, and teas as well as alcoholic drinks in an old-fashioned wooden decor, without accompaniment of video games, TV, etc.

To walk the final distance from Biniaraix to central Sóller should require no more than 25 minutes, for a total of just under five hours for the day, excluding stops.

VALLDEMOSA LOOP

This fairly strenuous hike takes you across the 'roof of the island', via a wonderful 19th-century Romantic curiosity: the 'Camino del Archiduque'. This private bridle path was constructed at the behest of Luis Salvator, an eccentric Austrian noble who had an estate down at Son Marroig. It's clearly visible from the middle of the itinerary and still (indirectly) linked to the high ridge by a minor path.

After traversing the engineered trail from the Mirador de ses Puntes, you have the opportunity to bag Teix summit (1063 metres), rounding off views which are already perhaps superior to those on the Cornadors circuit, before descending through the Valle de Cairats. This is now an ICONA sanctuary with outstanding examples of devices used in now-extinct rural industries, and has the only dependable water en route – take enough to last up to this point.

Rating
This walk is moderate.

Map
Again use SGE No 38-26 (670), *Sóller* (1:50,000).

Getting to/from the Trailhead
Autocares Llompart runs year-round morning services out of Puerto de Sóller, Sóller, and Deià to Valldemosa. The most convenient departure (though not on Sundays in winter) occurs at approximately 9.30 am from the first-named endpoints (variable start from either the harbour or Sóller proper); in winter there is no Sunday or holiday service at this hour. In Sóller the round Plaza America, 600 metres down the Gran Via from the post office, serves as the terminal.

Coming back from Valldemosa, you should aim for the services run by the same company which pass through at 4.45 and 5.30 pm (summer) and 3.30 and 7.30 pm (winter) on their way to Deià and Sóller.

Route Directions
From the bus stop in Valldemosa, walk on the road toward Palma; just past a zebra crossing, turn left up a street skirting left of a large manor (Son Gual) with a tower. Go right at the first intersection, then take a left to a

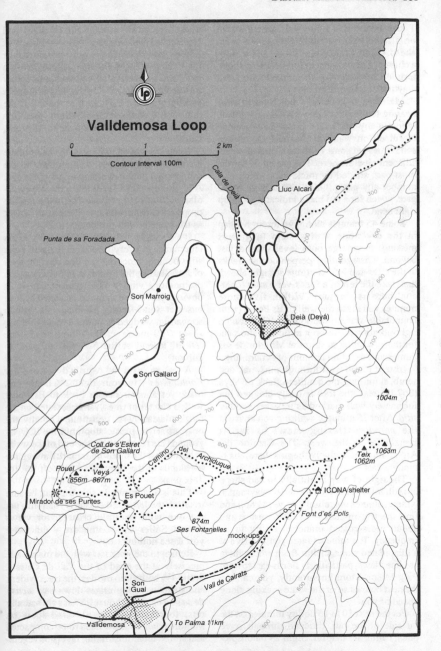

T-intersection at a stone wall, where a sign on a lamppost lists highlights of the route ahead. Circle a house clockwise, and aim for a cluster of pines – just before reaching them, turn left up a stony path marked with a red waymark and a yellow 'V'.

Maintain a generally north-north-west bearing toward the piney saddle just ahead, ignoring any side trails. If you've neglected to fill up on water at the outset, you can sometimes get some from take-outs along an adjacent pipeline here. The ascent is, for the most part, shaded by thick oaks which outnumber any pines. Once past a large metal gate, watch for a red blaze indicating a sharp right bend.

Some 45 minutes along, go through a gap in the dry-stone wall system (a gate is missing) to emerge onto level ground just beyond. Disregarding perpendicular tracks to the right and left, continue straight ahead, then take the left of a fork over a *sitja* (charcoal-burners' cirque). Within five more minutes you reach the well of Es Pouet (with nonpotable water); the legend '*Coll*' and a right-pointing arrow on it indicate a short cut for those wishing to skip the Mirador de ses Puntes and a certain amount of scrambling.

Instead climb west through pine, oak and scrub, skimming the southern flank of Veyá (867 metres); the trail is badly clogged but fortunately well marked as it passes another *sitja*. After 75 minutes' walking you arrive at the *mirador* offering views as far as Bañalbufar to the west. The Camino del Archiduque effectively begins here, hairpinning east.

The right of way is initially in bad shape but still followable with the aid of waymarks. Ninety minutes out, climb the Veyá knoll and find the trig marker – even if mist is not about, moss-coated branches testify to its frequency. Ten minutes later you'll arrive at a dilapidated stone shelter from where there are fine views, particularly north-east toward Puig Maior. More importantly, you can see the next hour or so of the route snaking along ahead of you.

For the next 10 to 15 dodgy minutes on the far side of the hut, descend through scree piles; cairns are helpful. Shun an inconspic-uous left, down toward Son Gallard and (indirectly) Son Marroig. After two hours of hiking, you'll reach the big 'crossroads' of the Coll de s'Estret de Son Gallard; here's a gate, and a bench labelled '*Teix*' and, rather misleadingly, '*Deya*'. On the right is the path coming up from Es Pouet; to the left is the main route down to Son Gallard (then Son Marroig and eventually, via the C-710 road, Deià).

Keep straight on to pick up the heart of the archduke's promenade, a monument to the sentimental nature-worship of a bygone age. A 15-minute climb leads to the most spectacular portion of the causeway; although the drops are sheer to one side, there is no danger as the route is well protected.

It's a simple matter to distinguish various landmarks in every direction. Galatzó peak slips behind, blocking the line of sight west of Bañalbufar; the Punta de sa Foradada, the promontory with a hole punched in it, is obvious just above the villa besieged by tour buses at Son Marroig. Deià is a bit slow in appearing, wedged in at the bottom of those sheer 700-metre cliffs which made the '*Deya*' legend at the Son Gallart pass so dubious.

A cairn and a toppled sign ('*Ses Fontanelles*'), to your right 2¾ hours out, mark yet another detour back to Es Pouet well; a cluster of trees, rather isolated on the bleak plateau here, constitute virtually the only attractive picnic stop until the ICONA grounds are reached near the end of the walk. Proceed past the three-hour mark through the highlands to the signposted turn off left for Teix peak.

This is a worthwhile side trip, but be sure to climb the left-hand (easterly) summit, not the one with multiple crosses, for views toward Sóller and Cornadors – otherwise you'll see nothing new.

Return to the junction with the main path, precisely at the head of the Vall de Cairats. Some 4½ hours into the day, the track widens and steepens as it plunges down past a *casa de sa neu* or 'snow house'. These are actually pits, found at various elevated spots on Mallorca, where snow used to be compacted and stored under insulating layers of vegetation, to provide a source of refrigerant in the warmer months.

Soon after, a sumptuous ICONA shelter straddles the trail; there are benches and a hearth inside, and it's pleasantly cool and dark on a hot day. But resist the temptation to lunch here if you've held out this far, because the Font d'es Polls (4 hours 40 minutes), with passably drinkable water, beckons just beyond.

Below the spring, ICONA has signposted a mock-up 'working' charcoal *sitja* and a *forn de calc* (lime kiln). Five hours along, pass through a first gate near the edge of the ICONA property, then a second by a cottage, and finally a third one by a Y-fork. Bear right here, and soon you'll hit the asphalt above Son Gual. Allow an hour from the fountain to the Valldemosa bus stop, for a total of just over 5½ walking hours. The final section is rather anticlimactic but it's probably better appreciated last, rather than first.

SÓLLER TO CALA TUENT VIA THE VALL DE BALITX

This is one of the most varied and beautiful walks on the island, with almost symmetrical altitude changes out and back, plus the chance to break the journey for a swim at one of the north-west coast's more serviceable beaches. Other sources have underestimated the grandeur of the coastal sections of the outing, which is long rather than difficult. In summer the daunting heat is compensated for by the possibility of catching a boat back from Sa Calobra, one cove beyond Cala Tuent (see the next hike description).

Rating

The hike is of moderate difficulty.

Map

Again it's SGE No 38-26 (670), *Sóller*, plus No 38-25/39-25 (643/644), *Pollensa* 1:50,000.

Route Directions

Leave the Plaza de sa Constitució, Sóller's main square, on Carrer de Sa Lluna. Turn left onto Carrer de la Victoria 11 Maig, and bear right when the first sign points left toward

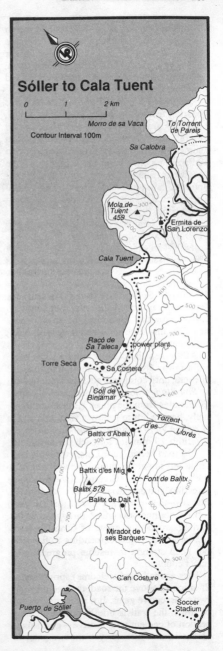

Sóller to Cala Tuent

0   1   2 km

Contour Interval 100m

Morro de sa Vaca

To Torrent de Pareis

Sa Calobra

Mola de Tuent 459

Ermita de San Lorenzo

Cala Tuent

Racó de Sa Taleca — power plant

Torre Seca — Sa Costera

Coll de Biniamar

Torrent d'es Llorés

Baltix d'Abaix

Baltix d'es Mig — Font de Balitx

Baltix 578
Baltix de Dalt

Mirador de ses Barques

C'an Costure

Puerto de Sóller

Soccer Stadium

Start of the trail through the Vall de Balitx

Puerto de Sóller. Cross the Torrent de Fornalutx and its parallel road perpendicularly; pass the high wall of the soccer stadium, this time following a second sign indicating the port.

At the next junction bearing a sign, veer right (away from it) onto the Camino de la Figuera, until coming to a T-intersection with a *'Son Blanco'* legend pointing uphill some 20 minutes from the plaza. Almost immediately, hang a left to follow a sign indicating *'Camino Viejo de Balitx-Tuent-Sa Calobra'*.

Climb 10 minutes to reach the asphalted C-710 road heading for Lluc; cross this and angle left toward a ramp-driveway adorned with a blue arrow. (Coming in the opposite direction, you must watch for a *'C'an Bisbal'* placard – the route is not blazed going downhill.) Continue ascending through a gate, curling around the estate of C'an Costure. Ignore all side trails descending to the left, but keep straight to resume progress over intact cobbles.

Pass a small (and welcome) spring about 25 minutes above the road, then go through two consecutive gates. Just over an hour out of town, the trail is briefly buried under a section of cement tractor drive – go straight across it, and through yet another gate, to enter olive terraces and adopt an east-northeast bearing. Blue waymarks are helpful since the trail is vague at the margin of the pines and olives.

Some 45 minutes above the asphalt highway, you meet a dirt drive; a sharp left leads quickly to the main track toward Balitx. Heading to the right brings you to the Mirador de ses Barques (with a view and a café) within a few minutes; if you detour to it, use the white-signed steps to resume the onward route – they're more scenic than the jeep track done twice.

Most will opt to carry on directly toward Balitx, at least on the outbound leg. Just under 90 minutes out of Sóller and 10 minutes after meeting the track coming directly from below, a green double-gate marks the start of an extensive olive plateau. Some 10 minutes later you've almost reached the farm of Balitx de Dalt, when the track forks at an unlocked gate; turn right, following the legend *'Cala Tuent'*, to enter the Shangri-La-like Vall de Balitx.

About 400 metres into the valley, an obvious cobbled trail emerges to the right of a curve, soon passing the Font de Balitx; this provides reliable water except perhaps in late summer. You must rejoin the tractor track just before Balitx d'es Mig (forlornly abandoned), and continue on it until a peculiar cinder-block oddity, again labelled '*Cala Tuent*', signals the re-eruption of the old path to the left.

This finely engineered way descends to Balitx d'Abaix to complete approximately two hours of walking out of Sóller; in season, fresh orange juice from the surrounding orchards will be on sale here.

The track, now cart-wide, crosses the Torrent d'es Llorés stream bed and once through an iron gate begins climbing in earnest. Blue arrows stay with you as you toil upward, and roughly 2½ hours along you should reach the Coll de Biniamar. Thick tree foliage obscures views in any direction, but within five minutes a red-blazed side trail meanders off left to the lonely estate at Sa Costera, a 20-minute (one-way) detour.

The half-ruined farm overlooks the bay of Racó de sa Taleca, tantalisingly inaccessible some hundreds of metres below. The grounds themselves make an excellent picnic stop, with year-round water available from a spring in a cave up on a terrace behind the house to the right.

Once back on the main trail, descend (within 20 minutes) past a side trail headed for an old seaside power plant; the water is easily reached here but with Cala Tuent so close it's probably not worth the detour.

The main path persists, sometimes overgrown, at other moments a fine corniche route, through successive stone gates until turning down and right past a lone farm 90 minutes past Biniamar and some four hours beyond Sóller. Soon you meet a wider track, which quickly hairpins left to let you face the Tuent cove. Descend to a *bar/restaurante* on a knoll and the final stretch of bona fide trail down to the beach.

There you'll find lots of room to spread out on the mix of sand and pebbles, and another watering-hole, but be warned that the bay catches a lot of drifting trash. If you have come to Cala Tuent for the first time from Sa Calobra and wish to walk back to Sóller via Balitx, the following will set you in the right direction.

From the west end of the beach and its boundary track, a path leads uphill for a few minutes to an asphalt road near the previously mentioned restaurant. Turn left, then veer right, following a blue arrow, onto a dirt track heading up by a villa. Double back

Balitx d'es Mig farm, Coll de Biniamar rear

Final approach to Cala Tuent

toward the sea on the noted hairpin, reaching the end of the jeep track and the above-cited farm a half-hour above the beach. In this direction, various blue arrows point toward the trail which (within 15 minutes) slips through the stone gates for a startling look at the Sa Costera coastline.

Total time from Cala Tuent to the Coll de Biniamar will be just under two hours, the increased time reflecting the uphill grade – hard work in the heat and best saved for late in the day. From Biniamar to Sóller should take about two hours (ie the same as the outward leg), assuming no dawdling or mistakes.

It's possible to continue onward from Cala Tuent to Sa Calobra, though most of the trail within the Tuent valley has been destroyed by new roads and villa development. Short cuts of the road system are possible but the most important thing is to reach the Ermita de San Lorenzo, up on the saddle separating the Tuent area from Sa Calobra. A good trail, to the right of the gate as you enter the chapel

grounds, descends to the first bend in the road from Sa Calobra to Escorca. Allow 80 minutes to reach Sa Calobra, and enough leeway to catch the late afternoon boat back to Sóller (see the Getting to/from the Trailhead section of the next walk).

If for any reason you are walking *from* Sa Calobra *to* Cala Tuent, it's easy enough to see the beginning of this path about a km above Sa Calobra, just before the noted bend. A sign just past a group of farms (20 minutes along) helpfully points toward San Lorenzo and Tuent.

TRAVERSE OF THE TORRENT DE PAREIS
This opportunity to clamber down the deepest and wildest gorge on the island makes perhaps the most popular and sensational trek on Mallorca. Fit individuals of all ages tackle it, and the route's difficulty has been grossly overestimated in existing English-language sources. True, there is some boulder-hopping to be done, occasionally involving eight-foot drops and the assistance of chocks and *clavijas*, but actual exposure is minimal, the difficult spots are few, and the traverse should present no problems as long as the rocks are dry.

Rating
It's on the challenging end of moderate.

Season
Because of the desirability of a dry surface, this is the one Mallorcan walk that's probably better done between May and September, when rain is unlikely; another exceptional recommendation is to wear shorts for maximum freedom of movement – no thornbushes to worry about in the canyon.

Map
SGE Nos 38-25 & 39-25 (643/644), *Pollensa* (one sheet) and No 39-26 (671) *Inca*, both 1:50,000.

Getting to/from the Trailhead
The bus line heading north-east on the C-710 toward Pollensa has its terminal by the Sóller train station, just at the start of the tram

tracks. Currently this leaves daily at 9 am from April to September, weekends only during the cooler months. At about 10.30 am it reaches Escorca, where there's a restaurant and the adjacent church of St Pere.

Once down to the mouth of the gorge at Sa Calobra, you should immediately book a place on the boat back to Sóller which departs daily at 4.30 pm between May and October. There is no public bus service out of Sa Calobra, so if you miss the boat, or there isn't one, you'll probably have to walk back to Sóller by reversing the Balitx itinerary already described.

Route Directions

Walk past the small 13th-century chapel of St Pere and bear left up steps past an *in situ* sculpture fashioned from an olive stump. Take a path to the right, leading up to two gates – go through the left-hand one, and bear sharply left again at a round garbage bin.

Now follow a low stone wall to a small iron gate 10 minutes from the chapel, and five minutes later make a sharp left at an olive tree painted with a faint black circle. Another left, then a right turn are necessary until the head of the gorge itself comes into view.

The trail improves a half-hour along at the so-called *voltes llargues* (long bends or switchbacks); complete an hour of downhill hiking by passing under a fig tree. Twenty metres beyond this, a faint trail without waymarks descends through rock and long grass to the gorge bed. Angle up onto the true left bank to find a path similar to the one you've just left; this takes you (within 20 minutes more) to S'Entreforc. Here the ravines of Lluc and Sa Fosca, the 'pair' of the Mallorquín *pareis*, meet to form a single gorge.

A large rock bears a cruciform legend, with labels as follows: *'Lluch* (ie Lluc)', back upstream; *'Sa Fosca'*, left and for experienced cavers only; *'Millor no eneri'* ('best

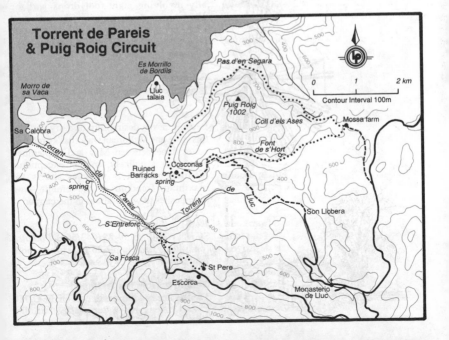

not to enter' in Mallorquin), right toward a cliff; and *'Calobra'*, straight on.

From the signpost-rock, 40 minutes will be enough to get through the first series of pitches, drops and tight spots. Blazes are present but really superfluous, and in the warmer months you'll probably have some company. After the two-hour mark comes an easy stretch before the *torrent* narrows drastically.

Some 2 hours 40 minutes out, you work around a second huge monolith on its right (courtesy of two *clavijas*) then a third giant with the help of a strap anchored by a peg. Your reward is a dripping spring on the rock wall to the left. The gorge finally opens about 3½ hours into the day. A few minutes later a large, late-persisting pool (a dip may be possible) spreads just below the last, easy boulder.

From here on crowds of people, coached or shipped in, are the norm. A final flat stretch

(for a total of four hours) should see you to the eastern Calobra cove, with a 'bar' to one side of its popular pebbles. It may be better to continue an extra quarter of an hour through a pedestrian tunnel to the boat-dock cove – though heavily commercialised, it may paradoxically be quieter.

PUIG ROIG CIRCUIT

This loop-hike allows fine views of the sea and Puig Mayor, the summit of the island but unfortunately off-limits owing to military security. Much of the route follows an old corniche path used by smugglers in past eras. If you do the walk as a not-quite-perfect circuit, you can finish at the famous monastery of Lluc, but it must be said that such a detour ends extremely dully on several km of dirt track and tarmac. Also, those dependent on public transport must be warned that, if they dawdle, they may easily miss the bus back to Sóller.

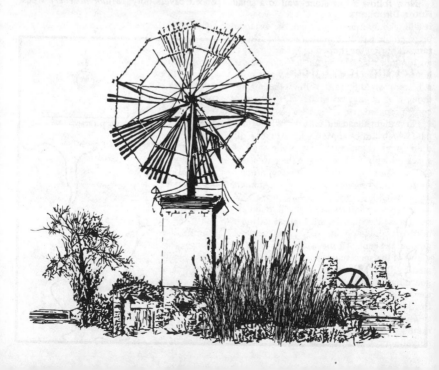

Rating
This is an easy trek, except for the need to hurry.

Map
Use SGE Nos 38-25 & 39-25 (643/644), *Pollensa* and 39-26 (671), *Inca*, both 1:50,000.

Getting to/from the Trailhead
Use the same bus service as for the Torrent de Pareis hike, except this time alight at the Km 15.8 marker (measured from Pollensa – 46 km out of Sóller), next to the driveway with a gate serving the Mossa farm. It will be about 11.10 am.

If you make a true circuit to this point, you need to be back to catch the Sóller-bound bus at 4.25 pm (difficult if not impossible); this leaves Puerto Pollensa at 4 pm. If you decide to end the day at Lluc, the bus passes there at 4.45 pm.

Route Directions
It will take 30 minutes to cover the distance between the Km 15.8 marker and the Mossa farm. Ignoring the (hopefully) chained dogs, go through the gate on the left side of the house; you may be able to obtain water from a cistern on the right behind the manor though, as always on Mallorca, it's best to come prepared.

Go straight ahead and onto the old revetted path which climbs appealingly up to the Coll d'els Ases (Donkeys' Pass). The way is speckled with red blazes, and the pass itself (50 minutes out) tufted with the droopy *Amplodesmus mauritanica* 'grass' common on the island.

Just over 1½ hours along you'll round the bend at the Pas d'en Segara, highest and most northerly point on the route, and begin a gradual descent. All the while you drink in views of the spectacular coast here, accentuated by Puig Mayor, the Morro de sa Vaca guarding Sa Calobra, and the *talaia* (watchtower) of Lluc on top of Es Morrillo de Bordíls.

This tower, like all such Mallorcan monuments, is visually coordinated with its neighbours – in this case one above Cala

Bed of the Torrent de Pareis, halfway along

Tuent and another, the Torre Seca, above Sa Costera. These *talaias*, many now crumbling and/or inaccessible, date primarily from medieval times. Just a handful, strategically placed on various exposed capes and elevated points, could pass signals inland and to each other, thus warning the islanders of approaching pirates or navies.

Clamber over a stile slightly less than 2½ hours along. The old ruined barracks of the customs officers, who were usually in cahoots with the smugglers, appear below and to the right. Within 15 more minutes, the path slips through a gap in a dry-stone wall running down to the ruins and becomes confusing; drop down as best you can to a spring near a clump of trees, reached less than three hours out. Look for a low shed, actually a water tank, with a corrugated roof; the vegetated area makes a fine place for lunch.

Resume progress from in front of the tank along a wide track which has come up from the old barracks; S'Entreforc and the upper reaches of the Torrent de Pareis are clearly

Torrent de Pareis - skirting the last boulder slide

visible on the right. Within a few moments you reach Cosconás, a bizarre settlement whose few houses are tucked under a rock overhang – ignore the red arrow indicating the direct way back to the gap in the fence.

From Cosconás onwards, you face a very dull track-walk of 90 minutes to the grounds of the Monasterio de Lluc (Lluch), for a total of 4 hours 40 minutes of hiking, not including rests. The road beyond Son Llobera is asphalted, and the 90-minute duration applies only if you stride out and take every available short cut. At least you may have the opportunity to look around the monastery

before the bus arrives, but it's not quality hiking and if you can it's preferable to return to Mossa.

To do this more 'sporting' option, bear left onto a cairned path just five minutes past Cosconás which skims the southern base of Puig Roig for 1¾ hours en route to the Mossa farm. The countryside is wooded much of the way, the trail is usually blazed and there is one recessed spring. Obviously you'll need your own vehicle to accomplish this, or trust to a thumbed ride, as you'll almost certainly miss the late afternoon bus by the time you get from Mossa to the Km 15.8 marker.

Index

MAPS

Temperature

To convert °C to °F multiply by 1.8 and add 32
To convert °F to °C subtract 32 and multiply by .55

Length, Distance & Area

	multiply by
inches to centimetres	2.54
centimetres to inches	0.39
feet to metres	0.30
metres to feet	3.28
yards to metres	0.91
metres to yards	1.09
miles to kilometres	1.61
kilometres to miles	0.62
acres to hectares	0.40
hectares to acres	2.47

Weight

	multiply by
ounces to grams	28.35
grams to ounces	0.035
pounds to kilograms	0.45
kilograms to pounds	2.21
British tons to kilograms	1016
US tons to kilograms	907

A British ton is 2240 lbs, a US ton is 2000 lbs

Volume

	multiply by
imperial gallons to litres	4.55
litres to imperial gallons	0.22
US gallons to litres	3.79
litres to US gallons	0.26

5 imperial gallons equals 6 US gallons
a litre is slightly more than a US quart, slightly less than a British one

Walking guides

Bushwalking in Australia
Two experienced and respected walkers give details of the best walks in every state, covering many different terrains and climates.

Tramping in New Zealand
Call it tramping, hiking, walking, bushwalking, or trekking — travelling by foot is the best way to explore New Zealand's natural beauty. Detailed descriptions of 20 walks of varying length and difficulty.

Trekking in the Indian Himalaya
The Indian Himalaya offers some of the world's most exciting treks. This comprehensive guide gives advice on planning and equipping a trek, as well as detailed route descriptions.

Trekking in the Nepal Himalaya
Complete trekking information for Nepal, including day-by-day route descriptions and detailed maps — a wealth of advice for independent and group trekkers alike.

Trekking in Turkey
Among Turkey's best-kept secrets are its superb treks, which rival those of Nepal. This book, the first trekking guide to Turkey, gives details on treks that are destined to become classics.

Lonely Planet Guidebooks

Lonely Planet guidebooks cover every accessible part of Asia as well as Australia, the Pacifi, Central and South America, Africa, the Middle East and parts of North America. There ar four main series: *travel survival kits*, covering a single country for a range of budge *shoestring* guides with compact information for low-budget travel in a major region; *trekki guides* ; and *phrasebooks*.

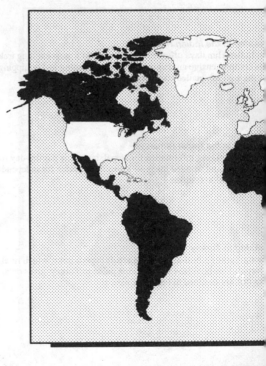

Mail Order

Lonely Planet guidebooks are distributed worldwide and are sold by good bookshops everywhere. They are also available by mail order from Lonely Planet, so if you have difficulty finding a title please write to us. US and Canadian residents should write to Embarcadero West, 112 Linden St, Oakland CA 94607, USA and residents of other countries to PO Box 617, Hawthorn, Victoria 3122, Australia.

Lonely Planet

Lonely Planet published its first book in 1973. Tony and Maureen Wheeler had made an overland trip from England to Australia and, in response to numerous 'how do you do it?' questions, Tony wrote and they published *Across Asia on the Cheap*. It became an instant local best seller and inspired thoughts of a second travel guide. A year and a half in South-East Asia resulted in their second book, *South-East Asia on a Shoestring*, which they put together in a backstreet Chinese hotel in Singapore in 1975. The 'yellow book', as it quickly became known, soon became the guide to the region and has gone through six editions, always with its familiar yellow cover.

Soon other writers came to them with ideas for similar books - books that went off the beaten track, books that 'assumed you knew how to get your luggage off the carousel' as one reviewer put it. Lonely Planet grew from a kitchen table operation to a spare room and then to its own office. Its international reputation began to grow as the Lonely Planet logo began to appear in more and more countries. In 1982 *India - a travel survival kit* won the Thomas Cook award for the best guidebook of the year.

These days there are over 70 Lonely Planet titles. Over 40 people work at our office in Melbourne and another half dozen at our US office in Oakland, California.

At first Lonely Planet specialised in the Asia region but these days we are also developing major ranges of guidebooks to the Pacific region, to South America and to Africa. The list of walking guides is growing and Lonely Planet now has a unique series of phrasebooks to 'unusual' languages. The emphasis continues to be on travel for travellers and Tony and Maureen still manage to fit in a number of trips each year and play a very active part in the writing and updating of Lonely Planet's guides.

Keeping guidebooks up to date is a constant battle which requires an ear to the ground and lots of walking, but technology also plays its part. All Lonely Planet guidebooks are now stored on computer, and some authors even take lap-top computers into the field. Lonely Planet is also using computers to draw maps and eventually many of the maps will be stored on disc.

The people at Lonely Planet strongly feel that travellers can make a positive contribution to the countries they visit both by better appreciation of cultures and by the money they spend. In addition the company tries to make a direct contribution to the countries and regions it covers. Since 1986 a percentage of the income from each book has gone to aid groups and associations. This has included donations to famine relief in Africa, to aid projects in India, to agricultural projects in Central America, to Greenpeace's efforts to halt French nuclear testing in the Pacific and to Amnesty International. In 1989 $41,000 was donated by Lonely Planet to these projects.